CHOICE MENUS
COOKING FOR ONE OR TWO

Quick and Easy Meals and Menus to
Help You Prevent or Manage Diabetes

Marjorie Hollands, M.Sc., RD

Margaret Howard, B Sc., RD, P.H.Ec.

An Imprint of HarperCollinsPublishers

Choice Menus: Cooking for One or Two
© 2000, 2008 by Marjorie Hollands and Margaret Howard.
All rights reserved.

Published by Collins, an imprint of HarperCollins Publishers Ltd.

Originally published in Canada by Macmillan Canada, an imprint of CDG Books
Canada: 2000
Revised and updated Collins edition: 2008
This trade paperback edition: 2011

HarperCollins books may be purchased for educational, business,
or sales promotional use through our Special Markets Department.

HarperCollins Publishers Ltd
2 Bloor Street East, 20th Floor
Toronto, Ontario, Canada
M4W 1A8

www.harpercollins.ca

Library and Archives Canada Cataloguing in Publication information
is available upon request.

Hollands, Marjorie and Margaret Howard
Choice Menus: Cooking for one or two.
Quick and easy meals and menus to help you prevent or manage diabetes

ISBN: 978-1-44340-505-8

PP 9 8 7 6 5 4 3 2 1

Printed and bound in China

Photography by Hal Roth/Assisted by Paolo Christante
Food styling by Julie Zambonelli/Prop styling by Maggie Jones
Design by Sharon Kish
Photograph on page 55, 167 by Christine Balderas/iStockphoto
Photograph on page 103 by Westmacott Photography/iStockphoto

CONTENTS

INTRODUCTION

Cooking for One or Two   1
Prevention and Management of Diabetes   2
The Importance of Meal Planning   6
Eating Well with Canada's Food Guide   9
Guidelines for the Nutritional Management of Diabetes   11
Meal Planning and Shopping Tips For One or Two   16

HOW TO USE THIS BOOK   17

A Month of Menus   19

FOOD CHOICE VALUES OF MENUS   20
MEAL PLANNING MENUS   TABS

RECIPES

Breakfast   21
Lunch   48
Dinner   94
Snacks   163
Special Meals for Special Occasions   178

APPENDICES

  I   Beyond the Basics: Meal Planning for Healthy Eating   216
 II   Breakfast Cereals of Your Choice   223
III   Fruits of Your Choice   224
 IV   The ABCs of Nutrition and Diabetes   225
  V   Food Definitions and Procedures   229
 VI   Common Herbs and Spices   231
VII   The Well-Stocked Diabetes Kitchen   232
VIII Recommended Storage Times for Refrigerator and Freezer Food 233
 IX   Nutrient Analysis of Recipes and Menus   237

ACKNOWLEDGEMENTS   239
RECIPE INDEX   240
DIABETES AND NUTRITION INDEX   249

INTRODUCTION

Maybe you have just learned you have diabetes or that your blood glucose is a bit too high. Maybe you have been told to lose some weight because there is a good chance you'll develop type 2 diabetes if you don't. Maybe it's a family member or a friend you're worried about. Maybe you want to be healthier and need to change your eating habits. Whatever the case, *Choice Menus: Cooking for One or Two* comes to your rescue.

COOKING FOR ONE OR TWO

If you have always cooked for one or two, or if cooking for fewer people is new to you, you have undoubtedly encountered some challenges. Few recipes are written for only one or two servings, and by now you are probably tired of eating leftovers from larger recipes. When we wrote *Choice Menus*, we were thinking of family meals, with recipes generally for four to six servings. We wanted people newly diagnosed with diabetes (or trying to avoid diabetes) to realize that they could eat much the same way as the rest of the family did, the main difference being how much to eat at a meal, not what.

If you thought you would never find a book that would show you how to cook for only one or two people, think again. This book was created just for you. After all, it's important to eat well no matter how many people gather around the table. Singles, couples and empty nesters will all enjoy these varied, fresh-tasting recipes tailored for just one or two.

Choice Menus: Cooking for One or Two offers tantalizing selections for daily eating from breakfast through lunch, dinner and snacks. And for special occasions, be sure to refer to the eight Special Meals for Special Occasions in the recipes section (see page 178)—and all fit into a diabetes meal plan.

As in *Choice Menus*, this unique meal planner focuses on menus that are based on single servings but supported by recipes created for one or two servings. The result? Fewer leftovers to crowd the fridge and freezer.

Symptoms of Diabetes

- Unusual thirst
- Frequent urination
- Weight change (gain or loss)
- Extreme fatigue or lack of energy
- Blurred vision
- Frequent or recurring infections
- Cuts or bruises that are slow to heal
- Tingling or numbness in hands or feet
- Sexual difficulties

We have worked hard to create easy-to-follow recipes that minimize kitchen time but still result in great homemade meals. (Most of the recipes take no longer than 30 minutes to prepare.) The majority of them contain readily available ingredients. We have tried to give you meals that offer a variety of interesting smaller-scale recipes with taste, texture and eye appeal. Notes included after some of the recipes offer additional guidance and tips for novice and experienced cooks alike.

The Canadian Diabetes Association has published a new meal planning guide called *Beyond the Basics: Meal Planning for Healthy Eating, Diabetes Prevention and Management* (see page 216). We have used this in the planning of our menus. They are planned especially for someone with type 2 diabetes (although many people with gestational or type 1 diabetes will find them very helpful as well). All recipes include carbohydrate choices so you can use them in menus you plan yourself. Meal planning and food choices can be confusing at first. The goal of *Choice Menus: Cooking for One or Two* is to take the guesswork out of meal planning.

Our menus do not replace nutritional counselling by a registered dietitian who is a diabetes educator. You are an individual with your own food preferences and lifestyle. A dietitian can help you identify problem areas and set goals, then work with you to prepare an individualized meal plan. But our menus and recipes are always there to give variety and fresh ideas.

If you have type 2 diabetes and wish to follow our menus, speak to your diabetes educator about appropriately matching your insulin to the meals.

Prevention and Management of Diabetes

More than 2 million Canadians have diabetes (although 3 out of 10 don't know it) with an estimated 60,000 new cases diagnosed every year. Of those diagnosed, 90 per cent have type 2 diabetes and 10 per cent have type 1. It is a condition to be taken seriously.

The good news is that the onset of type 2 diabetes can be delayed successfully and sometimes prevented, and a diagnosis of type 2 diabetes does not need to lead to complications. The key is to keep blood glucose and cholesterol levels controlled and near normal.

Many diabetes pills, or oral hypoglycemic drugs, have been developed to increase insulin production or decrease insulin resistance. Most people with type 2 diabetes will need either pills or insulin eventually to maintain near normal blood glucose levels. But exercise, diet (meaning the food you eat) and glucose monitoring are still the cornerstones of diabetes management and are important whether or not diabetes medication is prescribed. We hope that with the help of *Choice Menus: Cooking for One or Two*, you will find it a bit easier to manage your diabetes effectively.

What is diabetes?

There are really three kinds of diabetes: type 1, type 2 and gestational.

Type 1 diabetes is usually, but not always, diagnosed in children and teenagers and occurs when the pancreas is unable to produce insulin. Insulin is a hormone that allows muscle cells to get the glucose they need for energy, so those with type 1 diabetes must take insulin daily, either by injection or by insulin pump, in order to survive. Only about 10 per cent of diabetes is type 1.

Type 2 diabetes, which is the type most people have, occurs when the pancreas over a period of time, does not produce enough insulin or when the body cannot effectively use the insulin it does produce. It is usually diagnosed in overweight adults, although increasing numbers of children are being diagnosed in high-risk populations such as Aboriginal, Hispanic, Asian, South Asian and African.

Gestational diabetes is a temporary form of diabetes that can occur during the last part of a pregnancy when hormonal changes increase the body's demand for insulin. It affects over 3 per cent of pregnancies and increases the chance that both mother and child may develop type 2 diabetes later in life.

Prevention of type 2 diabetes

About 80 per cent of people with type 2 diabetes are overweight at diagnosis. Current research suggests that most cases of type 2 diabetes might be prevented or delayed by early and effective weight management. This is best achieved by strategies that promote gradual rather than quick weight loss. The focus should be on healthy food choices and regular physical activity along with reduced fat intake. Even a small weight loss can make a big difference. Losing just 5 to 10 per cent of your body weight has been shown to improve blood glucose and

ARE YOU AT RISK FOR DIABETES?

- I'm age 40 or older.
- I'm of Aboriginal, Hispanic, Asian, South Asian or African descent.
- I'm overweight, especially around the middle.
- I have a parent, brother or sister with diabetes.
- I gave birth to a baby that weighed more than 4 kilograms (9 pounds).
- I had gestational diabetes during pregnancy.
- I have high cholesterol or triglycerides.
- I have high blood pressure.
- I have impaired glucose tolerance (IGT) or impaired fasting glucose (IFG).

cholesterol levels as well as lower high blood pressure. If you weigh 68 kg (150 pounds), that would be 3.5 to 7 kg (8 to 15 pounds).

Before people develop type 2 diabetes, they often have higher-than-normal blood glucose levels, but not high enough for a diagnosis of diabetes (7 mmol/L fasting). Studies show that people with prediabetes can cut in half their risk of progressing to full-blown diabetes by making changes in exercise and eating habits—and the earlier the better.

Maybe you don't have diabetes—but there is a history of diabetes in your family—and you've been thinking that you really should lose some weight and improve your eating habits. Maybe none of the above describes you but you've just been thinking it's time to eat in a healthier way and you're looking for some direction. Whatever your goal, planning healthy meals that help you lose weight is very important. A healthier lifestyle helps you feel better, have more energy and decreases your risk for chronic diseases such as diabetes, heart disease and cancer.

HOW IS DIABETES TREATED?

- Physical activity
- Healthy eating
- Weight management
- Medication
- Stress management
- Blood pressure control

Achieving a healthy weight

There are many ways to assess your present body weight. Height/weight tables are the easiest way but they don't allow for body composition. BMI or body mass index measures your weight as it relates to your height but it doesn't measure the amount of body fat directly. [To calculate your BMI, divide your weight (in kilograms) by the square of your height (in metres). If your BMI is over 30, you are at increased risk.]

Measuring waist circumference provides a more specific measure of health risk because waist circumference indicates harmful abdominal fat. Incidence of diabetes and high blood pressure are much higher in those who store excess body fat around their middle, commonly called a "pot belly," "beer belly" or "apple shape."

To measure your waist circumference (WC), place the tape measure, not too tightly, around your torso midway between your lowest rib and the top of your pelvic bone. A normal WC is less than 40 inches (100 cm) in men and less than 35 inches (87.5 cm) in women. More than this raises your health risk. Fortunately abdominal fat is often the first to go with weight loss.

Strategies for successful weight loss

The desire to lose weight must come from within. Only you can change your attitudes towards eating and exercise. You must be motivated enough to change habits not for a few weeks or months, but for a lifetime. Researchers have been studying the experiences of successful dieters (those who have lost 30 pounds or more and have kept it off for at least a year). These are some of their key strategies:

- Set realistic goals. Instead of trying to lose a specific number of pounds, make it your goal to adopt healthier eating and exercise habits. The safest rate of weight loss is ½ to 2 pounds (¼ to 1 kg) per week.
- Seek support from family and friends. It will be easier to stick to your new eating plan if everyone in the household eats the same type of foods. If you're cooking for just one or two, you have a real advantage. You may be more motivated to exercise if you work out with a friend or family member.
- Make changes gradually. Ease into exercise and don't overdo it. Switch to lower-fat eating in stages. For example, if you usually drink whole milk, switch to 2%, then 1%, then finally to skim.
- Eat slowly. Since it takes about 20 minutes for the stomach to signal the brain that it's full, slowing down helps you feel satisfied with less food and allows you to better appreciate the flavours and textures of your food.
- Eat three meals a day, plus snacks. Skipping meals is not a good idea. And people were more successful if they kept to a regular eating plan rather than dieting on weekdays and splurging on weekends or holidays.
- Be active every day. You don't have to be an exercise fanatic to attain and maintain weight loss. The most common exercise reported was plain old walking, which can be done anywhere by almost everyone.
- Make time for exercise. Choose activities that are convenient and enjoyable for you to do. Treat it like any other appointment—set a time and jot it down in your calendar.
- Record your progress. You may choose to start a food diary and exercise log to keep track of your accomplishments. Monitor your blood glucose regularly and record that as well. Take both to your diabetes health professional so you can identify any problem areas.
- Think about how you relate to food. Overeating or the "munchies" are often triggered by stress, boredom, sadness, loneliness or the

use of food as a reward. It may temporarily make you feel better, but it does not solve any problems.

- Don't try to be perfect. Losing weight requires major changes in eating and exercise habits but not every favourite high-calorie food must be banished forever and you don't need to exercise vigorously every day. But the longer you maintain weight loss, the easier it becomes.

THE IMPORTANCE OF MEAL PLANNING

For the person who has diabetes, or is trying to avoid diabetes, careful meal planning has never been more important. Over the long term, too much blood glucose can lead to changes in the small blood vessels supplying the nerves and eyes and kidneys, and lead to the serious complications of diabetes. Research makes it clear that keeping blood glucose levels as close to normal as possible can prevent and possibly delay these complications.

With the increasing use of glucose monitors to measure blood glucose before and after meals, it is now possible to fine-tune meal plans and medication to preferences and lifestyles in a way that was not possible 10 or 15 years ago.

The person with type 1 diabetes needs to balance carbohydrate intake with insulin and exercise to achieve good control. Someone with gestational diabetes is usually treated with a meal plan and careful blood glucose monitoring, and sometimes insulin, to make sure both mother and baby get the nutrients they need for the duration of the pregnancy. For those who are overweight and have type 2 diabetes or prediabetes, a combination of healthy eating with a daily exercise like walking is the key, or as the British Diabetic Association says so well, "Eat less, walk more!"

If you are a lean person with type 2 diabetes, weight maintenance is likely your goal and you need to carefully balance food intake and exercise with your available insulin supply. Planning five or six small meals over the day is one strategy.

In every case we're talking what to eat, how much to eat and even when to eat—in other words, meal planning.

Glycemic index

At one time, it was believed that all starchy carbohydrates digested slowly and all sweet foods containing sugar digested more rapidly. We understand much more about food and diabetes now thanks to "glycemic index" (GI) research. Recognizing that carbohydrate has a major impact on blood glucose, and that we were being encouraged to eat less fat and more carbohydrate, Dr. David Jenkins and Dr. Tom Wolever, in their University of Toronto laboratories, addressed this question: Are all carbohydrate foods created equal? Their research studied the effect that various carbohydrate-rich foods had on after-meal blood glucose in an individual, then compared it to how that same individual responded to a standard meal of glucose or white bread.

In other words, glycemic index, or GI, measures how quickly or slowly a carbohydrate food is digested—and carbohydrate foods are definitely not all the same.

GI rates foods from 0 to 100, with glucose rated at 100 and white bread at 71. High-GI foods score 70 and above, medium-GI foods between 56 and 69 and low-GI foods 55 and below.

Foods with a high-GI value contain carbohydrate that is quickly digested and absorbed, resulting in a fast and high rise in blood glucose after a meal, followed by a rapid fall. Foods with a low-GI value contain carbohydrate that is digested and absorbed more slowly, resulting in a slower, lower rise in blood glucose followed by a more gradual decline.

Many factors decide what the glycemic index of a food will be; here are some of them:

- *Food form.* Drinking a glass of fruit juice will raise blood glucose more quickly than eating a solid whole fruit (see page 23).
- *Degree of processing.* The starch in a highly processed breakfast cereal such as cornflakes digests faster than the starch in a whole grain cereal such as oatmeal. Parboiled or converted rice digests more slowly than quick-cooking rice.
- *Cooking method.* Starch in a mashed potato digests more rapidly than starch in a boiled or new potato cooked in its skin.
- *Cooking time.* Overcooked pasta and vegetables digest more quickly than those cooked al dente (tender but firm).

Choosing low-GI foods along with a heart healthy diet has obvious benefits for people with diabetes whose goal is a slower rise in blood glucose after a meal. Another benefit is that low-GI foods are bulkier, take longer to eat, and are digested more slowly. This can increase your feeling of satiety or fullness so that you eat less, and this is a plus whether your goal is weight loss or weight maintenance.

Go for Lower-GI foods

- Choose at least one low-GI food at each meal.
- Eat fresh fruits and vegetables.
- Choose parboiled brown rice more often than instant rice.
- Cook pasta just until al dente (tender but firm).
- Choose baked potatoes more often than mashed, boiled or instant.
- Eat whole grain, pumpernickel and oat bran bread more often than white.

With obesity on the rise and a major risk factor for heart disease and diabetes, it makes sense to include more low GI foods in meals and snacks. When you look at foods in the low GI group—split pea soup, baked beans, oatmeal porridge—it looks like good old-fashioned healthy eating.

The following table illustrates how different foods with the same carbohydrate content are rated.

LOW-GI FOODS 55 OR LESS CHOOSE MOST OFTEN	MEDIUM-GI FOODS 56 TO 69 CHOOSE MORE OFTEN	HIGH-GI FOODS 70 OR MORE CHOOSE LESS OFTEN
skim milk	banana	watermelon
plain yogurt	pineapple	dried dates
soy beverage	raisins	instant mashed potatoes
apple, plum, orange	whole new potatoes	baked white potato
sweet potato	popcorn	parsnips
oat bran bread	split pea or green pea	rutabaga
rolled oats (large-flake)	soup	instant rice
All-Bran	brown rice	cornflakes
converted or parboiled rice	couscous	Rice Krispies
cooked firm (al dente) pasta	basmati rice	Cheerios
lentils	shredded wheat cereal	bagel, white
kidney beans	whole wheat bread	soda crackers
navy beans	rye bread	jelly beans
chickpeas	pita bread	ice cream
		french fries
		digestive cookies
		table sugar

Glycemic Index: A New Way of Looking at Carbs, published by the Canadian Diabetes Association (2005). Reprinted with permission.

How to plan meals that raise blood glucose more gradually

Including more lower glycemic index foods in your meals is one way to raise your blood glucose more gradually, and here are some others. We have planned the menus and recipes in *Choice Menus: Cooking for One or Two* with these principles in mind.

• Choose carbohydrates that digest slowly. Vegetables and fruits rich in fibre take longer to digest than do their juices; foods containing soluble sticky fibre (oats, barley, legumes, pectin) as well as insoluble bran fibre digest even more slowly.

- Eat carbohydrate foods as part of a mixed meal, one that contains protein and fat as well as fibre. Most carbohydrate-based foods already contain some protein or fat. Meats, alternatives, fats and oils digest very slowly and slow the digestion of the starches and sugars eaten with them. However, an excessive amount of fat or oil in a meal can make it difficult for the insulin supply to work effectively; so can too much carbohydrate at one meal.
- Don't overcook vegetables and pasta. Let your body do the processing.
- Space meals at regular intervals throughout the day to make better use of a limited insulin supply. Skipping meals, then overeating at the next meal, is not a good idea. Research has shown that spreading food over several small meals a day can result in better blood glucose and cholesterol values after meals.
- Limit the *amount* of carbohydrate (starch and sugar) you eat at each meal. This is the most important factor if you are to achieve improved blood glucose control. You need a certain amount of carbohydrate in each meal to encourage your pancreas to produce insulin. And the brain requires a steady supply of glucose fuel to think clearly. But too much starch or sugar at one time may be too much for your insulin supply to handle. Balance and moderation are the key.

EATING WELL WITH CANADA'S FOOD GUIDE

The revised *Canada's Food Guide* (2007) translates the science of nutrition and health into healthy eating for Canadians, not just what *type* of food to choose but also the *amount*. It emphasizes the importance of combining healthy eating with physical activity to reduce the risk of obesity and chronic disease. These nutrition principles apply to people with diabetes as much as to other Canadians. They are the basis for *Beyond the Basics* as well as our recipes and menus in the *Choice Menus* series.

What type of food should people choose?

Vegetables and fruit:
- Eat at least one dark green and one orange vegetable each day.
- Have vegetables and fruit more often than juice.
- Choose vegetables and fruit, ideally fresh, prepared with little or no added fat, sugar or salt.

Grain products:

- Make at least half of your grain products whole grain each day.
- Choose grain products that are lower in fat, sugar and salt.

Milk and alternatives:

- Drink skim, 1% or 2% milk each day.
- Choose lower fat dairy products or milk alternatives.
- Men and women over 50 need a supplement of 400 IU or more vitamin D per day in addition to following *Canada's Food Guide.*

Meat and alternatives:

- Have meat alternatives such as beans, lentils and tofu often.
- Eat at least two servings of fish each week.
- Choose lean meat and alternatives prepared with little or no added fat or salt.

Oils and fats:

- Include a small amount of unsaturated fat each day.
- Use vegetable oils such as canola, olive and soybean.
- Choose soft margarines low in saturated and trans fats.

Beverages:

- Satisfy your thirst with water.
- Limit beverages high in calories, fat, sugar or salt.

What amount of food should people eat?

Since some serving sizes in *Beyond the Basics* are based on servings that contain 15 grams available carbohydrate, they may differ slightly from those in the Food Guide but the recommended number of servings per day will be the same.

RECOMMENDED NUMBER OF FOOD GUIDE SERVINGS PER DAY FOR ADULTS

	19 TO 50 YEARS		51+ YEARS	
	Females	Males	Females	Males
Vegetables and Fruit	7–8	8–10	7	7
Grain Products	6–7	8	6	7
Milk and Alternatives	2	2	3	3
Meat and Alternatives	2	3	2	3

GUIDELINES FOR THE NUTRITIONAL MANAGEMENT OF DIABETES

Every few years The National Nutrition Committee of the Canadian Diabetes Association publishes guidelines for diabetes and healthy eating based on a review of current research on food and diabetes. Current nutritional guidelines stress the importance of near-normal blood glucose and cholesterol levels as well as the importance of healthy eating and a healthy weight. The *Choice Menus* series has always followed these guidelines. A few are summarized below.

Carbohydrate

When you have diabetes, the kind and amount of carbohydrate you eat in a meal is very important, since it has the most effect on the rise in blood glucose that occurs after eating. Digestion releases starch and sugar from carbohydrate-rich foods and breaks them down into glucose, the simplest form of sugar and our main source of energy. Glucose passes into the bloodstream after meals, which results in a rise in blood glucose (or "blood sugar") and a release of insulin hormone by the pancreas. So the total amount of carbohydrate you eat at a meal is very important (see Appendix I, page 216).

Carbohydrate counting

Carbohydrate counting is one of several meal planning tools developed to help you manage your blood glucose levels. For most people with diabetes, carbohydrate counting is more flexible and simpler to use than an exchange system of meal planning where foods are grouped into specific categories. With "carb counting" you keep track of the amount of carbohydrate eaten at each meal with the goal of staying within a planned amount. In this way, carbohydrate intake is consistent throughout the day, and from one day to the next, making it easier to adjust your medication or insulin to match your activity and eating patterns.

So how do you count carbs? One way is the Plate Method, a simple visual guide to meal planning. Picture your plate half filled with vegetables and the other half filled with equal portions of grains or starches, and meat or alternatives. Add a glass of milk and fruit to complete your meal

Some people use food tables (such as Nutrient Value of Some Common Foods, available at www.hc-sc.gc.ca, to identify

BLOOD GLUCOSE TESTING

- Blood glucose is measured in millimoles of glucose per litre of blood and can be determined with a glucose meter. Blood glucose is usually tested just before and after meals. The recommended blood glucose level for all kinds of diabetes is 4 to 7 mmol/L before meals and 5 to 10 mmol/L two hours after meals.
- Your diabetes health professional will help you decide what pattern of blood glucose testing works best for you. What's important is not how many tests you do, but how you use the information they provide. The goal is to make changes to your lifestyle or treatment that keep your diabetes well controlled.

carbohydrate content. Labels also provide information (see www.healthyeatingisinstore.ca). When reading a food label, keep in mind that the amount of carbohydrate listed is for the serving size described. Does it match the portion you're having? Note, too, that the total carbohydrate stated includes sugar and fibre. Since fibre does not raise blood glucose levels, subtract it from the total carbohydrate. The result will give you the amount of carbohydrate "available" to raise blood glucose.

Beyond the Basics, published by the Canadian Diabetes Association, is another meal planning tool that can be used to keep carbohydrate consistent from meal to meal. A serving of carbohydrate, or a carb choice, is defined as a portion of food containing 15 grams of available carbohydrate, with so many carb choices planned for each meal (see Appendix I, page 216).

You may find that using a combination of all the above methods works best for you. Carbohydrate counting is an option for anyone with diabetes. However, for it to be effective, you must be willing to work closely with your dietitian and/or diabetes educator and test your blood glucose levels several times a day, before and after meals, on a regular basis. By keeping a precise record of your results, you can track what's happening and look for patterns. Understanding how meals, activity and medication affect your blood glucose levels means you will be able to lead a more flexible lifestyle.

We have tried to take the guesswork out of "carb counting," making it easier for you to get started. In *Choice Menus: Cooking for One or Two*, each meal menu contains a consistent planned amount of carbohydrate, less at breakfast and more at lunch and dinner. Snacks vary in carbohydrate content according to size (see page 20 for details). Menus for Special Occasions have the same amount of carbohydrate but sometimes a few extra calories. We have included weights and measures in both menus and recipes wherever we thought they would be useful, especially for high carbohydrate foods. This should help those of you "counting carbs" to keep your carbohydrate intake planned and consistent (for further information see Appendix I, Beyond the Basics, page 216).

Perhaps you have different carbohydrate goals than we have used in our menus. You may want to discuss this with your dietitian. Since each recipe shows carbohydrate choices as well as other nutrition information, you can plan your own menus, but let ours provide inspiration for variety and healthy eating.

What about sugars and diabetes?

Sugar appears in many different forms in the foods we eat: glucose and fructose in honey and corn syrup; glucose, fructose and sucrose in fruits and vegetables; lactose in milk; maltose in beer. The sugar in the sugar bowl is sucrose, a sugar that occurs naturally in all living plants, and especially in sugar beets and cane sugar. When the juice from these plants is extracted and crystallized, the result is table sugar, which has been the sweetener of choice for generations.

Sugar has been seen as a forbidden food and a guilty pleasure for those with a sweet tooth and diabetes. People with diabetes have traditionally been told to avoid anything sweet because of the popular belief that it worsens diabetes control. This is just one of the myths about sugar and diabetes. Here are two others:

MYTH: Eating too much sugar causes diabetes.
FACT: There is no scientific evidence that links sugar intake with the development of diabetes. However, overweight people have an increased risk of developing type 2 diabetes whether they eat sugar or not, especially when there is diabetes in the family.

MYTH: Sweet foods are fattening because sugar is high in calories.
FACT: Any food eaten in excess of your energy needs can be fattening and cause weight gain.

Sugar itself is not fattening, nor are other carbohydrate-rich foods. The villain in high-calorie foods is usually fat, not sugar. Carbohydrate has less than half the calories of fat: 4 calories per gram versus 9 calories per gram for fat. Anyone who needs to lose weight to avoid diabetes or to bring diabetes under better control would be wise to limit fat and increase exercise rather than act as if only sugar mattered.

The position of the Canadian Diabetes Association is that sugar need not be completely avoided but should be used carefully. The secret is to work it in, not add it on. Research shows that sugar can take the place of other carbohydrate in a slowly digested mixed meal without upsetting diabetes control. (See Appendix I, Other Choices, page 219). The *total amount of carbohydrate* eaten in a meal is more important than whether or not a food contains some sugar.

Our recipes call for a variety of nutritive and non-nutritive sweeteners (see Appendix I, pages 221–222). Sugar is used

in some recipes, but in small amounts—for flavour or texture—and counts as part of the carbohydrate in that meal.

Fibre

Increasing fibre intake can reduce your risk of coronary heart disease by lowering the "bad" cholesterol in your blood, especially if it is high, and may also reduce your risk of type 2 diabetes and certain cancers.

There are two kinds of fibre in foods, insoluble and soluble. Both types have a special role to play. Foods that contain insoluble fibre are full of "roughage," so they are great laxatives that help keep bowels healthy and regular and may help prevent certain kinds of cancer. Insoluble fibre also acts as a barrier to digestive enzymes, thus slowing the digestion of a meal. Key sources of insoluble fibre are wheat bran and foods made with whole wheat, whole grains and seeds, and the skins of fruits and vegetables.

Soluble fibre is a bit different. After it is eaten, soluble fibre forms a sticky gel. This also slows the digestion of the starch in food, thus slowing the rise in blood glucose after the meal. Key sources are oat bran and barley, legumes such as lentils, dried beans and dried peas, and pectin-rich fruits such as apples, peaches, pears, strawberries and citrus fruits.

Getting 25 to 50 grams of fibre a day may seem a challenge (especially when the average Canadian gets no more than 15 grams a day). If you wish to increase fibre, consider using more of the high fibre recipes (page 249) and add a high fibre cereal most days (page 223)— have it for breakfast or sprinkle it over a salad, counting one serving as 1 carbohydrate choice. Remember to drink more water as you slowly increase your fibre intake.

Protein

People with diabetes do not need any more (or less) protein than those without diabetes, but excessive intake should be avoided. However, anyone following a weight loss plan must be sure to get enough protein, as must vegetarians (see page 105). Vegetarian recipes are listed in the index under the heading Vegetarian.

Fats and oils

Many studies indicate that high-fat diets can impair glucose tolerance and promote obesity, high cholesterol levels and heart disease.

FRUITS WITH THE MOST FIBRE:
- apples
- blueberries
- cherries
- peaches
- pears
- plums
- raspberries
- strawberries

VEGETABLES WITH THE MOST FIBRE:
- broccoli
- carrots
- cauliflower
- corn
- green beans
- green peas
- rutabaga
- tomatoes

When saturated fat is reduced, all these problems reverse or improve. Thus the emphasis continues to be on reducing intake of *saturated fat* in meat, poultry and dairy products by choosing lower-fat foods more often. And there is even more emphasis on avoiding foods that contain *trans fatty acids*, processed foods such as fast foods, packaged snacks and baked goods. This fat is even more harmful than saturated fat since it not only raises the "bad" LDL cholesterol but also lowers the "good" HDL cholesterol. That's yet another good reason to read labels when shopping; look for low fat and 0 grams trans fat.

Some fats are better for diabetes than others. *Omega–3 fatty acids*, found in fatty fish (see page 220), are linked to heart health and may reduce serum triglyceride, a type of blood fat often elevated in diabetes. For that reason, current guidelines recommend eating fish such as salmon or sardines at least twice a week.

Research indicates that *monounsaturated fats* (such as canola and olive oils) may have a beneficial effect on both triglycerides and glycemic control. Current guidelines recommend that these oils, and the soft non-hydrogenated margarines containing them, be used in amounts that avoid weight gain. Our recipes and menus do this.

Sodium and hypertension (high blood pressure)

It is important to keep hypertension (high blood pressure) under control, especially if you have type 2 diabetes. The body uses sodium to regulate blood pressure and keep muscles and nerves operating properly, but too much sodium can lead to high blood pressure in some individuals. The recommendation is to limit sodium to 1500–2300 mg per day (about the amount in a teaspoon of salt). However, the salt shaker is probably not your main source of sodium. Most of the sodium in our diet is hidden in packaged and processed foods, another reason to read labels and compare—or avoid the food in question. Attaining a healthier weight through balanced eating and regular physical activity is often enough to bring high blood pressure back to normal. Guidelines also advise avoiding or limiting alcohol and smoking as ways to reduce blood pressure.

Our recipes give the sodium content per serving as well as many tips on how to reduce salt intake. Few recipes need the addition of salt. Yeast breads are the exception as the addition of salt makes the dough more elastic, improving the volume of the finished loaf.

WAYS TO CUT DOWN ON SALT

- Choose fresh or frozen vegetables rather than canned.
- Look for canned foods with less sodium or rinse canned food to remove some of the salt.
- Choose hard brick cheeses rather than processed cheese slices and spreads.
- Choose unsalted popcorn and fruits and vegetables rather than salty snacks.
- Flavour food with herbs, spices, garlic, onion, lemon and lime rather than processed salt.
- Limit bologna, wieners, bacon, ham, salami, pepperoni and luncheon meats.

Meal Planning and Shopping Tips for One or Two

The key to efficient food shopping is effective meal planning. The meal planning process goes like this:

- Start by choosing the menus you plan to use during the week.
- Make a list of the groceries you need to buy for the menus you've chosen.
- Organize the list in the order you will shop. Or organize by store departments (for example, dairy, meat, etc.).
- Plan your shopping trip for after a meal so you won't give in to impulse buying.

Shopping tips

As you push your grocery cart through the store, you will realize that it is no longer impossible to shop for one or two. Most grocery stores have individual chicken breasts wrapped and priced alongside the typical packages of three or four. There are some other things to keep in mind when you are shopping for the smaller amounts you need:

- The butcher will make up smaller portion sizes if you ask.
- Check the deli section for cooked meat cuts and cheeses, cut and weighed in just the amount you want.
- Watch for products packaged in individual servings.
- The produce section has vegetables and fruits in bulk bins where you can choose just what you need. Smaller portions of vegetables such as broccoli and cauliflower florets and cut-up squash are often available as well, or ask, and staff will often divide a large package for you.
- Bags of frozen vegetables can be very economical—sometimes even fresher than the real thing.
- Many stores have salad bars where you can buy small amounts of vegetables for salads or stir-frying.
- Bulk food bins allow you to choose the exact amount you want.
- Eggs, the original natural single portion, can be purchased in half-dozen cartons.

HOW TO USE THIS BOOK

In the section that follows, you will find 30 healthy breakfast menus, 30 appetizing lunches, 30 delectable dinner menus and a variety of snacks in different shapes and sizes to fill the gaps between meals. Any combination of breakfast, lunch, and dinner menus (one of each) will together add up to about 1,300 calories. Then add in one or more snacks during the day to fit your lifestyle and energy needs (see below).

First, decide how many calories you want your meals to provide each day. Are you trying to trim away a few extra pounds? Or do you simply want to maintain your present healthy weight? Your age, sex, body metabolism and active or inactive lifestyle determine how many calories of food energy you use each day. No two people are alike, so it is difficult to say exactly how much you need. Ask your dietitian if you're not sure.

The table below shows estimated energy needs at different stages in life (based on *Canada's Food Guide*, 2007).

ESTIMATED ENERGY REQUIREMENTS
CALORIES NEEDED PER DAY

AGE	SEX	SEDENTARY	LOW ACTIVE	ACTIVE
19 to 30 years	Males	2,500	2,700	3,000
	Females	1,900	2,100	2,350
31 to 50 years	Males	2,350	2,600	2,900
	Females	1,800	2,000	2,250
51 to 70 years	Males	2,150	2,350	2,650
	Females	1,650	1,850	2,100
71 and over	Males	2,000	2,200	2,500
	Females	1,550	1,750	2,000

If your goal is a healthier weight, the safest rate of weight loss is ½ to 2 pounds per week. Since one pound of body fat is equal to 3,500 calories, eating 500 calories a day less than your body needs should result in a weight loss of one pound per week. For a sedentary man over 50, with an estimated need for 2,150 calories per day, this would be 1,650 calories per day. For a low active woman over 50, who needs 1,850 calories per day, this would be 1,350 calories per day.

For 1,300 to 1,500 calories:
- Choose three meals (any breakfast, lunch and dinner)
  = 1,300 calories (and 11 CARB CHOICES)
- Choose three meals plus one 75-calorie snack
  = 1,375 calories (and 12 CARB CHOICES)

OR

- Choose three meals plus one 150-calorie snack
  = 1,450 calories (and 13 to 15 CARB CHOICES)

For 1,600 to 1,800 calories:
- Choose three meals plus two 150-calorie snacks OR three meals plus two 75-calorie snacks and one 150-calorie snack
  = 1,600 calories (and 13 to 15 CARB CHOICES)
- Choose three meals plus snacks worth 450 calories
  = 1,750 calories (and 16 to 18 CARB CHOICES). You get the idea.

The snack menus come in three different sizes:
- 75 calories when you just want a bite
- 150 calories to fit in mid-morning, afternoon or as a bedtime snack
- 300-calorie ones that are really small meals, great for snacks on active days

If you are a carbohydrate counter, you may want to consider how many carbs a snack contains as well. Look on the coloured tab of each snack menu for the CARB CHOICES.

When you eat is up to you and what's convenient. Most people find that spacing meals at even intervals over the day helps keep energy levels high—and hunger pangs low. This pattern of eating also helps you avoid hypoglycemia or low blood sugar, often a concern if you are on medication for diabetes.

When meals are more than four or five hours apart, snacks come in handy. A planned snack is better than an unplanned snack. Ask a dietitian to help you map out a meal plan based on your usual day's routine. If weekends are a lot different than weekdays, you may want to have another plan in mind for then. If you work different shifts, many people find it makes life simpler to have a plan in mind for each shift worked, as well as one for days off.

Everyone's different. Blood glucose monitoring may suggest that the amount of carbohydrate in the breakfast menus is a little too much for you and your insulin supply. No problem—just save part of breakfast and eat it a couple of hours later.

Each menu provides the following nutrients within a 10% deviation.

Menu	Carbohydrate (g)	Protein (g)	Fat (g)	Calories
Breakfast	45 g	18 g	8 g	318
Lunch	60 g	29 g	11 g	450
Dinner	60 g	36 g	14 g	505
Total	165 g	83 g	33 g	1273

SNACKS:

75 calories	10–15 g carbohydrate
150 calories	15–20 g carbohydrate
300 calories	35–45 g carbohydrate

A Month of Menus

The book's mix-and-match format allows you to plan meals to suit each particular day, at the same time keeping carbohydrate contents consistent. You probably won't use the numbered menus in sequence, although we tried to avoid repeating the same foods—except when you'd have leftovers on hand. You will, no doubt, find favourite menus to repeat over and over, or you may have the same breakfast two or three days in a row. It's your choice. Each menu describes one serving. Although most of the time you will be cooking for one or two, it is not always possible or practical to make just enough food for two servings. Many recipes yield more than this, providing you with extra portions that you can refrigerate or freeze.

The first menus you'll encounter either need no special recipes or only simple ones that are right in the menus. Further along, menus call for recipes found in the recipe chapters. Rather than grouping recipes as in a traditional cookbook, we have done so according to the meals in which they are used. So you'll find chapters for "Breakfast," "Lunch," "Dinner" and "Snacks." That way, all the recipes you need for a menu are together for easier use.

Although this book is geared towards meals for one or two people, we have also considered special occasions, such as when you're having company. So we have included the "Special Meals for Special Occasions" chapter, which is full of recipes that everyone will enjoy. Each menu in this chapter still fits into a meal plan.

FOOD CHOICE VALUES OF MENUS

Each breakfast menu provides about 350 calories* and is based on:

3 Carbohydrate choices (45 grams carbohydrate)
 2 Grains & Starches choices
 ½ Fruits choice
 ½ Milk & Alternatives choice
1 Meat & Alternatives choice
1 Fats choice

Each lunch menu provides about 450 calories* and is based on:

4 Carbohydrate choices (60 grams carbohydrate)
 2 Grains & Starches choices
 1 Fruits choice
 1 Milk & Alternatives choice
2 Meat & Alternatives choices
1 Fats choice

Each dinner menu provides about 500 calories* and is based on:

4 Carbohydrate choices (60 grams carbohydrate)
 2 Grains & Starches choices
 1 Fruits choice
 1 Milk & Alternatives choice
3 Meat & Alternatives choices
1 Fats choice

Snack menus provide:
- 75 calories (and **1 carbohydrate choice**)
- 150 calories (and **1 or 2 carbohydrate choices**)
- 300 calories (and **2 or 3 carbohydrate choices**)

*when using skim milk
For more about Food Choice Values, see Appendix I (page 216).

1 small peach (85 g), sliced OR fruit of your choice (page 224)

½ cup (125 mL) wheat bran flakes OR cereal of your choice (page 223) with
½ cup (125 mL) low-fat milk

1 slice whole wheat toast (30 g) with
1 tbsp (15 mL) each peanut butter and reduced sugar fruit spread

coffee or tea (with or without milk)

Stacked Turkey Sandwich:
    2 slices rye bread (60 g)
    thinly sliced cooked turkey (50 g)
    2 tsp (10 mL) light mayonnaise
    1 tbsp (15 mL) grainy mustard
    1 slice mild onion, sliced tomato and shredded lettuce

2 medium plums OR fruit of your choice (page 224)

1 cup (250 mL) low-fat milk

1 serving *Asian Grilled Pork Tenderloin* (page 122)

⅔ cup (150 mL) cooked parboiled brown rice with sliced green onion

Vegetable Kebabs:
    3 zucchini cubes, 2 cherry tomatoes, 2 mushrooms
Toss in 1 tbsp (15 mL) low-fat Italian dressing. Thread on skewer; broil until cooked.

⅔ cup (150 mL) sliced mango OR papaya with
½ cup (125 mL) low-fat vanilla yogurt with aspartame, sprinkled with ground nutmeg

coffee or tea (with or without milk)

assorted raw vegetables dipped in 2 tbsp (25 mL) *Curried Lentil Dip* (page 171)
OR ··
6 low-fat round tortilla chips (10 g) with ⅓ cup (75 mL) *Fresh Cucumber Salsa* (page 168)
OR mild or medium salsa
OR ··
½ cup (125 mL) O-shaped oat cereal with ¼ cup (50 mL) low-fat milk
OR ··
2 oblong whole wheat Melba toasts (10 g) with 2 tbsp (25 mL) *Salsa Cheese Spread* (page 172)

Waffles with Fresh Applesauce:
    1 small apple, sliced
    1 tsp (5 mL) water
    ground cinnamon and sweetener
Microwave for about 2 minutes. Serve over 2 frozen oat bran waffles (35 g each), toasted.

Café au Lait:
    ½ cup (125 mL) each strong hot coffee and hot low-fat milk

Peanut Butter and Banana Sandwich:
    2 slices whole wheat bread (60 g)
    1½ tbsp (22 mL) crunchy peanut butter
    1 small banana (100 g peeled), sliced

1 cup (250 mL) low-fat milk

1 whole wheat hamburger bun (50 g)
1 grilled hamburger patty (90 g) (½ cup/125 mL raw) with
tomato slices, sliced onion, mustard, lettuce

raw baby carrots with cucumber slices

¼ small cantaloupe with
½ cup (125 mL) light vanilla ice cream

coffee or tea (with or without milk)

2 gingersnaps (15 g)
coffee or tea (with or without milk)
OR ·
1 small banana (100 g peeled)
OR ·
3 cups (750 mL) air-popped popcorn
OR ·
1 medium apple (150 g)

1 cup (250 mL) cubed cantaloupe or honeydew melon OR fruit of your choice (page 224)

⅔ cup (150 mL) O-shaped toasted oat cereal OR cereal of your choice (page 223) with
½ cup (125 mL) low-fat milk

Egg in a Hole:
Cut a circle from 1 slice whole wheat toast (30 g). Melt ½ tsp (2 mL) soft margarine or butter in a non-stick skillet; place bread and bread round in skillet, break 1 egg into the hole, cover skillet and cook until egg is set; top with bread round.

coffee or tea (with or without milk)

1 medium (170 g) microwave-baked potato topped with
½ cup (125 mL) shredded light Cheddar cheese
sliced green onion

1 tangerine or mandarin orange OR fruit of your choice (page 224)

1 cup (250 mL) low-fat milk

1 serving *Calf's Liver with Onion and Herbs* (page 125)

1 small baked potato (85 g)

steamed green beans with chopped sweet red pepper
lemon wedge

Baked Apple:
   1 medium cored apple (150 g) sprinkled with cinnamon
Bake in 350°F (180°C) oven until tender. Serve warm with 1 tbsp (15 mL) low-fat plain yogurt and sweetener to taste.

⅔ cup (150 mL) low-fat milk

15 thin pretzel sticks (12 g)
Minted Limeade (page 170)
OR ···
¾ cup (175 mL/175 g) low-fat yogurt sweetened with aspartame
OR ···
1 large or 2 small mandarin oranges
OR ···
Pudding Sundae:
   ½ cup (125 mL) light vanilla pudding made with low-fat milk topped with 1 tbsp (15 mL)
   Light Raspberry Blueberry Spread (page 47) OR reduced sugar fruit spread

Pineapple and Cheese English Muffin:
    1 whole wheat English muffin (65 g), halved and toasted
    ¼ cup (50 mL) low-fat cottage cheese
    ground cinnamon
    1 slice fresh or canned pineapple, diced

1 serving light hot chocolate made with ¾ cup (175 mL) hot low-fat milk (see package directions)

Tomato, Bean and Mozzarella Salad:
    ½ cup (125 mL) drained and rinsed kidney beans
    2 tbsp (25 mL) diced part-skim mozzarella cheese
    4 cherry tomatoes, halved
    ¼ cup (50 mL) chopped cucumber
    1 green onion, minced, toss with
    1 tsp (5 mL) olive oil and 1 tbsp (15 mL) balsamic vinegar

4 whole wheat Melba toasts

I medium peach OR ½ cup (125 mL) sliced peaches canned in juice

1 cup (250 mL) low-fat milk

Pasta and Salad Dinner:
    ½ cup (125 mL) uncooked cheese tortellini cooked according to package directions, with
    ¾ cup (175 mL) *Tomato Mushroom Pasta Sauce* (page 131)
    2 tbsp (25 mL) grated Parmesan cheese

tossed green salad with
sliced mushrooms and cucumber with
1 tbsp (15 mL) low-fat Italian dressing

1 cup (250 mL) low-fat milk

1 medium orange
OR ···
1 *Chocolate Chip Oatmeal Cookie* (page 176) OR 1 wholemeal digestive cookie
½ cup (125 mL) low-fat milk
OR ···
⅔ cup (150 mL) cubed cantaloupe with
¼ cup (50 mL) vanilla yogurt with aspartame
OR ···
¾ cup (175 mL) *Frozen Melon Smoothie* (page 169)

½ small banana (50 g peeled), sliced
½ cup (125 mL) spoon-size shredded wheat cereal OR cereal of your choice (page 223) with
½ cup (125 mL) low-fat milk

1 soft cooked egg
1 slice whole wheat toast (30 g)

coffee or tea (with or without milk)

Greek Salad in a Pita (page 79)

1 sliced orange, sprinkled with ground cinnamon

1 cup (250 mL) low-fat milk

Chicken Breast in Wine Sauce:
   1 boneless, skinless chicken breast (100 g)
   1 tbsp (15 mL) white wine or chicken broth
   pinch dried oregano or basil
Bake in 350°F (180°C) oven for about 20 minutes. Sprinkle with chopped fresh parsley.

steamed cauliflower or broccoli with 2 tbsp (25 mL) *Creamy Ranch Dressing* (page 109)

½ cup (125 mL) cooked corn niblets

1 serving *Warm Cranberry Fall Fruit Compote* (page 147)
2 gingersnaps (15 g)
1 cup (250 mL) low-fat milk

1 medium pear
1 cube (20 g) light Swiss cheese

OR ⋯⋯⋯⋯⋯⋯⋯⋯⋯⋯⋯⋯⋯⋯⋯⋯⋯⋯⋯⋯⋯⋯

3 whole wheat soda crackers (10 g)
with 1 tbsp (15 mL) peanut butter

½ cup (125 mL) low-fat milk

BREAKFAST · 6

1 orange, sliced OR fruit of your choice (page 224)

Tomato Bagel Melt:
    1 small whole wheat bagel (60 g), halved and toasted. Top each half with
    1 tsp (5 mL) light mayonnaise
    tomato slices
    2 tbsp (30 mL) shredded mozzarella cheese made with skim milk
Broil until the cheese melts.

coffee or tea (with or without milk)

LUNCH · 6

1 serving *Spicy Beans on Toast* (page 64)

sliced tomato and cucumber

1 cup (250 mL) low-fat milk

DINNER · 6

Spanish Omelette:
    1 sliced green onion
    ½ small tomato, chopped
    2 medium mushrooms, sliced, with ½ tsp (2 mL) soft margarine or butter
Sauté for 5 minutes. Set aside.
    2 eggs beaten with 2 tbsp (25 mL) water
Cook in a non-stick skillet until the egg is set. Top with the cooked vegetables and fold over.

1 toasted cinnamon raisin English muffin (65 g)

½ cup (125 mL) sliced peaches canned in light syrup OR fruit of your choice (page 224)

1 cup (250 mL) low-fat milk

SNACKS · 6
1 CARB CHOICE
150 CALORIES

½ cup (125 mL) light ice cream

OR ···

1 *Oatmeal Date Muffin* (page 174)

coffee or tea (with or without milk)

½ red grapefruit OR fruit of your choice (page 224)

½ cup (125 mL) high-fibre wheat bran cereal OR cereal of your choice (page 223) with ½ cup (125 mL) low-fat milk

Breakfast Alaska:
    1 slice whole wheat toast (30 g), topped with 1 strip cooked, crumbled bacon-style turkey
    1 egg white beaten until stiff
Spoon the egg white over bacon, seal to the edge of the toast. Sprinkle with 1 tbsp (15 mL) grated Parmesan cheese. Bake in 350°F (180°C) oven for about 10 minutes or until golden.

coffee or tea (with or without milk)

1 serving *Seasonal Fruit Plate with Ricotta Cheese* (page 88)

½ toasted medium whole wheat bagel (45 g) with ½ tsp (2 mL) soft margarine or butter

coffee or tea (with or without milk)

Sautéed Shrimp:
    8–10 large shrimp (80 g), marinated for up to 2 hours in 1 tbsp (15 mL) orange juice,
        2 tsp (10 mL) chili sauce,1 small garlic clove, minced, 1 tsp (5 mL) canola oil,
        1 tsp (5 mL) minced gingerroot
Sauté in a non-stick skillet on medium heat until shrimp are pink and opaque.

⅔ cup (150 mL) cooked parboiled brown or white rice
steamed broccoli with lemon wedge
assorted salad greens with 1 tbsp (15 mL) *Warm Sherry Vinaigrette* (page 110)

½ cup (125 mL) seedless grapes OR fruit of your choice (page 224)
1 cup (250 mL) low-fat milk

2 oblong rye crackers (20 g) with
¼ cup (50 mL) *Salsa Cheese Spread* (page 172)

1 cup (250 mL) *Minted Limeade* (page 170) OR diet soft drink

OR ···

1 medium apple (150 g)
1 cube (25 g) light Cheddar cheese

BREAKFAST · 7

LUNCH · 7

DINNER · 7

SNACKS · 7
1 CARB CHOICE
150 CALORIES

1 mandarin orange OR fruit of your choice (page 224)

Creamy Rolled Oats:
> ¼ cup (50 mL) large-flake rolled oats cooked with ¾ cup (175 mL) water (see page 28 for cooking directions) with granulated brown low-calorie sweetener
> ½ cup (125 mL) low-fat milk

½ toasted cinnamon raisin English muffin (30 g) with
1 tbsp (15 mL) each light cream cheese and reduced sugar fruit spread

coffee or tea (with or without milk)

1 serving *Tuna Niçoise Salad* (page 80)

1 small crusty roll (30 g) with ½ tsp (2 mL) soft margarine or butter
1 pear OR ½ small papaya (150 g) with lime wedge OR fruit of your choice (page 224)

iced tea with lemon, sweetener, if desired

1 serving *Pork Chops Marinara with Mozzarella Cheese* (page 121)

Creamy Onion Fettucine:
> ⅔ cup (150 mL) cooked fettucine (40 g dry) with
> 2 tbsp (25 mL) light sour cream and chopped green onion

steamed spinach

1 cup (250 mL) assorted salad greens with
1 tbsp (15 mL) low-fat Italian dressing

1 peach sliced with ¼ cup (50 mL) blueberries

coffee or tea (with or without milk)

assorted raw vegetables with ¼ cup (50 mL) *Curried Lentil Dip* (page 171)

OR ···

½ toasted whole wheat English muffin (30 g) with
1 tbsp (15 mL) peanut butter

coffee or tea (with or without milk)

1 kiwi fruit, sliced OR fruit of your choice (page 224)

1 soft-cooked egg

1 toasted hot cross bun (50 g) with
1 tbsp (15 mL) reduced sugar fruit spread

Café au Lait:
  ½ cup (125 mL) each strong hot coffee and hot low-fat milk

Chicken in a Pita:
  1 whole wheat pita bread (65 g), halved
  ½ cup (125 mL) diced cooked chicken with
  1 tbsp (15 mL) light mayonnaise
  2 tbsp (25 mL) each diced sweet red pepper and cucumber
  shredded lettuce

¾ cup (175 mL) *Orange Stewed Rhubarb* (page 89) OR fruit of your choice (page 224)

1 cup (250 mL) low-fat milk

1 serving *Crispy Baked Chicken* (page 113)

1 serving *French-Style Green Peas with Lettuce* (page 136)

½ baked pepper squash

1 serving *Baked Sliced Apples* (page 148)

coffee or tea (with or without milk)

½ cup (125 mL) green or red seedless grapes
2 tbsp (25 mL) walnut halves (20 g)

OR ···

2 *Chocolate Chip Oatmeal Cookies* (page 176)

½ cup (125 mL) low-fat milk

1 orange, sliced OR fruit of your choice (page 224)

Cooked Multi-Grain Porridge:
  2 tbsp (25 mL) multi-grain cereal cooked with ½ cup (125 mL) water (see page 28 for cooking
    directions) with granulated brown low-calorie sweetener
  ½ cup (125 mL) low-fat milk

½ toasted whole wheat English muffin (30 g) with 2 tbsp (25 mL) light cream cheese and
1 tbsp (15 mL) reduced sugar fruit spread

coffee or tea (with or without milk)

1 cup (250 mL) *Shrimp Chowder* (page 57)

1 whole wheat roll (45 g) with
1 tsp (5 mL) soft margarine or butter
OR
1 piece *Herbed Cornbread* (page 173)

1 cup (250 mL) cubed honeydew or cantaloupe melon with lime wedge
    OR fruit of your choice (page 224)

coffee or tea (with or without milk)

Grilled or Broiled Salmon Fillet:
  1 salmon fillet (100 g), sprinkled with 1 tsp (5 mL) fresh lemon juice
  ¼ tsp (1 mL) grated lemon peel, freshly ground pepper
Broil or grill on medium-high for 10 minutes per inch (2.5 cm) thickness or until fish is opaque.

⅔ cup (150 mL) cooked parboiled brown or white rice
1 serving *Roasted Sweet Peppers with Parsley* (page 137)
steamed asparagus with balsamic vinegar

1 serving *Citrus Yogurt Jelly* (page 149) with 1 medium kiwi fruit, sliced

coffee or tea (with or without milk)

1 cup (250 mL) cubed melon OR ½ cup (125 mL) cut-up fresh or canned pineapple with
½ cup (125 mL) cottage cheese

OR ·

1 *Orange Date and Bran Muffin* (page 175)

coffee or tea (with or without milk)

½ cup (125 mL) blueberries OR fruit of your choice (page 224)
½ cup (125 mL) wheat bran flakes with ½ cup (125 mL) low-fat milk

Mushroom Omelette for One:
    ½ cup (125 mL) sliced mushrooms, ½ tsp (2 mL) soft margarine or butter
Sauté on medium heat in a small non-stick skillet. Set aside.
    1 egg beaten with 1 tbsp (15 mL) water
Cook in skillet until egg is set; top with the mushrooms and fold.
Serve on 1 slice whole wheat toast (30 g).

coffee or tea (with or without milk)

1 cup (250 mL) *Gingered Carrot Soup* (page 61)

½ toasted whole wheat English muffin (30 g) with
30g mozzarella cheese made with skim milk, sliced or shredded
Broil until cheese melts.

cherry tomatoes

1 medium apple (150 g) OR fruit of your choice (page 224)

1 cup (250 mL) low fat-milk

3 thin slices (60 g) lean roast pork loin

½ cup (125 mL) *Kasha and Red Pepper Pilaf* (page 129)

steamed green beans with ½ tsp (2 mL) soft margarine or butter

torn lettuce with 2 tbsp (25 mL) *Creamy Ranch Dressing* (page 109)

1 serving *Peach Cobbler* (page 151) with
¼ cup (50 mL) low-fat plain yogurt

coffee or tea (with or without milk)

1 *Autumn Pumpkin Cranberry Muffin* (page 42)

coffee or tea (with or without milk)

OR ···

2 tbsp (25 mL) dry-roasted peanuts (20 g)
2 tbsp (25 mL) raisins (20 g)

Summer Fruits with Yogurt:
    1 peach, sliced
    ¼ cup (50 mL) blueberries topped with
    ⅓ cup (75 mL) low-fat plain yogurt
    ¼ cup (50 mL) high-fibre wheat bran cereal with psyllium

½ toasted cinnamon raisin bagel (30 g) with
1 tbsp (15 mL) peanut butter

coffee or tea (with or without milk)

1 serving *Grilled Cheese French Toast Sandwich* (page 66)

2 slices fresh or canned pineapple with
⅓ cup (75 mL) *Orange Yogurt Sauce* (page 90)

1 serving light hot chocolate made with water (see package directions)
OR
½ cup (125 mL) low-fat milk

1 serving *Tomato and Basil Baked Eggs* (page 130)

steamed broccoli

1 serving *Oranges in Yogurt Cream* (page 152)

coffee or tea (with or without milk)

½ toasted whole wheat English muffin (30 g) with
2 tbsp (25 mL) cottage cheese
dash ground cinnamon
sliced strawberries OR 1 tbsp (15 mL) reduced sugar fruit spread

OR ···

2 *Peanut Butter Granola Cookies* (page 177)
½ cup (125 mL) low-fat milk

½ small banana (50 g peeled), sliced

1½ cups (375 mL) puffed wheat cereal OR cereal of your choice (page 223) with
½ cup (125 mL) low-fat milk

1 poached egg on
1 slice whole wheat toast (30 g)

coffee or tea (with or without milk)

1 serving *Curried Turkey Salad* (page 81) with
¼ cantaloupe (160 g)

1 *Buttermilk Tea Biscuit* (page 76) OR 1 serving *Red Pepper Foccacia* (page 77)

2 low-fat spice cookies (20 g)

1 cup (250 mL) low-fat milk

1 slice *Beef and Vegetable Meat Loaf* (page 119)

1 cup (250 mL) mashed squash

steamed snow peas

Pear Hélène:
½ cup (125 mL) light chocolate pudding made with low-fat milk served over
1 pear half canned, in juice

½ cup (125 mL) low-fat milk

1½ cups (375 mL) *Frozen Melon Smoothie* (page 169)

OR ···

1 shredded wheat biscuit OR cereal of your choice (page 223) with
½ cup (125 mL) low-fat milk

½ cup (125 mL) unsweetened applesauce

Bagel with Cheddar Cheese:
    1 small whole wheat bagel (60 g), halved, with sliced light Cheddar cheese (30 g)
Broil or microwave until cheese melts.

Café au Lait:
    ½ cup (125 mL) each strong hot coffee and hot low-fat milk

1 serving *Tomato and Goat Cheese Crostini* (page 69)

tossed green salad with 1 tbsp (15 mL) *Balsamic Vinaigrette* (page 84)

1 serving *Baked Fruit with Raspberry Sauce* (page 91)

Café au Lait:
    ½ cup (125 mL) each strong hot coffee and hot low-fat milk

Dilled Halibut:
    1 halibut fillet (100 g), sprinkled with 1 tsp (5 mL) fresh lemon juice and
    ¼ tsp (1 mL) dried dill weed
Broil or grill on medium-high for 10 minutes per inch (2.5 cm) thickness or until fish is opaque.

1 serving *Fresh Cucumber Salsa* (page 168)
½ cup (125 mL) cooked corn niblets
steamed broccoli

1 serving *Nutty Mango Crisp* (page 153)

1 cup (250 mL) low-fat milk

1 piece warmed *Herbed Cornbread* (page 173)

coffee or tea (with or without milk)

OR ·

⅓ cup (75 mL) *Power Granola* (page 31) with ½ cup (125 mL) low-fat milk

½ cup (125 mL) cut up cantaloupe or watermelon OR fruit of your choice (page 224)

Breakfast Tortilla Sandwich:
  2 small whole wheat flour tortillas (34 g each), microwaved for about 20 seconds
  1 egg, beaten with 1 tbsp (15 mL) water
Cook egg in a non-stick skillet until set. Fill warm tortillas with egg, top with mild or medium salsa.

Café au Lait:
  ½ cup (125 mL) each strong hot coffee and hot low-fat milk

1 cup (250 mL) *Turkey Minestrone* (page 60)

2 oblong rye crisp breads (20 g) OR 1 slice rye bread (30 g)
2 tbsp (25 mL) light cream cheese

2 medium plums OR fruit of your choice (page 224)

1 cup (250 mL) low-fat milk

1 serving *Roast Cornish Hen* (page 118) with
2 tbsp (25 mL) *Light Cranberry Sauce* (page 111)

1 serving *Scalloped Sweet and White Potatoes* (page 138)

½ cup (125 mL) green peas with sliced mushrooms, sautéed in
½ tsp (2 mL) soft margarine or butter

1 serving *Sautéed Spiced Fruits* (page 154)

coffee or tea (with or without milk)

3 graham wafers (20 g)

1 serving light hot chocolate made with water (see package instructions)

OR ·

½ cup (125 mL) fresh or frozen blueberries, topped with
½ cup (125 mL) low-fat plain yogurt
¼ cup (50 mL) high-fibre wheat bran cereal with psyllium

1 small peach OR fruit of your choice (page 224)

½ cup (125 mL) spoon-size shredded wheat OR cereal of your choice (page 223) with ½ cup (125 mL) low-fat milk

French Toast:
  1 egg, beaten with ⅓ cup (75 mL) low-fat milk, poured over 1 slice whole wheat bread (30 g) until all liquid is absorbed.
Cook on medium heat in a non-stick skillet in ½ tsp (2 mL) melted soft margarine or butter until golden brown. Sprinkle with ground cinnamon.

coffee or tea (with or without milk)

Tuna Sandwich:
  1 whole wheat pita bread (65 g), halved, with
  ½ cup (125 mL) *Tuna Sandwich Filling* (page 72)
  leaf lettuce

1 medium pear or apple OR fruit of your choice (page 224)

1 cup (250 mL) low-fat milk

1 lean sirloin steak (110 g boneless), broiled or barbecued

1 small baked potato (85 g cooked) topped with 2 tbsp (25 mL) light sour cream, chopped chives

Sautéed Mushrooms:
  8 medium mushrooms, sautéed in non-stick skillet in
  1 tsp (5 mL) soft margarine or butter, sprinkled lightly with
  pepper and dried tarragon

tomato slices

1 serving *Cranberry Almond Crumble* (page 155)

1 cup (250 mL) low-fat milk

Creamy Rolled Oats:
  ¼ cup (50 mL) large-flake rolled oats cooked with ¾ cup (175 mL) water (see page 28 for cooking directions) with granulated brown low-calorie sweetener
  ½ cup (125 mL) low-fat milk
OR ·
Cinnamon Toast:
  1 slice whole wheat toast (30 g) spread with 1 tsp (5 mL) soft margarine or butter
  ground cinnamon, granulated brown low-calorie sweetener

½ cup (125 mL) low-fat milk

Double serving (½ cup/125 mL dry mix) *Hot Cereal with Multi-Grains* (page 28) cooked with ½ medium apple, chopped, and dash cinnamon, with granulated brown low-calorie sweetener

1 cup (250 mL) low-fat milk

coffee or tea (with or without milk)

1 serving *Baked Bean Tortillas* (page 65)

sliced cucumber and cherry tomatoes

1 serving *Naturally Fresh Fruit Sorbet* (page 92)

1 cup (250 mL) low-fat milk

1 serving *Herbed Chicken and Vegetables* (page 114)

⅔ cup (150 mL) cooked parboiled brown rice

baby spinach leaves tossed with 2 tbsp (25 mL) pomegranate seeds and 1 tbsp (15 mL) *Warm Sherry Vinaigrette* (page 110)

1 serving *Raspberry Bavarian* (page 156)

coffee or tea (with or without milk)

1 frozen oat bran waffle (35 g) toasted, with
¼ cup (50 mL) *Honey Yogurt Sauce* (page 44)

coffee or tea (with or without milk)

OR ·

½ serving (2 tbsp/25 mL) *Salsa Cheese Spread* (page 172) with
2 thin slices French baguette (30 g)

½ cup (125 mL) low-fat milk

1 serving *Fruit Muesli* (page 30)

1 poached egg on
1 slice whole wheat toast (30 g)

coffee or tea (with or without milk)

3 *Cottage Cheese Pancakes* (page 87) with
⅓ cup (75 mL) *Strawberry Orange Sauce* (page 45)

1 *Orange Bran Flax Muffin* (page 43)

coffee or tea (with or without milk)

Grilled Sausage with Mustard Glaze:
   1 low-fat sausage (125 g)
   ½ tsp (2 mL) honey Dijon mustard
Cook sausage in water for 10 minutes; drain. Sauté in a non-stick skillet until brown. Spread with honey mustard and serve.

1 microwave-baked sweet potato (150 g)

1 serving *Apple Cabbage Slaw* (page 107)

1 serving *Balsamic Strawberries* (page 157)

coffee or tea (with or without milk)

½ cup (125 mL) bran flakes OR cereal of your choice (page 223) with
½ small banana (50 g peeled), sliced
½ cup (125 mL) low-fat milk

OR ···

½ cup (125 mL) *Microwave Cranberry Applesauce* (page 93)
2 low-fat spice cookies (20 g)

1 peach or nectarine, sliced OR fruit of your choice (page 224)

⅓ cup (75 mL) *Power Granola* (page 31) with
½ cup (125 mL) low-fat milk

1 slice whole wheat toast (30 g) with
1 tbsp (15 mL) crunchy peanut butter

coffee or tea (with or without milk)

1 serving *Open-Face Baked Cheese Tomato Tortillas* (page 73)
¼ cup (50 mL) *Fresh Tomato Salsa* (page 74)

1 cup (250 mL) cubed fresh pineapple OR fruit of your choice (page 224)

2 low-fat spice cookies (20 g)

1 cup (250 mL) low-fat milk

Baked Rainbow Trout:
   1 fillet rainbow trout (100 g), topped with 1 tbsp (15 mL) light mayonnaise,
      1 tsp (5 mL) fresh lemon juice, ¼ tsp (1 mL) grated lemon peel, freshly ground pepper
Bake on a non-stick pan in 400°F (200°C) oven for 10 minutes per inch (2.5 cm) thickness or until opaque.

1 serving *Baked Layered Tomato and Potato Slices* (page 139)
steamed snow peas with lemon
cooked sliced carrots

1 serving *Rosy Poached Pears* (page 158)

coffee or tea (with or without milk)

1 cup (250 mL) *Curried Vegetable and Split Pea Soup* (page 63)
6 whole wheat soda crackers (20 g)
1 cube (25 g) light Cheddar cheese

½ peach or ½ cup (125 mL) raspberries OR fruit of your choice (page 224)

1 shredded whole wheat biscuit OR cereal of your choice (page 223) with ½ cup (125 mL) low-fat milk

1 *Flax and Oat Bran Blueberry Muffin* (page 40)
½ tsp (2 mL) soft margarine or butter

coffee or tea (with or without milk)

1 serving *Toasted Vegetable Frittata Sandwich* (page 67)

Microwave-Baked Banana:
  1 small sliced banana (100 g peeled) topped with
  2 tbsp (25 mL) plain low-fat yogurt spiced with cinnamon and
  1 tsp (5 mL) granulated brown low-calorie sweetener
Microwave on high (100%) for about 1 minute.

1 cup (250 mL) low-fat milk

1 serving *Polenta Pie with Tomato Mushroom Pasta Sauce* (page 134)

mixed green salad with 1 tbsp (15 mL) *Balsamic Vinaigrette* (page 84)

½ cup (125 mL) low-fat frozen yogurt with
½ cup (125 mL) fresh or frozen raspberries

coffee or tea (with or without milk)

1 split and toasted hot cross or raisin bun (50 g) with
2 tbsp (25 mL) light cream cheese with grated orange peel, vanilla extract and sweetener to taste

coffee or tea (with or without milk)

1 serving *Baked Eggnog French Toast with Fruit Sauce* (page 37)

coffee or tea (with or without milk)

1 cup (250 mL) *Hearty Vegetable Barley Soup* (page 62)

1 cube (45 g) light Cheddar cheese
7 whole wheat soda crackers (21 g)

1 mandarin orange OR fruit of your choice (page 224)

1 cup (250 mL) low-fat milk

1 serving *Beef Strip Loin with Wine Sauce* (page 120)

¾ cup (175 mL) *Provençal Garlic Potatoes* (page 140)

cooked sliced beets, with beet greens if desired

assorted green salad tossed with 1 tbsp (15 mL) low-calorie dressing

1 serving *Pears with Raspberry Sauce* (page 159)

coffee or tea (with or without milk)

1 medium apple (150 g)
¼ cup (50 mL) dry roasted peanuts (35 g)
1 tbsp (15 mL) raisins (10 g)

½ cup (125 mL) orange and grapefruit sections

1 serving (¼ cup/50 mL dry mix) *Hot Cereal with Multi-Grains* (page 28) with granulated brown low-calorie sweetener
½ cup (125 mL) low-fat milk

½ toasted whole wheat English muffin (30 g) with
1 tbsp (15 mL) peanut butter

coffee or tea (with or without milk)

Salmon Pecan Sandwich:
    1 halved medium whole wheat bagel (90 g) with
    ½ cup (125 mL) *Salmon Pecan Sandwich Filling* (page 71)

sliced tomato and cucumber

1 cup (250 mL) *Lime Watermelon Splash* (page 56)
OR
½ cup (125 mL) low-sodium vegetable juice cocktail

1 serving *Mustard Baked Salmon* (page 127)

⅓ cup (75 mL) *Baked Rice* (page 141)

1 serving *Minted Carrots and Snow Peas* (page 142)

1 serving *Strawberry Bavarian* (page 156)

coffee or tea (with or without milk)

2 *Rhubarb Bran Muffins* (page 175)

coffee or tea (with or without milk)

1 cup (250 mL) whole strawberries OR fruit of your choice (page 224)

1 shredded whole wheat biscuit OR cereal of your choice (page 223) with ½ cup (125 mL) low-fat milk

1 *Bacon and Egg Muffin* (page 41)

coffee or tea (with or without milk)

1 serving *Vegetable Cheese Pie* (page 86)

cherry tomatoes

1 large kiwi fruit OR fruit of your choice (page 224)

1 cup (250 mL) low-fat milk

2 lean lamb chops (220 g with bone) sprinkled with chopped fresh or dried mint, and broiled

1 serving *Roasted Lemon Potatoes* (page 143)

steamed green beans OR Brussels sprouts

1 serving *Tuscan Tomato Salad* (page 108)

1 serving *Fresh Fruit Jelly* (page 160) with ¼ cup (50 mL) *Honey Yogurt Sauce* (page 44)

coffee or tea (with or without milk)

Tortilla Sandwich:
  2 small whole wheat flour tortillas (34 g each), microwaved for about 20 seconds
  1 egg, beaten with 1 tbsp (15 mL) water
Cook egg in a non-stick skillet until set. Fill warm tortillas with egg, top with mild or medium salsa.

coffee or tea (with or without milk)

½ red grapefruit OR fruit of your choice (page 224)

3 *Baker's Dozen Morning Multi-Grain Pancakes* (page 34) with
⅓ cup (75 mL) *Strawberry Orange Sauce* (page 45)

coffee or tea (with or without milk)

½ cup (125 mL) *Roasted Tomato Pasta Sauce* (page 75)
1 cup (250 mL) cooked fettucine (40 g dry)
2 tbsp (25 mL) grated Parmesan cheese

tossed green salad with 1 tbsp (15 mL) *Balsamic Vinaigrette* (page 84) OR low-calorie dressing

1 cup (250 mL) low fat milk

1 serving *Cheese and Spinach Lasagne Roll-Ups* (page 133)

large romaine lettuce salad tossed with 2 tbsp (25 mL) *Balsamic Vinaigrette* (page 84)

2 slices fresh or canned pineapple with juice

1 cup (250 mL) low-fat milk

4 *Peanut Butter Granola Cookies* (page 177)

1 cup (250 mL) low-fat milk

½ cup (125 mL) cut-up cantaloupe OR fruit of your choice (page 224)

3 sections *Make-Ahead Crispy Belgian Waffles* (page 35) with
¼ cup (50 mL) *Honey Yogurt Sauce* (page 44)

coffee or tea (with or without milk)

Crustless Asparagus Quiche For One (page 85)

tomato slices

1 medium pear OR 2 pear halves canned in light syrup

2 graham wafers (15 g)

coffee or tea (with or without milk)

1 serving *Veal Cutlet in Tomato Basil Sauce* (page 124)

1 serving *Corn and Zucchini Sauté* (page 144)

½ small banana (50 g peeled) sliced with ½ cup (125 mL) orange sections

1 cup (250 mL) low-fat milk

1 whole wheat English muffin (65 g), split and toasted, with
1 tbsp (15 mL) peanut butter

1 serving light hot chocolate made with water (see package instructions)

1 serving *Power Granola Fruit Parfait* (page 33)

1 slice whole wheat toast (30 g) with
2 tbsp (25 mL) *No-Cook Pineapple Orange Marmalade* (page 46) OR 1 tbsp (15 mL) reduced sugar fruit spread

coffee or tea (with or without milk)

Individual Turkey Quesadilla (page 78)

carrot and celery sticks

2 slices fresh or canned pineapple with juice OR fruit of your choice (page 224)

1 cup (250 mL) low-fat milk

1 cup (250 mL) *Mushroom Squash Bisque* (page 112)

2 slices (60 g) lean roast beef with 1 tbsp (15 mL) horseradish

⅔ cup (150 mL) *Cauliflower Potato Mash* (page 145) with
1 tsp (5 mL) soft margarine or butter

1 cup (250 mL) cooked peas and carrots

1 serving *Balsamic Peaches* (page 157)

coffee or tea (with or without milk)

3 *Tomato and Goat Cheese Crostini* (page 69)

1 cup (250 mL) low-fat milk

1 cup (250 mL) sliced strawberries and ¼ cup (50 mL) blueberries

1 serving *Overnight Ham and Asparagus Bake* (page 39)

½ whole wheat English muffin (30 g) with
1 tbsp (15 mL) *Light Raspberry Blueberry Spread* (page 47) OR reduced sugar fruit spread

coffee or tea (with or without milk)

1 cup (250 mL) *Curried Vegetable and Split Pea Soup* (page 63)

4 oblong whole wheat Melba toasts with
2 tbsp (25 mL) light cream cheese OR 2 tbsp (25 mL) *Salsa Cheese Spread* (page 172)

½ cup (125 mL) seedless grapes OR fruit of your choice (page 224)

1 cup (250 mL) low-fat milk

1 serving *Baked Fish en Papillote with Tomatoes and Herbs* (page 128)

1 small boiled new potato (85 g cooked) with chopped parsley

cooked baby carrots

Asian Steamed Green Beans:
    1 cup (250 mL) green beans steamed until crisp-tender with
    1 tsp (5 mL) soy sauce and ½ tsp (2 mL) minced gingerroot

1 serving *Mixed Berry Crisp* (page 153) with
¼ cup (50 mL) low-fat vanilla yogurt with aspartame

coffee or tea (with or without milk)

2 slices whole wheat bread (30 g each) OR 1 whole wheat pita bread (60 g) with
½ cup (125 mL) *Tuna Sandwich Filling* (page 72) OR *Salmon Pecan Sandwich Filling* (page 71)

1 cup (250 mL) low-fat milk

1 tangerine OR fruit of your choice (page 224)

½ cup (125 mL) wheat bran flakes OR cereal of your choice (page 223) with ½ cup (125 mL) low-fat milk

1 *Autumn Pumpkin Cranberry Muffin* (page 42)

1 cube (25 g) light Cheddar cheese

coffee or tea (with or without milk)

1 serving *Chicken Caesar and Potato Salad* (page 82) over shredded romaine lettuce

1 crusty whole wheat roll (30 g) with 1 tsp (5 mL) soft margarine or butter

½ cup (125 mL) *Microwave Cranberry Applesauce* (page 93)

1 cup (250 mL) low-fat milk

1⅔ cups (400 mL) *Pasta with Chickpea Garlic Sauce* (page 135)
2 tbsp (25 mL) grated Parmesan cheese

torn spinach, sliced mushrooms and red onion with 1 tbsp (15 mL) *Balsamic Vinaigrette* (page 84)

1 cup (250 mL) low-fat milk

2 *Buttermilk Tea Biscuits* (page 76) with
2 tbsp (25 mL) *No-Cook Pineapple Orange Marmalade* (page 46) OR 1 tbsp (15 mL) reduced sugar fruit spread

Café au Lait:
   ½ cup (125 mL) each strong hot coffee and hot low-fat milk

1 serving *Oven Puff Pancakes with Poached Apple Slices* (page 36)

Café au Lait:
½ cup (125 mL) each strong hot coffee and hot low-fat milk

1 serving *Cheesy Eggs and Asparagus on Toast* (page 70)

1 sliced kiwi fruit with 1 sliced orange OR fruit of your choice (page 224)

1 cup (250 mL) low-fat milk

1 cup (250 mL) *Sausage and Sweet Potato Chili* (page 123)

steamed spinach with 1 tsp (5 mL) each soft margarine or butter and fresh lemon juice

Fresh Fruit Cup:
¼ cup (50 mL) sliced strawberries
¼ cup (50 mL) halved green grapes
¼ cup (50 mL) honeydew melon cubes

2 *Chocolate Chip Oatmeal Cookies* (page 176) OR 2 digestive cookies

1 cup (250 mL) low-fat milk

½ cup (125 mL) *Curried Lentil Dip* (page 171) with
1 whole wheat pita bread (60 g), warmed, torn into pieces

½ cup (125 mL) cut up honeydew melon with lime OR fruit of your choice (page 224)

Creamy Rolled Oats:
 ¼ cup (50 mL) large-flake rolled oats cooked with ¾ cup (175 mL) water (see page 28 for cooking directions) with granulated brown low-calorie sweetener
 ½ cup (125 mL) low-fat milk

1 *Orange Bran Flax Muffin* (page 43)

coffee or tea (with or without milk)

1 serving *Tomato and Black Bean Salad* (page 83)

1 whole wheat roll (30 g) with ½ tsp (2 mL) soft margarine or butter

1 small banana (100 g peeled) OR fruit of your choice (page 224)

1 cup (250 mL) low-fat milk

2 slices (60g) *Roast Turkey Breast* with ½ cup (125 mL) *Dressing* (page 115)

2 tbsp (25 mL) *Light Cranberry Sauce* (page 111)

¼ cup (50 mL) *Light Turkey Gravy* (page 117)

1 serving *Cardamom-Scented Rutabaga* (page 146)

½ cup (125 mL) green peas

1 serving *Gingered Fruit Parfait* (page 161)

coffee or tea (with or without milk)

Toasted Tomato and Cheese Sandwich:
 2 slices toasted whole wheat bread (30 g each) with 1 tsp (5 mL) light mayonnaise, mozzarella cheese made with skim milk (30 g), sliced or shredded, and sliced tomato

1 cup (250 mL) low-fat milk

A Birthday Celebration (serves 4 or more)

1 cup (250 mL) *Rhubarb Punch* (page 184)
1 serving *Poached Chicken Breast* (page 185)
3 tbsp (45 mL) *Cranberry Citrus Coulis* (page 186)
steamed snow peas and julienned carrots
baby spinach leaves with 1 tbsp (15 mL) *Orange Vinaigrette* (page 187)

1 serving *Ice Cream Birthday Cake* (page 188)

coffee or tea (with or without milk)

Dinner with Friends (serves 4)

1 serving *Thai Peppered Shrimp with Leeks* (page 190)
1 serving *Stir-Fried Vegetables* (page 191)
½ cup (125 mL) *Fragrant Rice* (page 192)

⅓ cup (75 mL) *Mango Mint Sorbet* (page 193)

coffee or tea (with or without milk)

Gourmet Buffet Dinner (serves 6)

sparkling mineral water with a slice of lime
1 serving *Beef Burgundy* (page 194)
steamed thin green beans
sliced tomatoes with fresh basil

1 serving *Mocha Soufflé Dessert* (page 195) with
    ¼ small sliced banana and ½ cup (125 mL) sliced strawberries

coffee or tea (with or without milk)

A Spring Brunch (serves 4)

1 cup (250 mL) honeydew melon balls with lime juice and low-calorie sweetener, if needed
1 serving *Three Cheese Mushroom Risotto* (page 196)
1 cup (250 mL) sliced zucchini and 1 clove minced garlic sautéed in 1 tsp (5 mL) olive oil.
Season to taste with dried basil and freshly ground pepper.

1 cup (250 mL) *Balsamic Strawberries* (page 157)

Café au Lait:
    ½ cup (125 mL) each strong hot coffee and hot low-fat milk

A Spanish Lunch (serves 4)

1 serving *Gazpacho* (page 198)
1 serving *Tortilla Española* (page 199) with ¼ cup (50 mL) *Fresh Tomato Salsa* (page 74)
1 serving *Lemon Flan* (page 200)

Café con Leche:
 ½ cup (125 mL) each strong hot coffee and hot low-fat milk

A Romantic Dinner (serves 2)

1 cup (250 mL) *Golden Harvest Soup* (page 201)
1 serving *Roast Cornish Hen with Wild Rice Dressing* (page 202)
1 cup (250 mL) baby green peas

1 serving *Raspberry Fool* (page 203)

coffee or tea (with or without milk)

Passover Seder (serves 6)

Vegetable crudités
1 serving *Chicken and Matzo Ball Soup* (page 204)
1 cup (250 mL) *Spinach and Orange Salad* (page 205)
3 slices (90 g) *Spiced Beef Brisket* (page 206)
6 spears *Oven-Roasted Asparagus* (page 207)
1 serving *Potato Kugel* (page 208)

1 serving *Lemon Passover Cake* (page 209) with
 ½ cup (125 mL) sliced strawberries and ½ ripe kiwi fruit, quartered and diced,
 sweetened if desired, and chopped fresh mint (optional)

Harvest Thanksgiving (serves 6)

2 slices (60 g) *Roast Turkey Breast* (page 115)
½ cup (125 mL) *Vegetable Bread Stuffing* (page 210)
¼ cup (50 mL) *Light Turkey Gravy* (page 117)
2 tbsp (25 mL) *Fresh Cranberry Chutney* (page 212)
½ cup (125 mL) *Turnip Potato Purée* (page 213)
steamed broccoli with lemon wedge

1 serving *Spicy Pumpkin Pie* (page 214) with 2 tbsp (25 mL) light vanilla ice cream

coffee or tea (with or without milk)

BREAKFAST

RECIPES	CARBS	PAGE
Hot Cereal with Multi-Grains	1	28
Fruit Muesli	2	30
Power Granola	1	31
Power Granola Fruit Parfait	2	33
Baker's Dozen Morning Multi-Grain Pancakes	2	34
Make-Ahead Crispy Belgian Waffles	2	35
Oven Puff Pancakes with Poached Apple Slices	2½	36
Baked Eggnog French Toast with Fruit Sauce	3	37
Overnight Ham and Asparagus Bake	1	39
Flax and Oat Bran Blueberry Muffins	1	40
Bacon and Egg Muffins	1	41
Autumn Pumpkin Cranberry Muffins	1	42
Orange Bran Flax Muffins	1	43
Honey Yogurt Sauce	½	44
Strawberry Orange Sauce	½	45
No-Cook Pineapple Orange Marmalade	Extra	46
Light Raspberry Blueberry Spread	Extra	47

A HEALTHY START TO YOUR DAY

Did you know the word breakfast comes from *break* (meaning "to stop or interrupt") and *fast* (meaning "to go without food")? How apt. By morning, having fasted for 8 to 12 hours, your brain and muscles need a fresh supply of glucose energy. Eating a balanced breakfast helps your body refuel. You'll concentrate better, solve problems more effectively, have the energy you need to get through your morning without yielding to mid-morning hunger pangs, and have better control of your weight. Furthermore, studies show that breakfast eaters consume less fat and more nutrients each day than breakfast skippers. A healthy breakfast is truly a healthy start to the day.

Those of you who have diabetes shouldn't even think of skipping breakfast. If you have type 2 diabetes, you may have noticed your blood glucose is often higher before breakfast than before other meals—and eating breakfast helps bring blood glucose back to more normal levels.

In addition to the health aspects of breakfast, this first meal of the day can be an experience rich in flavours and variety. Our recipes and menus will help you achieve great breakfasts that are both enjoyable and healthy. Make breakfast so exciting that you could never think of missing it.

The Importance of Fruit

Fruits are packed with vitamins, minerals and fibre. They are also low in fat and calories and most have a low glycemic index (page 8). That's why fruits (and vegetables) make up the largest arc of the *Eating Well with Canada's Food Guide* rainbow. Those who eat at least one fruit (or vegetable) every meal and as a snack have a lower risk of heart disease, stroke, diabetes and some types of cancer. Our menus include plenty of fruit ideas to encourage you to eat more fruit, starting with breakfast.

We have a marvellous variety of healthy choices to choose from year-round, although fruits in season are usually more economical choices. The best vitamin C selections include oranges, grapefruit, tangerines, kiwi fruit, pineapple, honeydew melon, mangoes, apricots, cantaloupe and papaya. Fibre-rich, low-GI fruits include blueberries, strawberries, raspberries, apples, oranges, plums, pears and cherries. All are found in our menus. Realizing that you won't always have on

Opposite: Autumn Pumpkin Cranberry Muffins (page 42)

hand the fruit specified in a menu, we've included a list of alternate fruit portions in Appendix III (page 224), each equal to 1 Fruits or 1 Carb choice.

Fruit or juice?

"Eat your fruit, don't drink it." While fruit juices do contain vitamins and minerals, valuable fibre is lost during processing. Adding it back later isn't the same thing. Whole raw fruits contain both soluble and insoluble fibre. Since it takes more time to digest the fibre in raw fruit, the fruit's natural sugar is released more slowly and gradually than when you drink juice. This in turn results in a slower and more gradual increase in blood glucose levels. And there is an additional dividend: you'll feel more satisfied after eating a piece of fruit than after drinking a glass of juice. However, if fresh fruit is unavailable, orange juice is better than no fruit at all. If you do happen to drink a small glass of juice, sip it slowly.

WHOLE GRAIN CEREALS

Eating Well with Canada's Food Guide recommends that at least half our Grains & Starches choices each day be whole grain, and breakfast is a good place to start. Cereals are the foundation of a healthy breakfast. The whole grains found in cereals can be thought of as the "great regulators" because of their action on blood glucose and blood cholesterol, regularity and appetite. If ever there were a "magic bullet" food, cereals may be it.

Breakfast cereals containing whole grains, such as wheat, oats and barley, digest more slowly than refined rice or corn cereals. This results in a more gradual rise in blood glucose, giving you a more satisfied feeling. Wheat and oat bran (the outer layer of the whole kernel) add extra fibre to keep the digestive system healthy and to promote regularity. Eating oat bran or oatmeal as part of a low-fat diet helps lower cholesterol levels and may help reduce your risk for heart disease.

Being refined may be fine in some circles, but not if you're a breakfast cereal. Refining removes the fibre-rich bran coating of the grain, as well as the nutrient-packed germ, so the health benefits of whole grains are largely lost. Check labels; look for the words "whole grain" or "high source of fibre" when choosing a packaged ready-to-eat cereal. The first ingredient listed (the one that weighs the most) should be the whole grain part, not the sugar. The amount of fibre per serving is found on the Nutrition Facts panel. Compare when you shop. Our breakfast menus use a variety of packaged ready-to-eat whole grain and high-fibre cereals. Since everyone has a favourite, when you see the words "*or cereal of your choice*" in a menu, refer to Appendix II, page 223, for a listing of cereals with serving sizes equal to 1 Grains & Starches or 1 Carb choice. This is the amount of cereal containing 15 grams of available carbohydrate (total grams carbohydrate minus grams fibre).

Use our recipes for **Power Granola** (page 31) and **Hot Cereal with Multi-Grains** (page 28) to create your own "bulk mixes" rich in whole grain and bran. They are easy to prepare and all the ingredients can be found in bulk and health food stores, so you can buy just the amounts you need. A meal rich in whole grains can help you feel full and satisfied.

BREADS AND ALL THAT STUFF

Today there is an endless variety of breads, buns, bagels, muffins and the like available. When shopping for these bakery products, the words "whole wheat" and "high fibre" on the label suggest a wise choice. Those labelled "multi-grain," "100% wheat" or "seven grain" are often not whole grains but have white flour as their base. Colour is not an indication of whole grain content either, since molasses or caramel may have been added for colour. Enriched wheat flour is white flour with added nutrients. Check the ingredient list on labels and choose products listing whole grain flour first.

Having a small scale on your kitchen counter lets you judge serving sizes. 1 Grains & Starches choice (or 1 Carb choice) is equal to 1 ounce (30 grams) of bread containing 15 grams of carbohydrate (total minus fibre*). Some bagels, both whole wheat and white, weigh 2 ounces (60 grams), so they count as 2 Carb choices. Many weigh up to 4 ounces (120 grams) each, so they would count as 4 Carb choices. Since bagels tend not to be in labelled packages, it's best that you weigh them.

Margarine or butter?

Our breakfast menus don't use much of either. A good-tasting bread or warm muffin needs little if any margarine or butter for flavour—thus reducing both fat and calories. Non-stick pans can also help

Nutrition Facts
Per 70 g serving (2 slices)

Amount	% Daily Value
Calories 170	
Fat 2.7 g	4 %
Saturated 0.5 g + Trans 0 g	5 %
Cholesterol 0 mg	
Sodium 200 mg	8 %
Carbohydrate 36 g	13 %
Fibre 6 g	24 %
Sugars 3 g	
Protein 8 g	

Vitamin A	1 %	Vitamin C	0 %
Calcium	2 %	Iron	16 %

*Although fibre is listed as carbohydrate on a label, it does not raise blood glucose. So always subtract grams of fibre from grams of total carbohydrate to determine the grams of available carbohydrate that will increase blood glucose.

reduce both fat and calories. Each breakfast menu contains 1 Fats choice, but often it's hidden in other foods.

Non-hydrogenated soft tub margarine appears to be a better choice than butter because it contains much less saturated fat, but both have 45 calories per teaspoon. And whenever a recipe calls for melted margarine, use a healthy oil like canola or olive oil instead. But remember, even oils and margarine are fats that should be used in small amounts. Still want more flavour? Use a small amount of a reduced sugar fruit spread.

Fruit spreads with less sugar

A fruit spread labelled "lower in sugar" or "sugar reduced" must contain 25 per cent less sugar than a regular jam. A fruit spread labelled "no sugar added" has 50% less sugar than a regular jam. You may find more than one kind of spread at the grocery store. All will contain fruit sweetened with a combination of concentrated fruit juice (usually white grape juice) and a non-nutritive sweetener such as sucralose, aspartame or sorbitol. Check the Nutrition Facts panel for the *amount of carbohydrate per tablespoon (15 mL)*. To qualify as an Extra, a serving should not contain more than 5 grams of sugar and 20 calories. So read labels carefully. Remember that Extra doesn't mean "free."

Making your own fruit spreads can be rewarding, both for the taste and savings. Try **Light Raspberry Blueberry Spread** (page 47) and **No-Cook Pineapple Orange Marmalade** (page 46).

MILK AND YOGURT

Having fortified milk or soy beverages every day provides the nutrients that you need for healthy bones and optimal health and 2 cups (500 mL) of milk every day provides a lot of the vitamin D needed by most people (page 10). Fish, liver, and egg yolk are the only foods that naturally contain vitamin D.

Eating Well with Canada's Food Guide encourages us to use more milk and so do our menus. We have milk as a beverage, milk on cereal, milk as a recipe ingredient as well as milk in tea or coffee. In all instances, milk is no-fat skim milk or 1%, your choice. Or you may prefer a soy beverage, unflavoured and fortified with calcium and vitamin D. Either way, 1 cup (250 mL) milk is 1 Milk & Alternatives or 1 Carb choice.

FOOD SOURCES OF VITAMIN D

- 1 cup milk (vitamin D added) = 100 units
- 1 cup fortified soy beverage = 80 units
- 75 g herring or trout (cooked) = 156 units
- 75 g fresh salmon (cooked) = 225 units
- 75 g cooked salmon (canned) = 608 units
- 75 g Pacific sardines (canned) = 360 units
- 1 egg yolk = 25 units.

Along with its satisfying creamy texture and subtly tart flavour, yogurt offers an impressive nutritional profile of calcium, B vitamins and minerals. Many who cannot tolerate milk find they can eat yogurt. Low-fat yogurt appears in many of our menus. Try **Honey Yogurt Sauce** (page 44) with **Make-Ahead Crispy Belgian Waffles** (page 35). Or try **Power Granola Fruit Parfait** (page 33), where yogurt is layered with fresh fruit and granola.

THE BEST NUTRITIONAL BANG

Since breakfast is such an important meal, make it a healthy start to your day. For carbohydrate, fibre and vitamins B and C, include servings of fresh fruit along with whole grains, such as cereals, whole wheat toast or healthy muffins. Spread peanut butter on whole wheat toast for protein. Use a reduced sugar fruit spread instead of margarine or butter to reduce fat intake. Add milk to cereal for calcium and vitamin D. This kind of breakfast gives us nutrition while limiting total fat, saturated fat and sodium. Breakfast already has you on the road to healthy eating.

Hot Cereal with Multi-Grains

Breakfast Menus 17, 22

Prep • dry mix, 5 minutes
Cook • 1 serving, 3 to 5 minutes
Yield • 3¾ cups (925 mL)

Each Serving • ¹⁄₁₅ of recipe
        (¼ cup/50 mL dry mix;
        ¾ cup/175 mL cooked)
Carb choice   1
Fats choice   ½

Carbohydrate 19 g
    Fibre 3 g
Protein 4 g
Fat 2 g
    Saturated 0 g
Cholesterol 0 mg
Sodium 3 mg
Calories 111

It's hard to get the recommended daily amount of fibre without eating breakfast. This cereal mix is a source of fibre, has an attractive nutty taste and an overall "comfort food" appeal. All ingredients are found in bulk or health food stores and many supermarkets.

Dry Cereal Mix:

2 cups	large-flake rolled oats	500 mL
½ cup	rye flakes	125 mL
½ cup	cream of wheat or wheat flakes	125 mL
½ cup	oat bran	125 mL
¼ cup	flaxseeds (see Tips)	50 mL

In a large bowl, combine rolled oats, rye flakes, cream of wheat or wheat flakes and oat bran.

Place 2 tbsp (25 mL) flaxseeds in a small blender container or coffee grinder (see Tip). Process to a fine meal. Combine both the flaxseed meal and seeds with the rolled oat mixture. Store in a tightly sealed container.

Cooking Directions for Single Serving:

Microwave: In a microwave-safe serving bowl, combine ¼ cup (50 mL) cereal mix, ¾ cup (175 mL) water and a dash of vanilla or maple extract. Microwave, uncovered, on high (100%) for 2 minutes; stir. Microwave on low (30%) for 3 minutes. Let stand for 3 minutes. Stir and serve.

Stove top: In a saucepan, combine ¼ cup (50 mL) dry mix, ¾ cup (175 mL) water and a dash of vanilla or maple extract. Bring to a boil, reduce heat to medium-low; cook for 3 minutes or until desired consistency, stirring occasionally. Cover and remove from heat; let stand a few minutes. Stir and serve.

⊕ *Flaxseeds contain several essential nutrients, including calcium, iron, phosphorus and vitamin E, and are a source of omega-3 fatty acids. Generous amounts of both soluble and insoluble fibre are also present in flaxseed. But to reap the benefits of flaxseed, you'll need to grind it. Left whole, the seeds pass through the body undigested.*

- *Although you can buy ground flaxseed, flaxseeds last longer when stored whole and ground just before using.*
- *You can grind flaxseeds with a spice or coffee grinder. Simply process until the flaxseeds reach an almost flour-like consistency. One-quarter cup of whole flaxseeds yields about 6 tablespoons (⅓ cup/75 mL) of ground flaxseed.*
- *Because flaxseed is high in fat, store it (whether whole or ground) in the refrigerator or freezer to prevent spoilage. Whole seed will keep for up to one year, while ground flaxseed will keep for 3 to 4 months. Spoiled flaxseeds smell rancid.*

Fruit Muesli

Popular as a European breakfast, this version puts orange juice, fruit and rolled oats together for an easy start to the day. Muesli, mixed and refrigerated overnight, has the consistency of cooked cereal.

Prep · 10 minutes
Refrigerate · overnight
Yield · 2 servings

½ cup	large-flake rolled oats	125 mL
¼ cup	orange juice (see Tip)	50 mL
1 tbsp	chopped raisins	15 mL
1 tsp	liquid honey	5 mL
½ tsp	vanilla extract	2 mL
2	medium strawberries, sliced	2
¼ cup	mashed banana	50 mL
⅓ cup	low-fat plain yogurt or low-fat milk	75 mL

Each Serving · ½ of recipe

Carb choices	2
Fats choice	½

In a medium bowl, combine rolled oats, orange juice, raisins, honey and vanilla. Cover and refrigerate overnight.

In the morning, stir in strawberries, banana and yogurt. Spoon into cereal bowls and serve.

Carbohydrate 37 g
  Fibre 4 g
Protein 6 g
Fat 2 g
  Saturated 0 g
Cholesterol 1 mg
Sodium 31 mg
Calories 187

⊕ *Keep a can of concentrated orange juice in the freezer: 1 tbsp (15 mL) frozen concentrate with 3 tbsp (45 mL) water gives you the ¼ cup (50 mL) orange juice needed in this recipe. Keep the rest frozen for another use.*

POWER GRANOLA

Power-start your day with this rolled oat and bran cereal with flaxseed.

2 cups	large-flake rolled oats	500 mL
½ cup	natural bran	125 mL
⅓ cup	ground flaxseed (see Tip)	75 mL
⅓ cup	granular low-calorie sweetener with sucralose	75 mL
¼ cup	oat bran	50 mL
¼ cup	sliced almonds	50 mL
2 tsp	ground cinnamon	10 mL
⅓ cup	orange juice	75 mL
2 tbsp	liquid honey	25 mL
2 tsp	canola oil	10 mL
1 tsp	vanilla extract	5 mL
⅓ cup	dried cranberries, halved	75 mL

In a medium bowl, combine rolled oats, bran, flaxseed, sweetener, oat bran, almonds and cinnamon.

In a glass measure, combine orange juice, honey, oil and vanilla. Pour over rolled oat mixture; stir well.

Spray a baking pan with non-stick cooking spray. Spread the oat mixture in a thin layer on the pan. Bake in 300°F (150 °C) oven for 10 minutes; stir well. Bake an additional 8 minutes or until golden brown. Remove from oven; cool. Stir in cranberries and store in a tightly sealed container.

◉ To reap the benefits of flaxseed, you'll need to grind it. Left whole, the flaxseeds pass through the body undigested. Grind until it reaches an almost flour-like consistency. See pages 28–29 for more on flaxseeds.

◉ When a recipe contains both oil and honey, measure the oil first then the honey. The honey will slip out of the measuring cup or spoon more easily.

Breakfast Menus 19
Snack Menu 14

Prep • 15 minutes
Cook • about 18 minutes
Yield • 4⅓ cups (1.150 L)

Each serving • 1/14 of recipe
(⅓ cup/75 mL)
Carb choice   1
Fats choice   1

Carbohydrate 20 g
  Fibre 4 g
Protein 4 g
Fat 4 g
  Saturated 0 g
Cholesterol 0 mg
Sodium 3 mg
Calories 122

Power Granola Fruit Parfait

A breakfast fruit and granola parfait is such a great way to start the day.

1 cup	sliced fresh strawberries	250 mL
⅓ cup	low-fat plain yogurt	75 mL
⅓ cup	*Power Granola* (page 31)	75 mL
1	whole strawberry or slice of kiwi fruit	1
	mint leaf for garnish (optional)	

In a parfait or sherbet glass, layer half of the strawberries, half the yogurt and half the **Power Granola**; repeat layers.

Top with whole strawberry or slice of kiwi fruit and garnish with mint leaf.

VERY HIGH FIBRE

Breakfast Menu 26

Prep • 5 minutes
Yield • 1 serving

Each serving
Carb choices   2
Meat & Alternatives choice   ½
Fats choice   ½

Carbohydrate 39 g
  Fibre 8 g
Protein 9 g
Fat 5 g
  Saturated 0 g
Cholesterol 2 mg
Sodium 62 mg
Calories 222

BAKER'S DOZEN MORNING MULTI-GRAIN PANCAKES

Prep · 15 minutes
Cook · about 3 minutes per
pancake
Yield · 13 pancakes

Each Serving · 3 pancakes
Carb choices   2
Meat & Alternatives choice   ½
Fats choice   ½

Carbohydrate 33 g
  Fibre 4g
Protein 9 g
Fat 5 g
  Saturated 1 g
Cholesterol 3 mg
Sodium 312 mg
Calories 210

This flexible recipe provides a choice of different grains—cornmeal, millet or oats—as well as a choice of wheat germ or ground flaxseed. Serve with **Strawberry Orange Sauce** (page 45). The "baker's dozen" yield means leftovers to reheat in the toaster for another breakfast.

⅔ cup	whole wheat flour	150 mL
⅓ cup	all purpose flour	75 mL
¼ cup	large-flake rolled oats, cornmeal or millet	50 mL
3 tbsp	wheat germ or ground flaxseed	45 mL
2 tsp	granulated sugar	10 mL
1 tsp	baking powder	5 mL
½ tsp	baking soda	2 mL
1¼ cups	buttermilk (see Tip)	300 mL
2	egg whites or 1 egg	2
1 tbsp	canola oil	15 mL
1 tsp	vanilla extract	5 mL

In a bowl, combine flours, rolled oats, wheat germ, sugar, baking powder and soda. Stir to blend.

In a second bowl, whisk together buttermilk, egg whites, oil and vanilla. Pour into dry mixture; stir just until dry ingredients are moistened—don't worry about lumps (see Tip).

Heat a large non-stick skillet or griddle over medium heat until hot (a drop of water will sizzle). Spray with non-stick cooking spray. Drop batter by ¼ cup (50 mL) measure onto pan. Cook pancakes, turning once, for 1 to 2 minutes per side or until golden (see Tip).

⊕ *To replace buttermilk, simply add 1 tsp (5 mL) vinegar or lemon juice to each cup (250 mL) low-fat milk.*

⊕ *For the best pancakes, don't over-mix—they'll become tough. Let batter sit for a few minutes before cooking.*

⊕ *Be sure to cook all the batter. Batter refrigerated for even a day or two will yield thin, tough pancakes. Freeze extra cooked pancakes instead.*

MAKE-AHEAD CRISPY BELGIAN WAFFLES

This is such an easy way to have waffles for breakfast. The night before, make the batter, then in the morning add eggs and start cooking. Serve with **Honey Yogurt Sauce** (page 44) and a sprinkle of ground cinnamon.

½ cup	warm water	125 mL
½ tsp	dry yeast	2 mL
1 cup	warm low-fat milk	250 mL
2 tbsp	canola oil	25 mL
⅔ cup	all purpose flour	150 mL
⅔ cup	whole wheat flour	150 mL
½ tsp	granulated sugar	2 mL
1	egg	1
⅛ tsp	baking soda	0.5 mL

In a large bowl, combine warm water with yeast. Let stand for 5 minutes. Add warm milk, oil, flours and sugar. Beat until smooth and well blended. Cover the bowl; let stand at room temperature overnight. The batter will rise to double its size (see Tip).

Next morning, beat in the egg and baking soda. Using a preheated waffle iron, pour about ½ cup (125 mL) batter onto pan. Cover and bake until light comes on and waffles are crisp and golden. Serve at once (see Tip).

- *It's best to use a very large bowl since the batter does double in size.*
- *Keep cooked waffles warm in a low preheated oven until ready to serve. Leftover cooked waffles freeze well. Reheat in toaster for another breakfast.*

Breakfast Menu 25

....

Prep • 15 minutes plus overnight
Cook • about 4 minutes
    per waffle
Yield • three 7-inch
    (17 cm) waffles,
    each with 4 sections

....

Each serving • ¼ of recipe,
    3 sections

Carb choices	2
Meat & Alternatives choice	½
Fats choices	1½

....

Carbohydrate 34 g
  Fibre 3 g
Protein 10 g
Fat 10 g
  Saturated 1 g
Cholesterol 109 mg
Sodium 106 mg
Calories 265

....

Prep • 10 minutes
Cook • 12 minutes
Yield • 2 servings

Each Serving • ½ of recipe,
        1 pancake
Carb choices   1½
(2½ with ¾ cup/175 mL
poached sliced apples)
Meat & Alternatives choice   1
Fats choice   ½

Carbohydrate 26 g
    Fibre 4 g
Protein 12 g
Fat 6 g
    Saturated 2 g
Cholesterol 217 mg
Sodium 91 mg
Calories 204

....

Prep • 5 minutes
Cook • 5 minutes
Yield • about 1½ cups (375 mL)

Each Serving • ¾ cup (175 mL)
Carb choice   1

Carbohydrate 19 g
    Fibre 2 g
Protein 0 g
Fat 0 g
Cholesterol 0 mg
Sodium 1 mg
Calories 73

Oven Puff Pancakes with Poached Apple Slices

On an annual spring getaway to Niagara-on-the-Lake, Margaret and her husband were served this awesome pancake. Anita, the B & B hostess, brought it piping hot from the oven at just the right time, topped with poached sliced apples. Pancake and apple recipes can be easily doubled.

Pancakes:

½ cup	low-fat milk	125 mL
2	eggs	2
½ cup	whole wheat flour	125 mL
1 tsp	vanilla extract	5 mL
	Poached Apple Slices (below)	

Heat two 1-cup (250 mL) oval or round single-serve baking pans in 425°F (220°C) oven for 5 minutes or until they are hot. Lightly spray with non-stick cooking spray.

Meanwhile, in a small bowl, whisk together milk, eggs, flour and vanilla (mixture will be lumpy). Divide batter between dishes. Bake for 12 minutes or until puffy and golden. Turn oven off and allow pancakes to stay in oven for 5 minutes or until set.

Invert each onto warm serving plates and serve at once with apple slices.

Poached Apple Slices:

2	sliced cored peeled apples (2½ cups/625 mL)	2
¼ cup	water	50 mL
1	cinnamon stick	1
	low-calorie granular sweetener with sucralose, to taste	

In a small covered saucepan, on medium heat, cook apples, water and cinnamon stick for 5 minutes or until apples are tender. Remove and discard cinnamon stick. Add some sweetener if desired and serve warm over **Oven Puff Pancakes**.

Baked Eggnog French Toast with Fruit Sauce

This is a complete, nutritious breakfast in one recipe made with a lighter version of eggnog. It uses baguette slices rather than the larger French bread slices.

French Toast:

½ cup	*Blueberry* or *Peach Sauce* (page 38)	125 mL
½ cup	low-fat milk	125 mL
2	eggs	2
2 tsp	granular low-calorie sweetener with sucralose	10 mL
½ tsp	vanilla extract	2 mL
8	slices (¾-inch/2 cm) whole wheat French baguette (120 g total)	8
	ground cinnamon	

Lightly spray an 8-inch (20 cm) baking pan with non-stick cooking spray. Pour prepared fruit sauce in the bottom of the pan.

In a shallow bowl, whisk milk, eggs, sweetener and vanilla until blended. Dip each bread slice into the egg mixture; turn to coat both sides. Carefully remove each bread slice with a spatula and place over sauce. Pour any remaining egg mixture over bread. Sprinkle bread lightly with cinnamon.

Bake in a 450°F (230°C) oven for 18 minutes or until bread is golden and toasted. Remove from oven and serve.

HIGH FIBRE
Breakfast Menu 21

....

Prep · 10 minutes if sauce is already prepared
Cook · about 18 minutes
Yield · 2 servings, 8 slices

....

Each serving · ½ of recipe
Carb choices   3
Meat & Alternatives choice   1
Fats choices   1½

....

Carbohydrate 49 g
  Fibre 5 g
Protein 14 g
Fat 10 g
  Saturated 3 g
Cholesterol 218 mg
Sodium 463 mg
Calories 341

Fruit Sauce Only

....

Prep · about 5 minutes
Cook · 10 minutes
Yield · ½ cup (125 mL)

Each Serving · ¼ cup (50 mL)
Carb choice   1

....

Carbohydrate 14 g
   Fibre 2 g
Protein 1 g
Fat 2 g
   Saturated 0 g
Cholesterol 0 mg
Sodium 29 mg
Calories 71

BLUEBERRY SAUCE:

1 cup	blueberries, fresh or frozen (see Tip)	250 mL
1 tsp	grated orange peel or grated fresh gingerroot (optional)	5 mL
¼ cup	granular low-calorie sweetener with sucralose	50 mL
1 tsp	soft margarine or butter	5 mL
Pinch	ground nutmeg	

In a small saucepan, combine berries, 2 tbsp (25 mL) water and orange peel (if using). Bring to a boil on medium heat, stirring occasionally. Reduce heat and simmer uncovered for 10 minutes or until berries are soft and syrupy. Stir in sweetener, margarine and nutmeg.
Makes ½ cup (125 mL).

VARIATION
Fresh Peach Sauce: Replace blueberries with 1 cup (250 mL) sliced peeled peaches and nutmeg with ½ tsp (2 mL) almond extract; omit orange peel and gingerroot.
Makes ½ cup (125 mL).

⊕ *Wild blueberries are smaller, but have the very best flavour and texture. We find it worthwhile buying and freezing them during the short time they are available in the summer. The larger cultivated ones should be cut in half before using.*

OVERNIGHT HAM AND ASPARAGUS BAKE

Whether looking for a make-ahead breakfast or a lunch masterpiece, this recipe definitely fills the bill. You can put ingredients together and refrigerate overnight and then bake in the morning. Not only is this a vitamin- and mineral-rich recipe with a divine taste, it is also low in carbohydrate and calories.

2	slices whole wheat bread (30 g each), torn into bite-size pieces	2
¼ cup	diced lean ham	50 mL
4	steamed asparagus stalks, cut diagonally, or ½ cup (125 mL) cooked chopped broccoli	4
¼ cup	shredded light Swiss cheese (25 g)	50 mL
1	egg	1
1	egg white	1
⅓ cup	low-fat milk	75 mL
2 tbsp	low-fat plain yogurt or light sour cream	25 mL
1	green onion, chopped	1
½–1 tsp	dry mustard	2–5 mL
Pinch	paprika	
Pinch	freshly ground black pepper	

Lightly spray two 4-inch (10 cm) round baking dishes with non-stick cooking spray. Place 1 slice whole wheat bread, torn into pieces, in each dish. Layer with ham, asparagus pieces and cheese. Top with remaining pieces of bread.

In a small bowl, whisk together egg, egg white, milk, yogurt, onion and mustard. Pour over layers in pan. Sprinkle with paprika. Cover and refrigerate for at least 2 hours or overnight.

Bake, uncovered, in 350°F (180°C) oven for 25 minutes or until golden brown and knife inserted in centre comes out clean. Remove from oven; let stand for 5 minutes before serving.

Breakfast Menu 27

Prep · 15 minutes
Cook · 25 minutes
Yield · 2 servings

Each serving · ½ of recipe
Carb choice   1
Meat & Alternatives choices   2

Carbohydrate 20 g
  Fibre 3 g
Protein 18 g
Fat 6 g
  Saturated 2 g
Cholesterol 121 mg
Sodium 475 mg
Calories 200

....

Prep · 15 minutes
Cook · about 18 minutes
Yield · 12 medium muffins

....

Each Serving · 1 muffin
Carb choice   1
Fats choices   1½

....

Carbohydrate 22 g
  Fibre 2 g
Protein 4 g
Fat 7 g
  Saturated 0 g
Cholesterol 18 mg
Sodium 144 mg
Calories 165

FLAX AND OAT BRAN BLUEBERRY MUFFINS

Luscious blueberries, along with the taste of oats and flax, make this muffin outstanding in both flavour and nutrition.

TOPPING:

¼ cup	lightly packed brown sugar	50 mL
2 tbsp	soft margarine or butter	25 mL
¼ tsp	cinnamon	1 mL
⅓ cup	rolled oats	75 mL

In a small bowl, cream sugar, margarine and cinnamon. Stir in the rolled oats; mix well. Set aside.

MUFFINS:

1½ cups	all purpose flour	375 mL
½ cup	ground flaxseed	125 mL
½ cup	granular low-calorie sweetener with sucralose	125 mL
1½ tsp	baking powder	7 mL
½ tsp	baking soda	2 mL
1 cup	low-fat milk	250 mL
2 tbsp	canola oil	25 mL
1 tbsp	fresh lemon juice	15 mL
1	egg	1
1 tsp	vanilla extract	5 mL
¾ cup	fresh or frozen blueberries	175 mL

In a bowl, combine flour, flaxseed, sweetener, baking powder and baking soda.

In a second bowl, whisk together milk, oil, lemon juice, egg and vanilla until well blended. Stir into flour mixture until dry ingredients are thoroughly moistened. Gently fold berries into batter (do not overmix). Divide batter evenly among 12 non-stick or paper-lined medium muffin cups, filling ¾ full. Sprinkle topping evenly over each muffin. Bake in 375°F (190°C) oven for 18 minutes or until the tops are lightly browned and firm to the touch.

Bacon and Egg Muffins

Have your bacon and egg along with Cheddar cheese in one hearty muffin. They freeze very well.

2	slices bacon-style turkey, crisp-cooked (see Tip)	2
1¼ cups	all purpose flour	300 mL
⅔ cup	oat bran	150 mL
¼ cup	granulated sugar	50 mL
2 tbsp	granular low-calorie sweetener with sucralose	25 mL
2½ tsp	baking powder	12 mL
½ tsp	baking soda	2 mL
¼ tsp	each dried oregano and paprika	2 mL
1 cup	shredded light Cheddar cheese	250 mL
2	green onions, thinly sliced	2
1¼ cups	buttermilk	300 mL
¼ cup	canola oil	50 mL
1	egg or 2 egg whites, slightly beaten	1

Crumble cooked bacon into small pieces. In a large bowl, combine bacon, flour, oat bran, sugar, sweetener, baking powder, baking soda, oregano, paprika, cheese and onions.

In a second bowl, combine buttermilk, oil and egg. Pour into the dry ingredients; stir until combined.

Divide the batter evenly among 12 non-stick or paper-lined medium muffin cups, filling ¾ full. Bake in 400°F (200°C) oven for 20 minutes or until the tops are lightly browned and firm to the touch. Serve warm.

◉ *Bacon-style turkey or chicken has the flavour of regular bacon but with 50 per cent less fat.*

Breakfast Menu 23

Prep · 15 minutes
Cook · about 20 minutes
Yield · 12 medium muffins

Each serving · 1 muffin

Carb choice	1
Meat & Alternatives choice	½
Fats choice	1

Carbohydrate 20 g
  Fibre 1 g
Protein 6 g
Fat 8 g
  Saturated 2 g
Cholesterol 25 mg
Sodium 235 mg
Calories 173

AUTUMN PUMPKIN CRANBERRY MUFFINS

Breakfast Menu 28
Snack Menu 11

Canned pumpkin keeps the muffins moist while reducing fat. Fresh or frozen cranberries give flavour and colour. For a snack, muffins are quicker and easier to make than cookies. Too many muffins? They freeze well.

Prep · 15 minutes
Cook · about 18 minutes
Yield · 12 medium muffins

1 cup	natural wheat bran	250 mL
½ cup	each all purpose and whole wheat flour	125 mL
¼ cup	lightly packed brown sugar	50 mL
¼ cup	granular low-calorie sweetener with sucralose	50 mL
1 tsp	each baking powder and baking soda	5 mL
½ tsp	each ground nutmeg and cinnamon	2 mL
1 cup	buttermilk	250 mL
½ cup	unsweetened canned pumpkin (see Tip)	125 mL
¼ cup	canola oil	50 mL
1	egg or 2 egg whites (see Tip)	1
½ cup	fresh or frozen cranberries, chopped	125 mL

Each Serving · 1 muffin

Carb choice	1
Fats choice	1

Carbohydrate 17 g
  Fibre 3 g
Protein 3 g
Fat 6 g
  Saturated 1 g
Cholesterol 19 mg
Sodium 156 mg
Calories 123

In a large bowl, combine bran, flours, sugar, sweetener, baking powder, baking soda, nutmeg and cinnamon.

In a second bowl, whisk together buttermilk, pumpkin, oil and egg. Pour into the dry ingredients; stir just until moistened. Stir in the cranberries.

Divide the batter evenly among 12 non-stick or paper-lined medium muffin cups, filling ¾ full. Bake in 400°F (200°C) oven for 18 minutes or until the tops are lightly browned and firm to the touch.

◉ *Freeze any leftover pumpkin in measured amounts for future use in soups, sauces and other baking. Cooked squash is a pumpkin replacement.*

◉ *Two egg whites can replace one whole egg when low-fat or low cholesterol is an issue. Small cartons of egg whites are found in the egg department of most food stores. They keep well in the refrigerator.*

Orange Bran Flax Muffins

A fresh orange gives these super-tasty muffins an exciting citrus flavour.

¾ cup	oat bran	175 mL
½ cup	each whole wheat and all purpose flour	125 mL
½ cup	ground flaxseed	125 mL
⅓ cup	natural bran	75 mL
1½ tbsp	baking powder	22 mL
½ tsp	each baking soda and ground nutmeg	2 mL
1	medium orange	1
¾ cup	buttermilk	175 mL
¼ cup	brown sugar, lightly packed	50 mL
¼ cup	granular low-calorie sweetener with sucralose	50 mL
¼ cup	canola oil	50 mL
1	egg	1

In a large bowl, combine oat bran, flours, flaxseed, bran, baking powder, baking soda and nutmeg. Set aside.

Cut unpeeled orange into pieces and remove seeds. In a blender container or food processor, blend orange, buttermilk, brown sugar, sweetener, oil and egg until orange is finely chopped. Pour orange mixture into flour mixture. Stir just until moistened.

Divide the batter evenly among 12 non-stick or paper-lined medium muffin cups, filling ¾ full. Bake in 375°F (190°C) oven for 18 minutes or until the tops are lightly browned and firm to the touch.

HIGH FIBRE

Breakfast Menu 30
Lunch Menu 18

....

Prep · 15 minutes
Cook · about 18 minutes
Yield · 12 medium muffins

....

Each serving · 1 muffin

Carb choice	1
Fats choices	1½

....

Carbohydrate 20 g
  Fibre 4 g
Protein 5 g
Fat 8 g
  Saturated 1 g
Cholesterol 19 mg
Sodium 118 mg
Calories 159

Honey Yogurt Sauce

Breakfast Menu 25
Dinner Menu 23
Snack Menu 17

Prep • 5 minutes
Refrigerate • for several days
Yield • 1 cup (250 mL)

Each Serving • ¼ cup (50 mL)

Carb choice   ½

Carbohydrate 10 g
   Fibre 0 g
Protein 3 g
Fat 0 g
Cholesterol 1 mg
Sodium 44 mg
Calories 52

This easy sauce goes well with **Make-Ahead Crispy Belgian Waffles** (page 35).

1 cup	low-fat plain yogurt	250 mL
1 tbsp	liquid honey	15 mL
½ tsp	vanilla extract	2 mL

In a small bowl, whisk together yogurt, honey and vanilla. Cover and refrigerate for up to several days.

STRAWBERRY ORANGE SAUCE

Fresh and tasty, this sauce is delicious served with *Baker's Dozen Morning Multi-Grain Pancakes* (page 34) or *Cottage Cheese Pancakes* (page 87).

1 cup	orange juice	250 mL
1 tbsp	cornstarch	15 mL
2 cups	sliced strawberries	500 mL
2 tbsp	soft margarine or butter	25 mL
2 tsp	liquid honey	10 mL
	low-calorie sweetener (optional)	

In a small saucepan, whisk together orange juice and cornstarch. Cook over medium heat until bubbly and thickened, stirring constantly. Add strawberries, margarine and honey. Cook until margarine has melted and strawberries have softened. Add sweetener, if desired. Serve warm.

Breakfast Menu 24
Lunch Menu 18

....

Prep · 5 minutes
Cook · 5 minutes
Yield · 2 cups (500 mL) sauce

....

Each serving · ⅓ cup (75 mL)
Carb choice   ½
Fats choice   1

....

Carbohydrate 12 g
  Fibre 1 g
Protein 1 g
Fat 4 g
  Saturated 1 g
Cholesterol 0 mg
Sodium 50 mg
Calories 83

No-Cook Pineapple Orange Marmalade

Breakfast Menu 26
Snack Menu 28

Prep • about 15 minutes
Chill or freeze • up to 3 weeks
     in the refrigerator or
     1 year in the freezer
Yield • 5 cups (1.25 L)

Each Serving • 2 tbsp (25 mL)
Extra

Carbohydrate 5 g
   Fibre 0 g
Protein 0 g
Fat 0 g
Cholesterol 0 mg
Sodium 3 mg
Calories 19

Pineapple, combined with orange and lime, delivers a fresh and lush taste of the tropics to this traditional preserve.

1	large orange	1
1	can (19 oz/540 mL) crushed unsweetened pineapple with juice	1
1 cup	granular low-calorie sweetener with sucralose	250 mL
½ cup	orange juice	125 mL
1 tsp	grated lime rind	5 mL
	juice of 1 lime	
1	box (49 g) powdered fruit pectin crystals (see Tip)	1
1 cup	water	250 mL
½ tsp	rum extract	2 mL

With a vegetable peeler, peel the thin outer rind from the orange and cut in very fine strips. Place in a large bowl. Remove and discard remaining white pith and seeds. Finely chop the orange and add to rind.

In a bowl, combine pineapple with juice, sweetener, orange juice, lime rind and juice. Add to orange. Let stand for 10 minutes to allow juices to develop.

In a small saucepan, whisk pectin gradually into water until well mixed. Bring to a full boil over medium-high heat; boil for 1 minute, stirring constantly. Gradually stir into fruit mixture. Add extract and let stand for 30 minutes, stirring occasionally.

Spoon spread into clean jars or plastic containers to within ½ inch (1 cm) of rim. Cover with tight-fitting lids. Label and refrigerate for up to 3 weeks or freeze for longer storage.

⊕ *Certo-brand regular pectin has directions for making spreads without sugar. The low-sugar pectin from Bernardin is referred to as "no-sugar-needed" pectin and, as the name implies, can be made using no sugar or using some sugar and sweetener. Use either pectin in this spread.*

LIGHT RASPBERRY BLUEBERRY SPREAD

This spread is so flavourful, it's hard to believe it's low in carbohydrate.

3 cups	raspberries, crushed	750 mL
2 cups	blueberries, crushed	500 mL
2 tbsp	fresh lemon juice	25 mL
1 tsp	grated lemon peel	5 mL
1 cup	water	250 mL
1	box (49 g) powdered fruit pectin crystals (see Tip)	1
2 tbsp	granulated sugar	25 mL
1 cup	granular low-calorie sweetener with sucralose (see Tip)	250 mL
¼ tsp	ground nutmeg	1 mL

In a medium stainless steel or enamel saucepan, crush raspberries and blueberries with a potato masher (you should have 3 cups/750 mL crushed fruit). Combine fruit, lemon juice and peel and water. Gradually stir in pectin. Bring mixture to a full boil over medium-high heat, stirring constantly. Gradually stir in sugar, sweetener and nutmeg; return to boil and boil hard for 1 minute, stirring constantly.

Spoon spread into clean hot jars to within ⅓ inch (1 cm) of rim. Cover with tight-fitting lids. Label and refrigerate for up to 3 weeks or freeze for longer storage.

- ⊛ See the Tip on the opposite page for information about pectins.
- ⊛ If you do not keep a bulk sweetener on hand, then 10 packages of low-calorie sweetener are a good replacement.

Breakfast Menu 27

....

Prep · about 15 minutes
Cook · about 10 minutes
Yield · 4¼ cups (1.05 L)

....

Each serving · 1 tbsp (15 mL)
Extra

....

Carbohydrate 3 g
  Fibre 0 g
Protein 0 g
Fat 0 g
Cholesterol 0 mg
Sodium 2 mg
Calories 11

LUNCH

Recipes	Carbs	Page
Lime Watermelon Splash	½	56
Shrimp Chowder	1½	57
Homemade Light Beef Broth	0	58
Homemade Light Chicken Broth	0	59
Turkey Minestrone	1	60
Gingered Carrot Soup	1	61
Hearty Vegetable Barley Soup	1½	62
Curried Vegetable and Split Pea Soup	1½	63
Spicy Beans on Toast	3	64
Baked Bean Tortillas	2	65
Grilled Cheese French Toast Sandwich	2	66
Toasted Vegetable Frittata Sandwich	2	67
Tomato and Goat Cheese Crostini	1½	69
Cheesy Eggs and Asparagus on Toast	1	70
Salmon Pecan Sandwich Filling	0	71
Tuna Sandwich Filling	0	72
Open-Face Baked Cheese Tomato Tortillas	1	73
Fresh Tomato Salsa	Extra	74

RECIPES	CARBS	PAGE
Roasted Tomato Pasta Sauce	½	75
Buttermilk Tea Biscuits	1	76
Red Pepper Focaccia	1	77
Individual Turkey Quesadilla	2	78
Greek Salad in a Pita	2½	79
Tuna Niçoise Salad	2	80
Curried Turkey Salad	½	81
Chicken Caesar and Potato Salad	1	82
Tomato and Black Bean Salad	1	83
Balsamic Vinaigrette	0	84
Crustless Asparagus Quiche for One	1½	85
Vegetable Cheese Pie	2	86
Cottage Cheese Pancakes	2	87
Seasonal Fruit Plate with Ricotta Cheese	2	88
Orange Stewed Rhubarb	1	89
Orange Yogurt Sauce	½	90
Baked Fruit with Raspberry Sauce	1½	91
Naturally Fresh Fruit Sorbet	1	92
Microwave Cranberry Applesauce	1	93

WHAT'S FOR LUNCH?

Soup, a sandwich and a salad are old standbys. And rightly so. Each makes an easily prepared nutritious meal to satisfy midday hunger pangs. Soups and sandwiches can be served hot in the winter and cold in the summer. But the same old selections day after day become oh, so dull. Our lunch recipes and menus offer new twists on old favourites as well as some nifty new ideas.

Lunch is a marvellous time to stock up on nutrition. Soup, depending on the variety, can have vitamins and minerals from vegetables, fibre and protein from barley, lentils and beans and protein from meat. Sandwiches made from whole wheat breads are full of fibre to say nothing of the fibre, protein, vitamins and minerals in the fillings. And a low-fat salad is really just a tasty medley of fibre, vitamins and minerals finished off with protein from any added meat, cheese or alternative.

A Bowl of Soup?

We think soup is one of the most perfect foods. It's economical, easy to make, gets better with each reheating and tends to be low in fat. A pot of soup simmering on the stove gives warmth and comfort to a cold, blustery winter day. And a lively, refreshing cold soup just makes a summer lunch sing. A nourishing lunch is not far away when you have a freezer full of assorted frozen soups.

Soup is best made with homemade broth and we think our recipes are pretty good ones (pages 58 and 59). Whenever you see a reference to broth in a recipe, think homemade. Your soup will taste better, plus you control the salt level, an important consideration if you are to limit sodium intake (see page 15). If you should decide to use a commercial broth instead, look for a lower-sodium choice. Read the labels before you buy. All commercial broths tend to be high in sodium content, even those claiming sodium reduction. Dehydrated broths tend to be even higher. See pages 58 and 59 for comparisons.

Many flavourful (though expensive) ready-to-serve soups are appearing in the grocery stores and taste almost homemade. Check the Nutrition Facts on the label for serving size, then subtract the fibre from the carbohydrate to see how it fits your meal.

Cooking for one or two, you may wonder if it's worth the bother to make your own soups. We say it is. Most soup recipes freeze well.

Opposite: Chicken Caesar and Potato Salad (page 82)

Ladle leftover soup into small airtight containers, leaving enough room at the top for expansion (usually 1 to 2 inches/2.5 to 5 cm). To reheat, thaw completely in the refrigerator or microwave; then place contents in saucepan and heat over low heat, adding liquid as necessary to thin.

This chapter offers several new and quite unusual hot soups, *Turkey Minestrone* (page 60) and *Hearty Vegetable Barley Soup* (page 62) are filled with plain old-fashioned goodness—as well as slowly digested low-glycemic carbohydrate. And if you want something more exotic, try spicy *Gingered Carrot Soup* (page 61), delicious whether served hot or cold.

A Sandwich?

Sandwiches are an ideal lunch for one- and two-person households. Each is a custom creation of just the right amount for a person to eat at one sitting.

Bread in a sandwich does more than just hold the filling; it adds fibre, texture and variety to the total sandwich. Breads come in all shapes and sizes, as do buns, bagels, baguettes, pita breads and wraps (flour tortillas). And they all come in whole wheat and multi-grain versions. Each gives the filling a different taste. How about our *Salmon Pecan Sandwich Filling* (page 71) or *Open-Face Baked Cheese Tomato Tortillas* (page 73) and *Individual Turkey Quesadilla* (page 78) for a different slant on the traditional sandwich?

But the variety of sizes in bread products can create a problem for those with diabetes. Since bagels and breads come in such a variety of sizes, how do you know what's intended in a certain menu? To deal with this, we have added weights to bread products used in our menus and recipes. Remember that a 30 gram roll or slice of bread contains 15 grams of available carbohydrate and is equal to 1 Grains & Starches choice OR 1 Carb choice (see pages 25 and 217).

A Salad?

A salad may be an addition to a meal, or it may be the meal itself. We have both kinds in our lunch menus. Main-course salads tend to be a meal in themselves. They are a refreshing, flavourful and healthy change from soups and sandwiches. Like sandwiches, they are also custom creations designed for the number of people eating lunch, be it one or two or more.

A lunchtime salad is a great way to add more vegetables to your day as well as an opportunity to include high-fibre low-glycemic foods. See **Tuna Niçoise Salad** (page 80), and **Tomato and Black Bean Salad** (page 83).

Some of our recipes add fresh fruit to a salad for a refreshing change—see **Seasonal Fruit Plate with Ricotta Cheese** (page 88). The easy-to-prepare **Greek Salad in a Pita** (page 79) is a different twist on the traditional Greek salad. All make the perfect lunch.

How to make a salad great

The profusion of ready-to-use salad greens now available gives us plenty of exciting choices with few calories and little carbohydrate. They can all be used generously in a diabetes meal plan. But a crisp, well-dressed salad doesn't happen by chance. Here are some ideas to make a salad work:

- Wash leafy greens and use a salad spinner to dry. They keep fresher if wrapped in paper or cloth towelling and stored in a tightly sealed plastic container in the refrigerator. Or use one of the new ventilated plastic storage bags. Lettuce and spinach in airtight packaging should be refrigerated as purchased. Wash before using.
- Tear greens, don't chop; that way you'll have crisper salads.
- Darker greens have more nutrients.
- Keep some raw vegetables on hand to use in a green salad. Small broccoli and cauliflower florets, shredded carrots and chopped bok choy are all ideal choices.
- Add fresh herbs such as basil, dill, oregano or tarragon.
- Toss greens with the dressing at the last minute.

Dressing light

A salad dressing can make or break a salad. When it comes to dressing salads, less is best. Our recipes provide a given amount, enough to lightly coat the greens. Be sure the greens are dry so the dressing will cling to the leaves and not slide off. A too heavy or boring dressing insults fresh greens. Of course the dressing should be low in fat. While canola oil and olive oil are both healthy oils to use in dressings, surveys show that salad dressings are one of the chief sources of added fat in the Canadian diet. So use those high-fat dressings in moderation.

Here are some tips for lowering fat in dressings:

- Choose light, reduced-fat mayonnaise and salad dressings.
- Use measuring spoons to measure even light dressings.
- Lighten mayonnaise with lemon juice, vinegar, low-fat plain yogurt or milk.
- Mix salsa into yogurt for a super-light and tasty dressing.
- When eating out, ask for a lower-fat dressing on the side and add just what you need.
- Make your own so you know what's in it. Try one of our home-made low-fat dressings like **Balsamic Vinaigrette** (page 84) or the creamy curried dressing we use in the **Curried Turkey Salad** (page 81).

A Nice Finish to Lunch

Lunchtime is a great time to add in fruit as a dessert. Fruit delivers the sweetness we expect from a dessert but with relatively few calories and lots of fibre, minerals and vitamins. Fruits are served either raw or in fruit-based recipes such as **Baked Fruit with Raspberry Sauce** (page 91) or **Microwave Cranberry Applesauce** (page 93). And if you don't have on hand the fruit suggested in a given menu, check Appendix III (page 224) for other choices. And what do you think of **Naturally Fresh Fruit Sorbet** (page 92) for dessert?

Lunch in the Fast Lane

A lunch away from home can still be a healthy lunch. Here are some tips to keep in mind, especially if you eat out frequently.

- The best option of all is to brown bag it. Take along your own healthy lunch. See Lunch Menus 4 and 13 for ideas.
- Downsize it. Consider sharing a large portion with someone else, or ask for a doggy bag to take home.
- Pick one of the healthy options offered at many fast food restaurants.
- Survey all the choices a cafeteria offers before making your selection.
- Opt for the salad bar's fresh fruit, vegetable, bean, lentil or mixed greens salads.

- Make your pizza choice a healthy one. Choose one with a thin, whole grain crust, topped with lots of roasted vegetables and light on the cheese. Steer away from higher-fat higher-sodium toppings such as pepperoni, sausage or bacon.
- Find a vending machine with offerings of raw fruit, water, milk and sandwiches.

LIME WATERMELON SPLASH

Lunch Menu 22

....

Prep · 10 minutes
Chill · about 1 hour
Yield · 1 serving, 1 cup (250 mL)

....

Each serving · 1 cup (250 mL)
Carb choice   ½

....

Carbohydrate 12 g
  Fibre 1 g
Protein 1 g
Fat 1 g
  Saturated 0 g
Cholesterol 0 mg
Sodium 10 mg
Calories 53

Coolers and summer picnics are just made for each other, but you can enjoy a cooler any time you feel the need for one.

1 cup	cubed, seeded watermelon	250 mL
½ cup	Diet 7UP or diet tonic water	125 mL
1 tbsp	fresh lime juice	15 mL
4	ice cubes	4

Freeze watermelon until firm (about 1 hour).

In a blender, combine watermelon, 7UP and lime juice. With the blender running, add ice cubes, one at a time; process until slushy. Serve immediately.

Shrimp Chowder

Our shrimp chowder is thick and chunky and full of shrimp flavour. Not only is it low in fat and high in nutrients, it is easily prepared by opening two cans and adding a few fresh vegetables. Using low-fat evaporated milk in soup gives it the delicious thickness of cream without the fat.

1 tsp	canola oil	5 mL
¼ cup	diced celery	50 mL
2 tbsp	finely chopped onion	25 mL
½ cup	water	125 mL
⅔ cup	cubed potato (about 1 medium)	150 mL
1 tbsp	fresh lemon juice	15 mL
⅛ tsp	each dried thyme leaves and freshly ground pepper	0.5 mL
⅔ cup	low-fat evaporated milk	150 mL
1	can (106 g) shrimp, drained and rinsed (see Tip)	1

In a non-stick skillet, heat oil on medium heat. Sauté celery and onion for 5 minutes or until tender. Add water, potato, lemon juice, thyme and pepper. Cover and cook over medium heat for 10 minutes or until the potato is tender. Add milk and shrimp Warm over low heat to serving temperature.

Before serving, stir and check seasonings. You may add extra water if the chowder is too thick. A little extra lemon juice or thyme may be needed.

◉ *If you prefer to use frozen shrimp rather than canned, replace with ⅔ cup (150 mL/90 g) frozen thawed shrimp (tails and shells removed).*

Lunch Menu 10

....

Prep · 15 minutes
Cook · about 15 minutes
Yield · 2 servings,
  2 cups (500 mL)

....

Each serving · ½ of recipe
  (1 cup/250 mL)
Carb choices   1½
Meat & Alternatives choices   2

....

Carbohydrate 22 g
  Fibre 1 g
Protein 18 g
Fat 5 g
  Saturated 1 g
Cholesterol 84 mg
Sodium 153 mg
Calories 202

Homemade Light Beef Broth

A bit more effort is required to make beef broth than chicken broth as the bones need to be browned, but it's well worth it.

4 lb	beef bones	2 kg
2	onions, coarsely chopped	2
3	carrots, coarsely chopped	3
3	celery stalks, chopped	3
2	parsley sprigs	2
2	bay leaves	2
1 tbsp	peppercorns	15 mL
3	cloves of garlic	3
1 tsp	dried thyme	5 mL

In a roasting pan, combine beef bones, onions, carrots and celery. Bake in 450° F (230°C) oven for 1 hour or until well browned, stirring occasionally. Transfer bones and vegetables to a large saucepan. Drain and discard fat from roasting pan. Add 2 cups (500 mL) water; cook and stir to scrape up brown bits on bottom of pan. Transfer contents to saucepan, along with parsley, bay leaves, peppercorns, garlic and thyme. Add enough cold water to cover the bones by 1 inch (2.5 cm); bring to a boil. Reduce heat and simmer, uncovered, for 2 hours or longer. Strain, discarding bones and vegetables. Chill. Refrigerate until cold. Remove congealed fat and discard. Measure stock and freeze in appropriate amounts to use as needed.

Prep · 15 minutes
Cook · about 3 hours
Yield · about 12 cups (3 L)

HOMEMADE LIGHT CHICKEN BROTH

Any recipe calling for chicken broth will only be as good as the broth you use. Our homemade broth will give your recipe maximum flavour with far less sodium than commercial varieties.

2–3 lbs	chicken bones	1–1.35 kg
1	onion, coarsely chopped	1
2	celery stalks, coarsely chopped	2
2	sprigs parsley	2
1	bay leaf	1

Store poultry bones in the freezer until you've saved enough to make a batch of broth. Then place the frozen bones, along with any fresh ones you may have on hand, in a large saucepan. Add onion, celery, parsley, bay leaf and enough cold water to cover the bones by 1 inch (2.5 cm); cover saucepan and bring to a boil. Reduce heat and simmer for 2 hours or longer. Strain, discarding the bones and vegetables. Refrigerate until cold.

Remove congealed fat and discard. Measure stock and freeze in appropriate amounts to use as needed. Freeze some in an ice cube tray too. Transfer frozen cubes to a resealable plastic bag so they're ready to use whenever you need only a small amount.

Prep · 15 minutes
Cook · about 2 hours
Yield · about 12 cups (3 L)

SODIUM TIP

How much sodium is in commercial chicken broth? It is not easy to read labels and compare since some labels describe a serving of ⅔ cup (150 mL), others ¾ cup (175 mL) and still others 1 cup (250 mL). We have done the math for you and compared 1-cup (250 mL) servings below. Again, the cans and cartons of chicken broth with 25% less salt appear to have the least sodium—but still much more than homemade.

Chicken Bouillon (cubes)
1,300 mg sodium

Chicken Bouillon, Regular (sachets)
960 mg sodium

Chicken Bouillon, 25% Less Salt (sachets)
720 mg sodium

Ready-to-Use Chicken Broth, 25% Less Salt (carton)
555 mg sodium

Condensed Chicken Broth, Fat Free (water added)
990 mg sodium

Condensed Chicken Broth, Fat Free, 25% Less Salt (water added)
670 mg sodium

Homemade Light Chicken Broth
115 mg sodium

TURKEY MINESTRONE

Lunch Menu 15

....

Prep · 15 minutes
Cook · about 20 minutes
Yield · 3 servings,
about 3 cups (750 mL)

....

Each serving · ⅓ of recipe
(1 cup/250 mL)
Carb choice   1
Meat & Alternatives choices 1½

....

Carbohydrate 20 g
    Fibre 4 g
Protein 13 g
Fat 3 g
    Saturated 0 g
Cholesterol 15 mg
Sodium 312 mg
Calories 151

Minestrone is a thick vegetable soup containing pasta. It's hearty enough to be considered a complete meal. Think of it when you have leftover cooked turkey. Beans and pasta add slowly digested carbohydrate and fibre.

1 tsp	canola oil	5 mL
½ cup	diced zucchini	125 mL
¼ cup	chopped onion	50 mL
1	clove garlic, minced	1
2 cups	*Homemade Light Chicken Broth* (page 59) or salt-reduced chicken broth	500 mL
⅔ cup	canned crushed tomatoes	150 mL
⅔ cup	drained and rinsed pinto or romano beans (see Tip)	150 mL
¼ tsp	each ground oregano and basil	1 mL
¼ cup	elbow macaroni	50 mL
½ cup	diced cooked turkey	125 mL
	chopped fresh parsley (optional)	

In a large saucepan, heat oil over medium heat. Add zucchini, onion and garlic. Cook for 5 minutes or until softened. Stir in broth, tomatoes, beans, oregano and basil. Bring to a boil, add macaroni, reduce heat, cover and simmer for 12 minutes or until macaroni is tender. Add the turkey; heat to serving temperature.

Before serving, stir the soup, taste and adjust seasonings. It may need extra oregano or basil. Sprinkle each serving with parsley (if using).

⊕ *Draining and rinsing canned beans lowers their sodium content.*
⊕ *Remember that on standing, pasta continues to soften and absorb liquid. If the soup is too thick after standing, add extra broth or water.*
⊕ *This soup doubles easily. Any beans left over after making this recipe will freeze well for another use.*

GINGERED CARROT SOUP

Spicy gingerroot adds zip to this heartwarming soup. Cooking enhances carrots' considerable vitamin A content. How? When boiled or steamed, carrot cell walls partially dissolve, making nutrients more available for processing in the body. We find it useful to make soup in sufficiently large amounts to have extra to freeze for another day.

1 tbsp	canola oil	15 mL
1 cup	finely chopped onion	250 mL
1	leek, white and light green part only, chopped	1
1	stalk finely chopped celery	1
1 tbsp	finely chopped gingerroot (see Tip)	15 mL
1	clove garlic, minced	1
6	large carrots, peeled and chopped	6
	(3¼ cups/800 mL) (see Tip)	
4 cups	*Homemade Light Chicken Broth* (page 59)	
	or salt-reduced chicken or vegetable broth	1 L
⅔ cup	low-fat evaporated milk	150 mL
	freshly ground pepper, to taste	
	chopped fresh parsley	

In a large saucepan, heat oil on medium heat. Add onion, leek and celery; sauté for 5 minutes. Add gingerroot and garlic; sauté for 1 minute. Add carrots and broth; bring to a boil, reduce heat, cover and simmer for 30 minutes or until vegetables are tender. Remove pan from heat and cool slightly.

In a food processor or blender, purée the soup in batches until very smooth. Return to saucepan, add milk and heat to serving temperature, stirring frequently. Before serving, season to taste with pepper, if required. Sprinkle with parsley and serve.

- ⊕ Extra **Gingered Carrot Soup** *can be refrigerated and served chilled.*
- ⊕ *Peeling fresh gingerroot can be a chore. Use a blunt-edged teaspoon to scrape away peel for speedy and efficient results.*
- ⊕ *To keep carrots moist and vitamin-rich, chop off their green tops before refrigerating in plastic bags.*

Lunch Menu 11

....

Prep · 20 minutes
Cook · about 30 minutes
Yield · 6 servings, 6 cups (1.5 L)

....

Each serving · ⅙ of recipe
   (1 cup/250 mL)
Carb choice   1
Fats choice   ½

....

Carbohydrate 17 g
  Fibre 3 g
Protein 5 g
Fat 3 g
  Saturated 0 g
Cholesterol 2 mg
Sodium 139 mg
Calories 114

HEARTY VEGETABLE BARLEY SOUP

....

Prep · 15 minutes
Cook · about 1 hour
Yield · 3 servings,
     3 cups (750 mL)

....

Each serving · ⅓ of recipe
     (1 cup/250 mL)
Carb choices   1½

....

Carbohydrate 26 g
   Fibre 5 g
Protein 4 g
Fat 1 g
   Saturated 0 g
Cholesterol 0 mg
Sodium 462 mg
Calories 120

A meal in a bowl, this soup shouts out "welcome home" on a cold blustery day. For a vegetarian, simply substitute vegetable broth for the beef broth. Barley, like oats, is an excellent source of carbohydrate and soluble fibre. Pot barley is less refined and more nutritious than pearl barley.

1	can (10 oz/284 mL) salt-reduced beef broth (see Tip)	1
1 cup	water	250 mL
½ cup	chopped onion	125 mL
¼ cup	pot barley	50 mL
⅔ cup	cubed potato	150 mL
½ cup	chopped carrot	125 mL
1	stalk celery, diced	1
½ cup	cut-up peeled rutabaga	125 mL
1	bay leaf	1
½ tsp	dried thyme leaves	2 mL
Pinch	freshly ground pepper	
	chopped fresh parsley (optional)	

In a medium saucepan, combine broth, water, onion and barley. Bring to a boil, reduce heat, cover and simmer for 45 minutes.

Add potato, carrot, celery, rutabaga, bay leaf, thyme and pepper. Cover and cook for 15 minutes or until vegetables are tender. Extra water may be required (about ⅔ cup/150 mL) before end of cooking since some of the water will have been absorbed by the barley during cooking.

Before serving, remove bay leaf and discard, taste and adjust seasoning. You may need to add extra thyme. Serve soup with parsley (if using).

⊕ *For less sodium, canned beef broth and water can be replaced by 2¼ cups (550 mL) **Homemade Light Beef Broth** (page 58). See page 58 for information on sodium in commercial broths.*

CURRIED VEGETABLE AND SPLIT PEA SOUP

This wonderful wintertime soup tantalizes the taste buds with its subtle aromas and flavours. Since this recipe has an ample yield, there should be some left over to freeze in single serving amounts.

1 tbsp	canola oil	15 mL
1 cup	chopped onion (about 1 medium)	250 mL
2	cloves garlic, minced	2
2 tbsp	minced gingerroot or 1 tsp (5 mL) ground ginger	25 mL
2	cinnamon sticks	2
2	bay leaves	2
1 tbsp	curry powder	15 mL
9 cups	*Homemade Light Chicken Broth* (page 59) or salt-reduced chicken broth	2.25 L
2 cups	dried yellow split peas	500 mL
1½ cups	chopped carrot (about 3 medium)	375 mL
2 cups	each finely chopped celery and cauliflower	500 mL
2 tbsp	tomato paste (see Tip)	25 mL
½ tsp	freshly ground pepper	2 mL

In a large heavy saucepan, heat oil over medium heat. Add onion, garlic, gingerroot, cinnamon sticks and bay leaves. Cover and cook for 5 minutes or until vegetables are tender. Stir in curry powder and cook for 2 minutes. Add chicken broth and split peas. Bring to boil, cover, reduce heat and simmer for 45 minutes or until peas are almost tender.

Add carrot, celery, cauliflower and tomato paste. Cover and simmer for 20 minutes or until peas and vegetables are tender. Add pepper, remove cinnamon sticks and bay leaves and discard.

⊕ *Since tomato paste is often needed in small amounts, freeze the paste that is remaining from this recipe in ice cube trays or small containers in 1 or 2 tbsp (15 or 25 mL) amounts for other recipes (see **Beef and Vegetable Meat Loaf**, page 119).*

Lunch Menu 27
Snack Menu 19

....

Prep · 20 minutes
Cook · 1 hour and 10 minutes
Yield · 12 servings, 12 cups (3 L)

....

Each serving · ¹/₁₂ of recipe (1 cup/250 mL)
Carb choices   1½
Meat & Alternatives choice   1

....

Carbohydrate 26 g
   Fibre 4 g
Protein 11 g
Fat 2 g
   Saturated 0 g
Cholesterol 0 mg
Sodium 117 mg
Calories 157

Lunch Menu 6

....

Prep · 10 minutes
Cook · about 5 minutes
Yield · 2 servings

....

Each serving · ½ of recipe

Carb choices	3
Meat & Alternatives choice	1

....

Carbohydrate 65 g
  Fibre 20 g
Protein 15 g
Fat 3 g
  Saturated 1 g
Cholesterol 0 mg
Sodium 421 mg
Calories 294

SPICY BEANS ON TOAST

Enhance a can of ordinary beans with spices and the flavours of onion and parsley. Beans are a satisfying and slowly digested form of carbohydrate.

1	can (14 oz/398 mL) low salt baked beans in tomato sauce	1
2	green onions, chopped	2
¼ cup	chopped parsley	50 mL
Pinch	each garlic powder and chili powder	
Dash	Worcestershire sauce	
2	slices whole wheat bread (30 g each)	2

In a small saucepan, heat the beans, onions, parsley, garlic and chili powder, and Worcestershire sauce on medium-low until hot enough to serve.

Toast bread. Serve half of bean mixture over each toast slice.

Baked Bean Tortillas

Salsa, kidney beans, onions and a melted cheese topping fills baked tortillas to create a very tasty lunch dish. Extra heat? Use medium or spicy (picante) salsa.

4	small whole wheat flour tortillas (34 g each)	4
1	can (19 oz/540 mL) kidney beans, drained and rinsed	1
¾ cup	salsa, mild, medium or picante	175 mL
1 tsp	chili powder	5 mL
¾ cup	shredded light medium Cheddar cheese	175 mL
1	green onion, sliced	1

Carefully press tortillas into four round 1-cup (250 mL) oval or round single-serve baking dishes. Bake in 350°F (180°C) oven for 10 minutes or until the tortillas are crisp and golden brown. Remove and store for up to 1 month in a closed container.

In a saucepan, using a potato masher, press beans until coarsely mashed. Stir in salsa and chili powder. Heat on low until warm.

Fill each crisp shell with one-quarter of the beans, top with one-quarter of the cheese and onions. Bake in 350°F (180°C) oven for 10 minutes or until the filling is heated through and the cheese melted. Serve warm.

VERY HIGH FIBRE

Lunch Menu 17

....

Prep · 20 minutes
Cook · about 20 minutes
Yield · 4 servings

....

Each serving · ¼ of recipe
Carb choices   2
Meat & Alternatives choices 1½
Fats choice   ½

....

Carbohydrate 38 g
  Fibre 8 g
Protein 15 g
Fat 7 g
  Saturated 2 g
Cholesterol 10 mg
Sodium 385 mg
Calories 267

Lunch Menu 12

. . . .

Prep · 5 minutes
Cook · about 5 minutes
Yield · 2 servings, 2 sandwiches

. . . .

Each serving · ½ of recipe
      (1 sandwich)
Carb choices   2
Meat & Alternatives choices 1½
Fats choice   1

. . . .

Carbohydrate 32 g
  Fibre 5 g
Protein 18 g
Fat 11 g
  Saturated 5 g
Cholesterol 124 mg
Sodium 544 mg
Calories 290

GRILLED CHEESE FRENCH TOAST SANDWICH

This is an interesting combination of French toast and a traditional grilled cheese sandwich. Using whole wheat bread makes it a high source of fibre.

4	slices whole wheat bread (30 g each)	4
1 tsp	light mayonnaise	5 mL
1 tsp	Dijon mustard	5 mL
	light Cheddar cheese (50 g), sliced	
4	tomato slices	4
1	egg or 2 egg whites	1
¼ cup	low-fat milk	50 mL
Pinch	freshly ground pepper	

Place bread slices on a cutting board. Combine mayonnaise and mustard; brush over 2 bread slices. Add cheese and 2 tomato slices and top with remaining 2 bread slices.

In a shallow bowl or pie plate, whisk egg, milk and pepper. Dip sandwiches in egg mixture; let the sandwiches remain in the mixture until all liquid is absorbed.

Heat a non-stick skillet on medium-high heat. Lightly spray with non-stick cooking spray. Place sandwiches in the skillet; cook for 3 minutes or until browned; flip and cook second side until brown and cheese melts.

Toasted Vegetable Frittata Sandwich

HIGH FIBRE

A frittata is an Italian omelette in which the ingredients are mixed with the eggs rather than folded inside like a French omelette. A frittata is also firmer because it's cooked very slowly over low heat.

½ cup	chopped zucchini	125 mL
2	large mushrooms, sliced	2
2 tbsp	chopped red or green sweet pepper	25 mL
1 tbsp	chopped onion	15 mL
1 tsp	canola oil	5 mL
4	egg whites or 2 eggs (see Tip)	4
¼ cup	low-fat milk	50 mL
1 tbsp	fresh basil or ½ tsp (2 mL) dried	15 mL
Pinch	freshly ground pepper	
4	slices whole wheat toast (30 g each)	4
	chopped fresh parsley	

In a non-stick skillet, on medium-high heat, sauté zucchini, mushrooms, red pepper and onion in melted margarine, stirring occasionally, for 5 minutes or until vegetable liquid has evaporated and vegetables are tender.

In a small bowl, whisk eggs, milk, basil and pepper. Reduce heat to low. Pour egg mixture into skillet; cook slowly until eggs are set, stirring occasionally.

Divide frittata over two toast slices; sprinkle with parsley. Top with remaining slices of toast and serve.

⊕ *Refrigerated egg whites are available in most supermarkets in small cartons near the eggs.*

Lunch Menu 20

....

Prep · 15 minutes
Cook · about 10 minutes
Yield · 2 servings

....

Each serving · ½ of recipe
Carb choices	2
Meat & Alternatives choice	1
Fats choice	½

....

Carbohydrate 33 g
 Fibre 5 g
Protein 15 g
Fat 5 g
 Saturated 1 g
Cholesterol 1 mg
Sodium 420 mg
Calories 225

TOMATO AND GOAT CHEESE CROSTINI

Crostini is Italian for "little toasts." The mixture of fresh tomatoes, goat cheese (chévre) and basil is a winning combination. They can be used for an appetizer, for a snack or for lunch. Any leftovers? Amazingly, these do not become soggy even when they are stored in a refrigerator overnight.

1	medium tomato, seeded and diced	1
2 tsp	chopped fresh parsley	10 mL
1	log goat cheese (140 g), softened (see Tip)	1
1 tbsp	chopped fresh basil or 1 tsp (5 mL) dried	15 mL
1 tsp	dried herbes de Provence (see Tip)	5 mL
Pinch	freshly ground pepper	
12	slices (¾-inch/2 cm thick) whole wheat French baguette loaf (180 g total)	12

In a bowl, combine tomato and parsley. Set aside.

In a second bowl, crumble cheese. Combine with basil, herbes de Provence and pepper. Set aside.

Place bread slices on a baking sheet. Toast in 350°F (180°C) oven for 2 minutes per side or until golden and crisp. Evenly spread cheese mixture over each bread slice. Top with tomato mixture. Serve immediately or cover and refrigerate for several hours.

◉ *To soften cheese, we find about 10 seconds on high (100%) in the microwave oven does the trick.*

◉ *If you do not have herbes de Provence, make your own by using an assortment of dried herbs including basil, marjoram, rosemary, thyme and sage.*

Lunch Menu 14
Snack Menu 26

....

Prep · 20 minutes
Cook · 4 minutes for toast
Yield · 12 pieces

....

Each serving · 3 slices (45 g) baguette, ¼ of recipe

Carb choices	1½
Meat & Alternatives choice	1
Fats choice	1

....

Carbohydrate 25 g
 Fibre 3 g
Protein 11 g
Fat 9 g
 Saturated 5 g
Cholesterol 16 mg
Sodium 406 mg
Calories 225

Cheesy Eggs and Asparagus on Toast

This is real comfort food. And what a simple way to have your milk, starch and protein choices all in one easy recipe.

Prep · 15 minutes
Cook · about 5 minutes
Yield · 2 servings and ⅔ cup
(150 mL) sauce

Each serving · ½ of recipe
Carb choice   1
Meat & Alternatives choices   2
Fats choice   1

Carbohydrate 22 g
  Fibre 2 g
Protein 16 g
Fat 11 g
  Saturated 4 g
Cholesterol 225 mg
Sodium 355 mg
Calories 248

2 tsp	cornstarch	10 mL
¼ tsp	dry mustard	1 mL
Pinch	freshly ground pepper	
¾ cup	low-fat milk	175 mL
¼ cup	shredded light Cheddar cheese	50 mL
1 tsp	soft margarine or butter	5 mL
2	hard-cooked eggs (see Tip)	2
10	asparagus spears	10
2	slices whole wheat toast (30 g each)	2
	paprika	

In a 2-cup (250 mL) glass measure, whisk together cornstarch, mustard and pepper. Slowly whisk in milk. Microwave on high (100%) for 1 minute; stir well. Microwave on medium-high (70%) for 2 minutes or until sauce begins to thicken. Add cheese and margarine; stir until melted.

Remove shell from eggs and slice. Steam asparagus. Divide eggs and asparagus over each toast slice. Spoon hot sauce over egg, sprinkle with paprika and serve.

⊕ *To hard-cook eggs, place eggs in saucepan and cover with cold water. Bring to boil; remove pan from heat. Cover and let stand for 20 minutes. Drain and rinse in cold running water.*

⊕ *For easy shelling, gently roll back and forth in the pan with a little water. The cold water seeps into the cracks to make peeling easier.*

SALMON PECAN SANDWICH FILLING

The toasted nutty flavour and crunch of pecans makes the difference in this version of salmon sandwich filling. You can store the filling for up to two days in the refrigerator so tuck away the extra for a sandwich or a salad. The omega-3 fatty acids in salmon make this filling "heart-healthy."

1	can (7.5 oz/213 g) salmon, undrained	1
2 tbsp	light mayonnaise	25 mL
1 tsp	horseradish	5 mL
2	green onions, finely chopped	2
1 tbsp	chopped toasted pecans (see Tip)	15 mL
	chopped fresh parsley (optional)	

In a bowl, flake salmon; mash bones with salmon (see Tip). Stir in mayonnaise, horseradish, onions, pecans and parsley (if using). Cover and refrigerate for up to 2 days.

◉ *For a calcium boost, mash the bones with the salmon. This provides as much extra calcium as a small glass of milk.*

◉ *Toast nuts to bring out their flavour. Place pecans in a microwave-safe dish and microwave on high (100%) for about 1 minute. Watch carefully as they will brown very quickly.*

Lunch Menu 22
Snack Menu 27

....

Prep · 10 minutes
Yield · 3 servings,
        1½ cups (375 mL)

....

Each serving · ⅓ of recipe
        (½ cup/125 mL)
Meat & Alternatives choices 1½

....

Carbohydrate 2 g
    Fibre 0 g
Protein 12 g
Fat 12 g
    Saturated 2 g
Cholesterol 20 mg
Sodium 352 mg
Calories 163

TUNA SANDWICH FILLING

Lunch Menu 16
Snack Menu 27

Prep · 10 minutes
Refrigerate · for up to 3 days
Yield · 1½ cups (375 mL),
    enough for 3 sandwiches

Each serving · ⅓ of recipe
    (½ cup/125 mL)
Meat & Alternatives choices 1½

Carbohydrate 2 g
  Fibre 0 g
Protein 11 g
Fat 3 g
  Saturated 0 g
Cholesterol 20 mg
Sodium 136 mg
Calories 82

It's so helpful to have "prepared at home" fillings ready to make a sandwich to take to work, to a church luncheon or on a picnic. Store the extra filling in the refrigerator for up to three days.

1	can (6 oz/170 g) water-packed tuna (see Tip)	1
¼ cup	diced yellow or red sweet pepper	50 mL
¼ cup	diced cucumber	50 mL
1	green onion, minced	1
2 tbsp	low-fat plain yogurt	25 mL
1 tbsp	light mayonnaise	15 mL
¼ tsp	each dried thyme and freshly ground pepper	1 mL

Drain tuna and flake. In a bowl, stir together tuna, yellow pepper, cucumber, onion, yogurt, mayonnaise, thyme and pepper. Cover and refrigerate for up to 3 days.

⊕ *Choose the water-packed tuna as a lower fat choice than oil-packed. Calories count.*

Open-Face Baked Cheese Tomato Tortillas

Salsa combines with the mild freshness of mozzarella cheese to make this oh-so-easy, open-face sandwich sing. Serve it to unexpected guests for lunch. Or make just one when you're alone and need a special lift.

2	small whole wheat tortillas (34 g each)	2
½ cup	*Fresh Tomato Salsa* (page 74)	125 mL
½ cup	shredded part-skim mozzarella cheese	125 mL
2 tsp	pine nuts (see Tip)	10 mL

Place tortillas on a large baking pan. Spread salsa over each tortilla almost to the edge. Sprinkle with cheese and pine nuts. Bake in 400°F (200°C) oven for 10 minutes or until the cheese is bubbly and tortillas are golden brown.

⊛ *Because of the high fat content of pine nuts and the fact you may use them only occasionally, pine nuts are best kept in the freezer until needed.*

Lunch Menu 19

....

Prep · 10 minutes
Cook · 10 minutes
Yield · 2 servings

....

Each serving · ½ of recipe
        (1 tortilla)
Carb choice   1
Meat & Alternatives choice   1
Fats choices   1½

....

Carbohydrate 21 g
   Fibre 2 g
Protein 11 g
Fat 10 g
   Saturated 4 g
Cholesterol 18 mg
Sodium 364 mg
Calories 210

Fresh Tomato Salsa

Since it's not cooked, this salsa is fresh tasting and is quick and easy to make. You can use it as a dip for crisp tortillas, a topping for baked potatoes, or as a condiment for egg dishes, grilled meat and in the recipe for **Open-Face Baked Cheese Tomato Tortillas** (page 73).

2	medium tomatoes, chopped	2
2 tbsp	chopped fresh basil or 2 tsp (10 mL) dried	25 mL
1 tsp	olive oil	5 mL
1	clove garlic, minced (optional)	1
¼ tsp	salt	1 mL
Pinch	freshly ground pepper	

In a bowl, combine tomatoes, basil, oil, garlic (if using), salt and pepper. Set aside for a short time to allow the flavours to blend.

Lunch Menu 19
Special Occasions Menu 5

Prep · 10 minutes
Yield · 1 cup (250 mL)

Each serving · ¼ of recipe
(¼ cup/50 mL)
Extra

Carbohydrate 3 g
   Fibre 1 g
Protein 1 g
Fat 1 g
   Saturated 0 g
Cholesterol 0 mg
Sodium 150 mg
Calories 24

ROASTED TOMATO PASTA SAUCE

The sweet taste of roasted plum tomatoes accented with basil and garlic is the perfect sauce for fettucine and easy to prepare in the oven. While the sauce can be made anytime, it is especially good in late summer when tomatoes and basil are at their freshest.

8	medium plum tomatoes	8
2 tbsp	olive oil	25 mL
4	cloves garlic, minced	4
½ cup	chopped fresh basil leaves or	125 mL
	2 tbsp (25 mL) dried	
½ tsp	freshly ground pepper	2 mL
¼ tsp	salt	1 mL

Remove stem end from each tomato; cut lengthwise into quarters. Place tomatoes in a bowl and toss with olive oil and garlic. Spread tomatoes in a single layer on a large rimmed baking pan.

Roast in 400°F (200°C) oven for 35 minutes or until tomatoes are squishy and the skins are starting to wrinkle and char. (Note: Don't stir or turn them while they're cooking.)

Stir basil, salt, pepper and roasted tomatoes together in a large bowl. Serve over cooked pasta.

⊕ *Any leftover sauce can be used in recipe for Pork Chop Marinara with Mozzarella Cheese (page 121). The sauce freezes well in ½ cup (125 mL) servings.*

Lunch Menu 24

Prep · 20 minutes
Cook · about 35 minutes
Yield · 4 servings,
    2 cups (500 mL)

Each serving · ¼ of recipe
    (½ cup/125 mL)
Carb choice   ½
Fats choices   1½

Carbohydrate 11 g
    Fibre 3 g
Protein 2 g
Fat 8 g
    Saturated 1 g
Cholesterol 0 mg
Sodium 131 mg
Calories 110

BUTTERMILK TEA BISCUITS

Lunch Menu 13
Snack Menu 28

Prep · 10 minutes
Cook · about 12 minutes
Yield · 6 biscuits

Each serving · ⅙ of recipe
        (1 biscuit)
Carb choice   1
Fats choice   1

Carbohydrate 18 g
    Fibre 1 g
Protein 3 g
Fat 4 g
    Saturated 1 g
Cholesterol 1 mg
Sodium 268 mg
Calories 123

These tea biscuits are a lovely accompaniment to a lunchtime salad. They also make a great snack with a cup of tea.

1 cup	all purpose flour	250 mL
1 tsp	baking powder	5 mL
¼ tsp	each baking soda and salt	1 mL
2 tbsp	soft margarine or butter	25 mL
½ cup	buttermilk (see Tip)	125 mL
1 tbsp	all purpose flour	15 mL

In a medium bowl, combine 1 cup (250 mL) flour, baking powder, baking soda and salt. Cut in margarine with 2 knives or a pastry blender until mixture is consistency of coarse crumbs.

Make a well in the centre of the dry ingredients and add buttermilk all at once. Stir with a fork until dry ingredients are just combined. Turn dough onto surface dusted with 1 tbsp (15 mL) flour; knead dough 20 times or until smooth. Roll or pat out to ½-inch (1 cm) thickness. Cut 6 rounds with floured 2-inch (5 cm) biscuit cutter. Transfer to an ungreased baking sheet.

Bake biscuits in 425°F (220°C) oven for 12 minutes or until lightly browned.

VARIATION

Red Pepper Focaccia: Light and airy, this delicious quick bread can be enjoyed as a snack, with soup at lunch or dinner.

To the recipe for **Buttermilk Tea Biscuits**, add 1 tsp (5 mL) crumbled rosemary, pinch freshly ground pepper and 2 cloves garlic, minced. Follow steps 1 and 2 on page 76.

Turn dough onto surface dusted with 1 tbsp (15 mL) flour; knead dough 20 times or until smooth. Roll or pat out to ½-inch (1 cm) thickness and place on ungreased baking sheet. Shape into 4- x 7-inch (10 x 18 cm) rectangle.

Top dough with ½ cup (125 mL) chopped, drained canned roasted red peppers. Bake as above. Cool slightly before cutting into 6 pieces.

⊕ *Don't have any buttermilk on hand? Add 1 tsp (5 mL) fresh lemon juice or vinegar to ½ cup (125 mL) low-fat milk to sour. Let stand for 5 minutes.*

Individual Turkey Quesadilla

Lunch Menu 26

....

Prep · 15 minutes
Cook · about 8 minutes
Yield · 1 serving

....

Each serving · 1 recipe
Carb choices   2
Meat & Alternatives choices   2
Fats choices   1½

....

Carbohydrate 37 g
   Fibre 4 g
Protein 22 g
Fat 13 g
   Saturated 3 g
Cholesterol 37 mg
Sodium 515 mg
Calories 347

This is a good use for any leftover cooked turkey breast from Dinner Menu 30. Or you can make this anytime with cooked turkey from the deli counter.

½ tsp	canola oil	2 mL
⅓ cup	cut-up cooked turkey (30 g)	75 mL
¼ cup	diced green sweet pepper	50 mL
¼ cup	diced red onion	50 mL
Pinch	each chili powder and freshly ground pepper	
Dash	hot pepper sauce	
2	small whole wheat flour tortillas (34 g each)	2
⅓ cup	shredded light Monterey Jack cheese salsa (optional)	75 mL

In a non-stick skillet over medium heat, heat oil; add turkey, green pepper, onion, chili powder and pepper. Cook for 3 minutes or until onion just begins to soften. Add hot pepper sauce. Remove turkey mixture to a bowl and clean the skillet.

Place one tortilla in the skillet. Spoon turkey mixture over tortilla and sprinkle with cheese. Place another tortilla on top. Cook on medium for 5 minutes or until lightly browned and cheese is melted; flip part-way through. Cut into wedges and serve with salsa (if using).

GREEK SALAD IN A PITA

During garden-fresh tomato season, we often make a Greek salad. For a change, you can fill pita bread with salad rather than serving the pita on the side. And without the pita, it's a great Greek salad.

1	tomato, diced	1
½ cup	diced cucumber	125 mL
2 tbsp	crumbled feta cheese (20 g)	25 mL
3	sliced kalamata olives (optional)	3
1 cup	shredded romaine lettuce	250 mL
1 tbsp	fresh lemon juice	15 mL
1 tsp	olive oil	5 mL
1	whole wheat pita bread (65 g), halved	1

In a small bowl, combine tomato, cucumber, cheese and olives (if using). Toss with lettuce, lemon juice and oil.

Open each half pita bread. Spoon in salad and serve.

VERY HIGH FIBRE

Lunch Menu 5

....

Prep · 15 minutes
Yield · 1 serving

....

Each serving · 1 recipe
Carb choices   2½
Meat & Alternatives choice   ½
Fats choices   2

....

Carbohydrate 46 g
  Fibre 8 g
Protein 12 g
Fat 11 g
  Saturated 4 g
Cholesterol 18 mg
Sodium 588 mg
Calories 311

Lunch Menu 8

. . . .

Prep · 20 minutes
Chill · up to 1 hour
Yield · 2 servings

. . . .

Each serving · ½ of recipe
Carb choices   2
Meat & Alternatives choices   2

. . . .

Carbohydrate 32 g
    Fibre 5 g
Protein 22 g
Fat 10 g
    Saturated 2 g
Cholesterol 235 mg
Sodium 258 mg
Calories 300

TUNA NIÇOISE SALAD

The classic Niçoise salad contains basic ingredients found in the Nice area of France—olives, tomatoes, green beans, potatoes and tuna. Fortunately, all can be found at grocery stores at home.

	torn iceberg lettuce	
½	can (184 g) water-packed tuna, drained and flaked	½
2 cups	cooked green beans	500 mL
2	small cooked potatoes, diced (85 g each)	2
2	hard-cooked eggs, cut into slices	2
8	black olives (optional)	8
1	medium tomato, diced	1
2 tbsp	*Balsamic Vinaigrette* (page 84) or low-calorie dressing	25 mL

Arrange lettuce on two serving plates. Top each with one-half of the tuna, beans and diced potatoes, 1 egg, 4 olives (if using) and half of the diced tomatoes. Refrigerate for up to 1 hour before serving.

At serving time, top with remaining tomato and drizzle each with 1 tbsp (15 mL) dressing.

CURRIED TURKEY SALAD

Fresh fruits in a curry and yogurt dressing add an Indian flavour to cooked turkey. In India, curry powder is actually a blend of 20 freshly ground seasonings. Most curry powders sold in North America aren't as sophisticated but are still flavourful. It replaces salt to add flavour to many foods.

1 cup	cubed cooked turkey or chicken	250 mL
½ cup	sliced celery	125 mL
½ cup	cubed cantaloupe	125 mL
¼ cup	fresh or canned pineapple chunks, drained	50 mL
1 tbsp	toasted slivered almonds	15 mL
2 tbsp	low-fat plain yogurt	25 mL
1 tbsp	light mayonnaise	15 mL
1 tbsp	fresh lemon juice	15 mL
¼–½ tsp	curry powder	1–2 mL

In a bowl, combine turkey, celery, cantaloupe, pineapple and almonds

In a second bowl, whisk together yogurt, mayonnaise, lemon juice and curry powder. Stir into turkey mixture, cover and refrigerate for about 1 hour.

Lunch Menu 13

....

Prep · 15 minutes
Refrigerate · 1 hour or longer
Yield · 2 servings,
  2 cups (500 mL)

....

Each serving · ½ of recipe
  (1 cup/250 mL)
Carb choice   ½
Meat & Alternatives choices 2½

....

Carbohydrate 11 g
  Fibre 2 g
Protein 20 g
Fat 6 g
  Saturated 1 g
Cholesterol 43 mg
Sodium 121 mg
Calories 176

Chicken Caesar and Potato Salad

Lunch Menu 28

Prep · 20 minutes
Refrigerate · for up to 3 hours
Yield · 2 servings

Each serving · ½ of recipe
Carb choice   1
Meat & Alternatives choices   2
Fats choice   ½

Carbohydrate 20 g
   Fibre 2 g
Protein 17 g
Fat 8 g
   Saturated 2 g
Cholesterol 38 mg
Sodium 253 mg
Calories 213

The low-fat version of the famous Caesar dressing peps up chicken and red-skinned potatoes and makes a delightful luncheon salad.

Dressing:

2 tbsp	each grated Parmesan cheese and light mayonnaise	25 mL
2 tsp	red wine vinegar	10 mL
½ tsp	Worcestershire sauce	2 mL
½ tsp	Dijon mustard	2 mL
1	small clove garlic, crushed	1
Pinch	freshly ground pepper	

In a bowl, whisk together cheese, mayonnaise, vinegar, Worcestershire sauce, mustard, garlic and pepper. Cover and refrigerate.

Salad:

4	small red-skinned potatoes (170 g)	4
1	boneless, skinless cooked chicken breast (120 g raw), cubed	1
1	green onion, thinly sliced	1
2 tbsp	finely chopped fresh parsley	25 mL

In a saucepan, cook unpeeled potatoes in boiling water until tender. Drain and cool. Slice potatoes into quarters and place in a large bowl.

Stir in chicken, onion, parsley and dressing; toss to coat well with dressing. Cover and refrigerate for up to 3 hours before serving.

Tomato and Black Bean Salad

VERY HIGH FIBRE

Here is a very tasty and satisfying luncheon salad. It makes enough to serve four or divides easily when serving two.

Lunch Menu 30

4 cups	mixed salad greens	1 L
1	can (19 oz/540 mL) black beans, drained and rinsed (see Tip)	1
1⅓ cups	shredded light Cheddar cheese (100 g)	325 mL
1 cup	cooked fresh or frozen corn kernels	250 mL
1 cup	chopped tomato	250 mL
¼ cup	each chopped red onion and cucumber	50 mL
2 tbsp	finely chopped fresh coriander or parsley	25 mL
¼ cup	*Balsamic Vinaigrette* (page 84) or light vinaigrette (see Tip) salsa (optional)	50 mL

Prep · 20 minutes
Cook · about 4 minutes
Yield · 4 servings

Each serving · ¼ of recipe
Carb choice   1
Meat & Alternatives choices 1½
Fats choice   ½

Carbohydrate 24 g
  Fibre 10 g
Protein 14 g
Fat 7 g
  Saturated 3 g
Cholesterol 15 mg
Sodium 334 mg
Calories 209

Divide greens over four salad plates.

In microwave-safe casserole, heat beans on high (100%) for 2 minutes or until hot. Top each salad with ½ cup (125 mL) warm beans, ⅓ cup (75 mL) cheese, ¼ cup (50 mL) corn, ¼ cup (50 mL) tomato, 1 tbsp (15 mL) onion, 1 tbsp (15 mL) cucumber, ½ tbsp (7 mL) coriander and 1 tbsp (15 mL) light vinaigrette.

⊛ *If you decide to cook dried black beans, ⅔ cup (150 mL) of dried beans should yield 2 cups (500 mL) cooked beans for this salad. And you'll have less sodium!*

⊛ *We used **Balsamic Vinaigrette** but any low-calorie vinaigrette will be fine.*

BALSAMIC VINAIGRETTE

Lunch Menus 14, 24
Dinner Menus 20, 28

....

Prep · 10 minutes
Refrigerate · until ready to use
Yield · about 1 cup (250 mL)

....

Each serving · ¹⁄₁₆ of dressing
          (1 tbsp/15 mL)
Fats choice   ½

....

Carbohydrate 1 g
   Fibre 0 g
Protein 0 g
Fat 3 g
   Saturated 0 g
Cholesterol 0 mg
Sodium 5 mg
Calories 32

Balsamic vinegar imparts a wonderful subtle sweetness to a dressing for green salads. This royalty of all vinegars from Italy is made from the white Trebbiano grape. Its dark colour and aroma comes from aging in wooden barrels over several years. While relatively costly, its flavour delivery is well worth the price. A little goes a long way. The older the balsamic, the better, and the more expensive it is. However, most of us are quite happy with a younger, less expensive one. Look on the label for "Aceto Balsamico di Modena" to get the real thing.

½ cup	balsamic vinegar	125 mL
⅓ cup	water	75 mL
2 tbsp	finely chopped red onion	25 mL
1 tsp	Dijon mustard	5 mL
1	clove garlic, finely minced	1
1 tsp	low-calorie sweetener	5 mL
Pinch	freshly ground pepper	
¼ cup	olive oil (see Tip)	50 mL

In a bowl, whisk together vinegar, water, onion, mustard, garlic, sweetener and pepper. Whisk in oil until well blended. Pour into a covered container and refrigerate until ready to use.

⊕ *For a fat-free dressing, use chicken or beef stock to replace oil. Then 1 tbsp (15 mL) vinaigrette may be considered an Extra.*

Crustless Asparagus Quiche for One

Eliminating the crust leaves us with all the flavour of a great quiche but without the fat. Using a lower-fat cheese further reduces calories.

2	egg whites or 1 egg	2
1 tsp	Dijon mustard	5 mL
¼ tsp	dried basil or 1 tsp (5 mL) chopped fresh basil	1 mL
Pinch	freshly ground pepper	
1 tbsp	each finely chopped onion and red sweet pepper	15 mL
¼ cup	shredded light Swiss cheese	50 mL
½ cup	low-fat milk	125 mL
½ cup	cut-up asparagus	125 mL
½ cup	cooked parboiled brown or white rice (see Tip)	125 mL

Lightly spray a shallow 2-cup (500 mL) casserole with non-stick cooking spray.

In a small bowl, whisk together egg whites, mustard, basil and pepper until well blended. Add onion, red pepper and cheese; mix well.

In a glass measure in a microwave oven, heat milk until very warm, but not boiling. In another bowl, combine the hot milk, asparagus and rice. Slowly add egg mixture, stirring constantly.

Pour into prepared pan. Bake in 350°F (180°C) oven for 30 minutes or until a knife inserted in the centre comes out clean. Let stand for 5 minutes before serving.

⊛ *Is parboiled (converted) rice better for you than plain white rice? Yes, in parboiling, rice is boiled or steam-heated for a short time before milling, driving the B vitamins (thiamin, riboflavin and niacin) from the outer bran into the centre of the grain, so parboiled white rice has more B vitamins than plain white rice.*

Lunch Menu 25

Prep · 15 minutes
Cook · about 30 minutes
Yield · 1 serving

Each serving · 1 recipe
Carb choices   1½
Meat & Alternatives choices 2
Fats choice   1

Carbohydrate 27 g
  Fibre 2 g
Protein 21 g
Fat 8 g
  Saturated 4 g
Cholesterol 229 mg
Sodium 183 mg
Calories 266

Vegetable Cheese Pie

Lunch Menu 23

....

Prep · 20 minutes
Cook · about 30 minutes
Yield · 3 servings

....

Each serving · ⅓ of recipe
Carb choices   2
Meat & Alternatives choices   2
Fats choices   1½

....

Carbohydrate 32 g
   Fibre 3 g
Protein 20 g
Fat 13 g
   Saturated 6 g
Cholesterol 232 mg
Sodium 462 mg
Calories 320

One day Margaret discovered that this recipe is a marvellous way to get grandchildren to enjoy vegetables along with the cheese they all love.

1½ cups	chopped cooked broccoli (see Tip)	375 mL
1½ cups	fresh or frozen corn kernels	375 mL
3	green onions, chopped	3
¾ cup	shredded light Cheddar or Monterey Jack cheese	175 mL
3	eggs	3
1 cup	low-fat milk	250 mL
½ cup	biscuit baking mix	125 mL
¼ tsp	each freshly ground pepper and dried basil paprika	1 mL

Spray a deep 9-inch (23 cm) deep pie plate with non-stick cooking spray (see Tip). Sprinkle broccoli, corn, onions and cheese into the dish.

In a medium bowl, whisk together eggs, milk, baking mix, pepper and basil until well mixed. Pour over broccoli mixture and sprinkle with paprika. Bake in 350°F (180°C) oven for 30 minutes or until a knife inserted in the centre comes out clean. Let stand for 5 minutes before serving.

⊕ *Replace broccoli with 8 asparagus spears cut in 2-inch (5 cm) lengths.*

⊕ *If you wish to make individual pies, use small foil containers. Cooking time will be less but if you are cooking for two, you will have an extra one to reheat for another day.*

COTTAGE CHEESE PANCAKES

Moist and delicious, these pancakes, served with **Strawberry Orange Sauce** (page 45), make an outstanding lunch or breakfast.

¾ cup	all purpose flour	175 mL
2 tbsp	granular low-calorie sweetener with sucralose	25 mL
¾ tsp	baking powder	4 mL
¼ tsp	baking soda	1 mL
1	egg or 2 egg whites	1
½ cup	low-fat cottage cheese	125 mL
½ cup	low-fat milk	125 mL
½ tsp	grated lemon peel	2 mL
½ tsp	vanilla extract	2 mL

In a bowl, combine flour, sweetener, baking powder and baking soda; set aside. In a second bowl, whisk together egg, cottage cheese, milk, lemon peel and vanilla extract. Stir in flour mixture.

Heat a medium non-stick skillet over medium-high heat; spray with non-stick cooking spray. Using a ¼-cup (50 mL) dry measure, drop batter into skillet and cook for about 3 minutes or until bubbles break on surface; turn and cook second side until golden.

Lunch Menu 18

....

Prep · 10 minutes
Cook · about 6 minutes
Yield · 3 servings, 9 pancakes

....

Each serving · ⅓ of recipe
(3 pancakes)
Carb choices   2
Meat & Alternatives choice   1

....

Carbohydrate 29 g
   Fibre 1 g
Protein 12 g
Fat 3 g
   Saturated 1 g
Cholesterol 74 mg
Sodium 376 mg
Calories 194

SEASONAL FRUIT PLATE WITH RICOTTA CHEESE

Lunch Menu 7

....

Prep · 20 minutes
Yield · 2 servings

....

Each serving · ½ of recipe

Carb choices	2
Meat & Alternatives choice	1
Fats choice	1

....

Carbohydrate 30 g
   Fibre 3 g
Protein 12 g
Fat 8 g
   Saturated 5 g
Cholesterol 28 mg
Sodium 124 mg
Calories 232

With a hint of orange, ricotta cheese is a tasty part of this very colourful fruit plate.

¾ cup	light ricotta cheese	175 mL
2 tsp	finely grated orange peel	10 mL
2 tsp	granulated sugar	10 mL
Pinch	each ground ginger and nutmeg	
10	strawberries, sliced	10
⅔ cup	cantaloupe balls	150 mL
½ cup	halved green grapes	125 mL
¼ cup	orange juice	50 mL
	shredded lettuce	

In a bowl, combine ricotta cheese, orange peel, sugar, ginger and nutmeg.

In a second bowl, combine strawberries, cantaloupe, grapes and orange juice.

Arrange a bed of shredded lettuce on each of two serving plates. Top each with half of fruit mixture and half of the ricotta cheese. Serve at once.

Orange Stewed Rhubarb

Eating a wonderfully tasty bowl of cooked rhubarb reminds us of spring. This recipe adds an orange as well as some sugar and sweetener to enhance the rhubarb flavour. If you have any left, reserve a cup to use in **Rhubarb Bran Muffins** (page 175).

1 lb	rhubarb, sliced (4 cups/1L)	500 g
1	medium orange, peeled and chopped	1
2 tbsp	water	25 mL
2 tbsp	brown sugar	25 mL
2 tbsp	granulated brown low-calorie sweetener, with sucralose, as required	25 mL

In a microwave-safe casserole, combine rhubarb, orange and water. Cover and microwave on high (100%) for 5 minutes; stir.

Microwave on medium (70%) for 4 minutes; stir in sugar and allow to cool. Taste and add sweetener as desired.

Lunch Menu 9

Prep · 10 minutes
Cook · about 10 minutes
Yield · 4 servings,
       3 cups (750 mL)

Each serving · ¼ of recipe
       (¾ cup/175 mL)
Carb choice   1

Carbohydrate 17 g
    Fibre 3 g
Protein 2 g
Fat 0 g
    Saturated 0 mg
Cholesterol 0 mg
Sodium 8 mg
Calories 70

Orange Yogurt Sauce

Lunch Menu 12

Prep · 5 minutes
Refrigerate · up to 5 days
Yield · 2 servings,
  ⅔ cup (150 mL)

Each serving · ½ of recipe
  (⅓ cup/75 mL)
Carb choice   ½

Carbohydrate 10 g
  Fibre 0 g
Protein 4 g
Fat 0 g
Cholesterol 2 mg
Sodium 58 mg
Calories 60

Orange juice and nutmeg add interest to this very easy-to-make sauce.

⅔ cup	plain low-fat yogurt	150 mL
4 tsp	frozen orange juice concentrate, thawed	20 mL
Pinch	ground nutmeg	
	sweetener to taste	

In a small bowl, combine yogurt, orange juice concentrate and nutmeg. Taste and adjust with sweetener as desired. Cover and refrigerate for up to 5 days.

Baked Fruit with Raspberry Sauce

Top microwave-baked warm fresh fruit with a creamy raspberry–sour cream sauce. Warming the fruit (but not cooking it) enhances its natural sweetness. It makes an outstanding dessert.

Sauce:

1 cup	light sour cream	250 mL
2 tsp	each liquid honey and frozen orange juice concentrate, thawed, or orange liqueur	10 mL
½ cup	whole raspberries or sliced strawberries	125 mL

In a bowl, whisk together sour cream, honey and orange concentrate. Carefully fold in the raspberries; set aside.

Fruit:

1 cup	cubed cantaloupe	250 mL
1	small banana	1
2	purple plums, halved, pitted and sliced	2
	ground cinnamon	

Divide cantaloupe, banana and plums between four small microwave-safe bowls. Sprinkle with cinnamon and cook at high (100%) for 2 minutes or until warm. Top with raspberry sauce and serve.

Lunch Menu 14

....

Prep · 15 minutes
Cook · about 2 minutes
Yield · 4 servings

....

Each serving · ¼ of recipe
Carb choices   1½
Fats choices   1½

....

Carbohydrate 25 g
  Fibre 2 g
Protein 3 g
Fat 8 g
  Saturated 4 g
Cholesterol 23 mg
Sodium 48 mg
Calories 169

Naturally Fresh Fruit Sorbet

Lunch Menu 17

....

Prep · 15 minutes
Freeze · up to 1 week
Yield · about 3 cups (750 mL)

....

Each serving · ¼ of recipe
(about ¾ cup/175 mL)
Carb choice   1

....

Carbohydrate 20 g
Fibre 3 g
Protein 0
Fat 0
Cholesterol 0
Sodium 1 mg

Calories 80

Enjoy this fruit sorbet as a light ending to a big, festive meal. Or use it in smaller amounts as a palate cleanser between courses.

	fresh fruits (see variations below)	
¼ cup	granulated sugar	50 mL
1 tsp	grated orange, lemon or lime peel	5 mL
1½ cups	mineral water	375 mL

In a blender or food processor, process fruit, sugar and peel until smooth. Add mineral water; process for 30 seconds.

Freeze in a metal pan for one hour or until frozen around the outside. Process in a food processor or beat with electric mixer until smooth. Return to pan and freeze until firm or freeze in an ice cream maker according to manufacturer's directions. Remove solid sorbet from freezer to refrigerator about one hour before serving to allow softening.

Fruit Variations

Raspberry: Use 2 cups (500 mL) whole fresh or unsweetened frozen raspberries.

Kiwi fruit: Use 2 large, peeled kiwi fruits.

Cranberry: Use 1 cup (250 mL) chopped cranberries and add extra low-calorie sweetener to taste.

Strawberry: Use 2 cups (500 mL) sliced fresh or frozen strawberries.

Microwave Cranberry Applesauce

Cranberries added to applesauce give a beautiful colour and an extra tanginess to this traditional apple dessert.

2 cups	sliced peeled apples (2 medium)	500 mL
½ cup	fresh or frozen cranberries (see Tip)	125 mL
1–2 tbsp	granular low-calorie sweetener with sucralose	15–25 mL
2 tbsp	water	25 mL
¼ tsp	each ground nutmeg and cinnamon	1 mL
2 tsp	fresh lemon juice	10 mL

In a microwave-safe bowl, combine apples, cranberries, sweetener, water, nutmeg, cinnamon and lemon juice. Cover and microwave on high (100%) for 6 minutes or until apples and cranberries are tender; stir after 3 minutes. Let stand for 5 minutes.

- *You can store fresh cranberries in a refrigerator crisper for up to 2 weeks. But if you don't plan to use them right away, cranberries may be frozen for up to a year.*
- *Fresh and frozen berries can be used interchangeably.*

Prep · 10 minutes
Cook · 6 minutes
Yield · 2 servings, 1 cup (250 mL)

Each serving · ½ of recipe (½ cup/125 mL)
Carb choice   1

Carbohydrate 22 g
  Fibre 4 g
Protein 0 g
Fat 1 g
  Saturated 0 g
Cholesterol 0 mg
Sodium 1 mg
Calories 86

DINNER

RECIPES	CARBS	PAGE
Apple Cabbage Slaw	½	107
Tuscan Tomato Salad	½	108
Creamy Ranch Dressing, Creamy Herb Dip	Extra	109
Warm Sherry Vinaigrette	0	110
Light Cranberry Sauce	Extra	111
Mushroom Squash Bisque	½	112
Crispy Baked Chicken	1	113
Herbed Chicken and Vegetables	1	114
Roast Turkey Breast with Dressing	½	115
Light Turkey Gravy	Extra	117
Roast Cornish Hen	0	118
Beef and Vegetable Meat Loaf	½	119
Beef Strip Loin with Wine Sauce	0	120
Pork Chops Marinara with Mozzarella Cheese	½	121
Asian Grilled Pork Tenderloin	0	122
Sausage and Sweet Potato Chili	1½	123
Veal Cutlet in Tomato Basil Sauce	0	124
Calf's Liver with Onion and Herbs	1	125
Mustard Baked Salmon	½	127
Baked Fish en Papillote with Tomatoes and Herbs	0	128
Kasha and Red Pepper Pilaf	1	129
Tomato and Basil Baked Eggs	2	130
Tomato Mushroom Pasta Sauce	½	131
Cheese and Spinach Lasagne Roll-Ups	1½	133
Polenta Pie with Tomato Mushroom Pasta Sauce	2	134
Pasta with Chickpea Garlic Sauce	2½	135
French-Style Green Peas with Lettuce	½	136

Recipes	Carbs	Page
Roasted Sweet Peppers with Parsley	Extra	137
Scalloped Sweet and White Potatoes	2	138
Baked Layered Tomato and Potato Slices	1	139
Provençal Garlic Potatoes	1	140
Baked Rice	1½	141
Minted Carrots and Snow Peas	1	142
Roasted Lemon Potatoes	1	143
Corn and Zucchini Sauté	2	144
Cauliflower Potato Mash	1	145
Cardamom-Scented Rutabaga	½	146
Warm Cranberry Fall Fruit Compote	1	147
Baked Sliced Apples	1	148
Citrus Yogurt Jelly	1	149
Peach Cobbler	2	151
Oranges in Yogurt Cream	2	152
Nutty Mango Crisp	2	153
Mixed Berry Crisp	1	153
Sautéed Spiced Fruits	1	154
Cranberry Almond Crumble	1	155
Raspberry Bavarian	½	156
Strawberry Bavarian	½	156
Balsamic Strawberries	1	157
Balsamic Peaches	1	157
Rosy Poached Pears	1½	158
Pears with Raspberry Sauce	1	159
Fresh Fruit Jelly	1	160
Gingered Fruit Parfait	1	161

THE MAJOR MEAL OF THE DAY

Dinner is a time to relax after the day's activities and wind down with a satisfying meal. For most, it is the major meal of the day, and that's the way our menus treat it. However, "major" doesn't mean big servings and an overload of calories. Rather it means having a major amount of our daily nutrition in vegetables, grains and fruit—to maintain a healthy lifestyle.

Our dinner menus and recipes are designed to help one- and two-member households who may sometimes think dinners are not worth the trouble to prepare. Our recipes and menus are designed to make meal preparation worthwhile. Most recipes are for two servings. If you need only one, the other serving can be refrigerated or frozen for another day. All our dinner recipes are chosen to be quick and convenient to make—and delicious to eat.

Our recipes follow the healthiest, lowest-fat cooking methods: broiling, microwaving, steaming and stir-frying (see Appendix V, page 229 for definitions).

Dinner is traditionally a meal of a meat or alternative (the protein), potatoes or rice or pasta (the starch), vegetables and a dessert. Planning dinner, we tend to think first of the protein portion of the meal—will it be poultry, fish, meat or a meat alternative? But remember that protein is only a small part of a healthy meal. Better we question what vegetables and whole grains and starches we will eat, and *then* fit in a suitable protein choice. Think of your dinner plate as half covered by vegetables, one-quarter covered by whole grains or starches, and one-quarter by meat or an alternative.

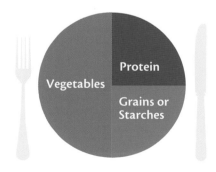

Opposite: Beef Strip Loin with Wine Sauce (page 120)

VEGETABLES

Let's start with how we fill half the plate. What are vegetables and why are they so important?

Eating Well with Canada's Food Guide considers vegetables so vital to our health that vegetables (and fruit) make up the largest arc of the rainbow.

Vegetables are the cornerstone of any healthy meal, especially if you have diabetes. They supply us with nearly all the vitamins, minerals and fibre essential to good health. Vegetables and fruits contain vitamin A (and beta-carotene that is converted to vitamin A), vitamin C and antioxidants that repair cell damage and protect the body against disease. Eating a variety of vegetables (and fruits), and having at least one serving at every meal, may help reduce your risk of some types of cancer as well as heart disease. Vitamin supplements do not seem to have the same effect.

All living plants produce carbohydrate and store it in their roots or fruit in the form of starches or sugars. Vegetables that are the leaf, stem or flower of a plant, or that are very young, contain only a small amount of carbohydrate and thus can be eaten freely by someone with diabetes. Sweet-tasting root vegetables and other vegetables that take longer to ripen contain more carbohydrate because they have more time to store it. They used to be grouped with fruit under the Fruits and Vegetables choice group. However, we know now that some root vegetables, such as carrots and beets, have much less available carbohydrate than was once thought because of the large amount of fibre they contain. In the new meal planning system all vegetables are classed as "free" with the exception of some of the sweeter vegetables (see page 101 and Appendix I, page 219).

Vegetables are considered to be "nutrient dense," that is, they have a high amount of nutrients for the number of calories they supply. Considering the cost of most vegetables relative to other foods, they are a magnificent nutrition bargain.

Vegetables: a quick guide to everything you need to know

Asparagus: Asparagus contains a good supply of vitamins and minerals. Microwave, roast or cook it, covered and upright in a small amount of boiling water, for 3 to 5 minutes.

VEGETABLES WITH THE MOST FIBRE:

- broccoli
- carrots
- cauliflower
- corn
- green beans
- green peas
- rutabaga
- tomato

Beets: Notable for their sweet, earthy flavour, beets are a rich source of fibre and are very low in calories. The best way to cook beets is to microwave or roast them whole with their skins on and stem and root ends untrimmed.

Bok choy: A mild versatile vegetable, it is a good source of vitamins A and C and calcium, and is very low in calories. Choose stalks with no sign of yellowing. Wash and chop as desired. Bok choy can be parboiled, steamed or stir-fried.

Broccoli and cauliflower: Some call broccoli "green goodness." This high-fibre food certainly boasts more nutrients than almost any other vegetable, especially calcium and beta-carotene (vitamin A). Peel stalks if they are tough, but be sure to include the tender leaves. Cauliflower is rich in vitamin C and very low in calories. Steam both vegetables, or microwave until tender-crisp.

Brussels sprouts and cabbage: Both of these vegetables contain fibre as well as vitamin C. The best way to cook them is as quickly as possible and in the least amount of liquid possible—microwave, steam or stir-fry.

Carrots: They are one of the best sources of beta-carotene and fibre and one of the least expensive vegetables. One Carb choice gets you 22 baby carrots—now that's a real bargain. **Minted Carrots and Snow Peas** (page 142) is a great way to serve this humble vegetable.

Green beans: Beans contain good amounts of beta-carotene and vitamin C and are rich in fibre. Since they grow quickly and are picked young, they are low in carbohydrate. Trim stem ends only; cover and steam or microwave for 3 to 5 minutes.

Leeks: They are prized for their subtle onion flavour and rich folic acid content. See **Thai Peppered Shrimp with Leeks** (page 190). Steam cut-up leeks for 3 to 5 minutes or steam whole for 10 to 15 minutes.

Mushrooms: Since mushrooms grow in the dark, they have little or no carbohydrate and few calories. Sauté mushrooms, uncovered, with a very small amount of broth or olive oil over medium-high for 3 to 5 minutes until all liquid is evaporated. Use as a great flavour addition to recipes or on their own. See **Mushroom Squash Bisque** (page 112).

Onions: Sliced, chopped, grated or diced, onions add flavour to a dish. They are cooked in many ways, based on the recipe being prepared. Since they are low in nutrients, the cooking method is not a concern.

Rutabagas: Some people still think of rutabagas as turnips, but they are two different vegetables. Rutabagas are larger, rounder and have a yellow flesh. Turnips are smaller and white-fleshed. Cut up rutabagas and steam or boil for 7 to 10 minutes. Of all the root vegetables, they are the best source of vitamin C and contain beta-carotene as well. Try our **Cardamom-Scented Rutabaga** (page 146) for a new twist.

Sweet and hot peppers: Like onions, peppers can be chopped, diced and sliced. Very rich in beta-carotene, they add flavour as well as colour. Peppers are great sautéed, stir-fried or stuffed. See **Roasted Sweet Peppers with Parsley** (page 137).

Snow peas: Snow peas should be shiny and flat. The smallest ones are sweetest and most tender. Remove tips and strings from both ends of the pod. Cover and steam for only a short time, 1 to 2 minutes, to retain vitamin C.

Spinach and Swiss chard: Select small leaves with good green colour and thin stems. Wash, but do not dry. Steam spinach for about 5 minutes, Swiss chard a bit longer. These greens are rich in vitamin A, folic acid and iron. You can increase iron absorption by serving with a source of vitamin C such as lemon or orange.

Tomatoes: Wonderful served raw with fresh basil, they can also be baked, broiled or sautéed. See **Baked Fish en Papillote with Tomatoes and Herbs** (page 128).

Zucchini: High in water content, zucchini is very low in calories. Eat raw or cut into slices and steam or sauté for 3 to 5 minutes. Try our **Corn and Zucchini Sauté** (page 144).

The sweeter vegetables

These are also packed with nutrients but have a significant amount of carbohydrate when eaten in larger portions. When you want to eat more than 1 cup (250 mL), count it as 1 Carb choice. Less than that, they can be eaten freely.

Green peas: Fresh peas have a very short season, and most of the ones we eat are sold frozen. It's best to quickly steam or microwave peas. They are a good source of protein and vitamin C. Frozen green peas retain their colour, flavour and nutrients better than canned and are low in sodium. Try **French-Style Green Peas with Lettuce** (page 136).

Parsnips: Considered a cold weather root vegetable and a cousin to the carrot, they are easy to prepare. They contain both vitamin C and folic acid. Steaming is the best way to cook them. Parsnips are also delicious dry-roasted alone or with other vegetables.

Winter squash: An excellent source of beta-carotene, these are hard-shelled and keep for a long time. A very versatile vegetable, squash can be baked, boiled, microwaved or steamed or added to a main dish as in **Herbed Chicken and Vegetables** (page 114). Cooking does not destroy vitamin A or beta-carotene since they are fat-soluble vitamins.

Fresh, frozen or canned?

Vegetables, fresh from the field and used as soon as possible, have the best flavour, texture and the most nutritional value. However, if they're wilted, pale or stored improperly, you're better off with frozen or even canned. Vegetables are flash-frozen soon after picking, so they retain most of their nutrients. Canned vegetables lose some vitamin C and often have large amounts of sodium and sometimes sugar added during processing, but much of this can be removed by rinsing before heating.

Are Some Vegetables Better for You Than Others?

The most nutritious vegetables are broccoli, spinach, Brussels sprouts, lima beans, peas, asparagus, artichokes, cauliflower and carrots, rated on their content of vitamin A, thiamin, niacin, riboflavin, vitamin C, potassium, iron and calcium.

What is the best way to cook vegetables?

Follow the "rule of least" when cooking vegetables to get the most out of your veggies: the least peeling, least amount of cooking water, least time to cook and least waiting time after cooking. Vegetable skins contain nutrients and fibre, so peeling should be done only when absolutely necessary.

Boiling, then draining vegetables, removes most, if not all, of the water-soluble vitamins such as vitamin C and folic acid. The longer vegetables are cooked, the more vitamin C is destroyed.

Microwave cooking is perfect for vegetables. More nutrients are retained, next to no water is required, and it's fast. Cover vegetables while microwaving to reduce cooking time and nutrient loss. Cook quickly on high (100%). Stir-frying is also excellent for the same reasons.

Steaming uses a minimum of water and is almost as good as the other two methods. Vegetables are at their flavour peak when cooked tender-crisp and served immediately.

Grains & Starches

Carbohydrate stored as starch in plants is the single most important source of food energy in the world and our body's principal source of energy. Since the carbohydrate we eat also has a major impact on blood glucose, this food group is very important for people with diabetes. It needs to be part of every meal, but in limited amounts. Our dinner menus and recipes use a variety of Grains & Starches with emphasis on slowly digested ones such as pasta, barley, corn and parboiled brown and white rice as well as sweet and white potatoes.

Rice and pasta

Rice and pasta are high in starchy carbohydrate. Both parboiled brown rice and whole grain pasta provide higher vitamin, mineral and fibre levels, and have a lower glycemic index. They all come in sufficient variety to delight the most adventurous cook and are economical food choices. Preparation of both is fast and easy; just follow the directions on the package.

Rice or pasta on call: We think having "rice on call" in the freezer is the ultimate home convenience food. You may well ask, What's that? It is simply cooking extra rice, then measuring it into small freezer bags in appropriate serving sizes. Seal, label and date the bags and pop them into the freezer. Rice will keep frozen for up to 6 months. To reheat rice, remove it from its bag to a small dish. Add 1 tbsp (15 mL) water, cover with waxed paper and reheat in a microwave oven on high (100%) for about 1 minute or until hot. Reheated rice makes a snap of Dinner Menus 1, 7 and 17.

Keep "pasta on call" in the same manner. To reheat pasta, remove it from its bag and lower it into a small saucepan of boiling water. Return to boil and cook for 1 minute; drain. It is amazingly convenient.

Potatoes

The potato is a tuber, a swollen underground stem that stores surplus starch in order to feed the above ground plants. Few foods are as wholesome as a potato. Carbohydrate, vitamins (particularly C) and minerals—the potato has them all in ample amounts and some protein as well. Many consider potatoes fattening. Not so, the only fat is what you add in cooking or at the table. Properly prepared, we feel potatoes taste so good they really don't need much of anything.

The best way to prepare potatoes is to cook them in their skins. The skin is an excellent source of fibre, with many nutrients just below it. So simply scrub unpeeled potatoes under cold water before cooking. Try to eat potatoes with their skin, which is where most of the iron and fibre are found. If you must peel them, use a vegetable peeler to remove the thinnest layer possible.

Potatoes are superb no matter how you cook them; boiled, grilled on the barbecue or baked in the oven as in **Scalloped Sweet and White Potatoes** (page 138).

Sweet potatoes are among the most nutritious foods in the vegetable kingdom, especially rich in vitamin A. Sweet potato is sensational baked, mashed or scalloped and with their dense, creamy texture, sweet potatoes cook well in the microwave. They have no more calories and carbohydrate than white potatoes but a much lower glycemic index (see page 8).

How much?

Some of the prepared foods in the menus and recipes need to be measured so you know you have the right amount on your plate. This is especially true for grains and starches. We suggest you have a set of graduated "dry" measuring cups—the ones in ¼-cup, ⅓-cup, ½-cup and 1-cup (or 50 mL, 75 mL, 125 mL and 250 mL) sizes. Having these measures at hand speeds up serving. These are also useful for measuring dry ingredients in recipes, so they do double duty. Two or three glass "liquid" measuring cups in 1-cup, 2-cup and possibly 4-cup (or 250 mL, 500 mL and 1 L) sizes come in handy as well.

MEAT & ALTERNATIVES

We have a wide variety of protein foods in our dinner menus. Some vegetarian, some chicken or meat, some fish or seafood. But they all provide about 21 grams of protein in each dinner or 3 Meat & Alternatives choices.

Protein is the basic building material of life and should be part of every meal. It provides us with the amino acid building blocks we need for growth and repair. Nine of these amino acids are called *essential*. They must come from our food because our bodies cannot make them. All animal sources of protein are *complete* proteins because they contain all nine essential amino acids. We get animal protein from meat, poultry, fish, eggs and dairy products. But you don't always need these foods to get the protein you require. It's possible to get all the necessary protein from a vegetarian diet and manage your diabetes effectively at the same time (see Meat Alternatives on page 105).

Meat

The saturated fat in meat is its one downside, but choosing leaner cuts of beef and trimming them well reduces the problem. When shopping for beef, choose cuts with the word *round* (top round, ground round) or *loin* (tenderloin, sirloin). These are among the leanest cuts. When buying pork and lamb, choose lean cuts labelled tenderloin, centre loin or extra-lean. Trim all visible fat before cooking.

Lean cooking methods include roasting, broiling, grilling, stir-frying, braising and stewing. Less tender cuts benefit from braising or stewing. More tender cuts can be roasted, broiled or barbecued as in *Beef Strip Loin with Wine Sauce* (page 120).

Poultry

Chicken and turkey breasts are extremely lean and low in calories. When cooking, be sure to remove the skin where most of the fat is. Use cooking methods similar to those for meat. See recipes for **Crispy Baked Chicken** (page 113) and **Roast Cornish Hen** (page 118).

Fish

Fast and easy to prepare, fish is a great substitute for higher-fat meats. Fish is delicate; if overcooked, it will be dry and tough. So use the "10-Minute Rule," also called the "Canadian Cooking Theory," devised by the Canadian Fisheries and Marine Service: measure the fish at its thickest point and cook at high heat (about 425°F/220°C) for 10 minutes for every inch (2.5 cm) of thickness. Fish can be baked, poached, grilled or microwaved. **Mustard Baked Salmon** (page 127) is a tasty and easy-to-prepare recipe.

Meat Alternatives

The term "meat alternatives," according to *Canada's Food Guide*, refers to eggs, dairy products, legumes, grains, nuts and seeds. Soy protein is the only *complete* plant-based protein. Other plant-based proteins are *incomplete* because they lack one or more of the nine essential amino acids. See index (page 248) for vegetarian recipes.

Lacto-ovo and lacto vegetarians add dairy products to meals in order to complete proteins, as we have in **Cheese and Spinach Lasagne Roll-Ups** (page 133). Total vegetarians or vegans eat only plant-based foods so they must balance grains with complementary legumes and seeds to obtain adequate protein. A general guide is to combine grains or nuts and seeds with legumes as in **Pasta with Chickpea Garlic Sauce** (page 135). And you don't have to combine complementary proteins at the same meal as long as you eat a variety over the day. A dietitian can help you plan a healthy vegetarian diet, adequate in all nutrients, that is also suitable for people with diabetes.

SUPERMARKET MEALS

In a hurry or want a break from cooking? Your local supermarket offers many frozen chicken, meat, fish or pasta entrées in single-serving sizes. Although many are high in sodium, they are fine for occasional use. They can be conveniently heated and combined with vegetables and a salad for a satisfying meal.

Just remember when shopping for frozen entrées to read labels carefully and compare. Look first at the amount of protein in one serving and then the amount of fat, sodium and calories. Choose the frozen entrée with the least fat and sodium and the most protein. Compare them to our dinner menus, which contain about 35 grams of protein, 15 grams of fat, 60 grams of carbohydrate and around 500 calories for an *entire meal*, not just one course.

DESSERTS

Fruit makes an excellent dessert. It tastes sweet, is relatively low in calories and is a major source of fibre, minerals and vitamins. Strawberries, pears and apples contain soluble fibre. Cantaloupe, oranges and bananas are rich in potassium. Most fruits are available all year long and can be purchased in small amounts. And if you don't happen to have the fruit suggested in a menu, check Appendix III, page 224, for other fruit choices.

We use fruit in some great-tasting and easy dessert recipes. Consider **Cranberry Almond Crumble** (page 155), **Nutty Mango Crisp** (page 153) and **Sautéed Spiced Fruits** (page 154).

Apple Cabbage Slaw

This variation of coleslaw is dressed with a cider vinegar and olive oil vinaigrette rather than the more commonly used mayonnaise-style dressing. We prefer its more refreshing taste and lower calories. Adding apples gives just that much more flavour as well as fibre. One of the family of cruciferous vegetables, cabbage is high on the list of anti-cancer foods.

2 cups	shredded green cabbage (see Tip)	500 mL
	or 1 cup (250 mL) each green and red cabbage	
1	green onion, thinly sliced	1
½	medium apple with skin, diced	½
2 tbsp	cider vinegar	25 mL
2 tsp	olive oil	10 mL
1 tsp	low-calorie sweetener	5 mL
Pinch	each celery seed and freshly ground pepper	

In a bowl, combine cabbage, onion and apple.

In a glass measure, whisk together vinegar, oil, sweetener, celery seed and pepper. Microwave on high (100%) for 30 seconds or until hot. Pour over cabbage mixture, toss well, cover and refrigerate for at least 1 hour before serving.

◉ *This salad keeps well for up to 2 days in the refrigerator. You can have a lot of fun with the colours of this salad: cabbage is available in green or red, as are apples—Granny Smith, red delicious—and even onions come in red. You can mix and match from all red to all green, or anywhere in between.*

Dinner Menu 18

....

Prep · 10 minutes
Refrigerate · for at least 1 hour
Yield · 2 servings,
      2 cups (500 mL)

....

Each serving · ½ of recipe
      (1 cup/250 mL)
Carb choice   ⅓
Fats choice   1

....

Carbohydrate 13 g
   Fibre 3 g
Protein 2 g
Fat 5 g
   Saturated 1 g
Cholesterol 0 mg
Sodium 22 mg
Calories 95

Tuscan Tomato Salad

Dinner Menu 23

····································

Prep · 15 minutes
Yield · 2 servings

····································

Each serving · ½ of recipe
Carb choice   ½
Fats choice   1

····································

Carbohydrate 9 g
  Fibre 1 g
Protein 2 g
Fat 5 g
  Saturated 1 g
Cholesterol 0 mg
Sodium 18 mg

Calories 83

The tomato is an important ingredient in Italian cuisine. This composed salad is easy to put together, yet yields abundant, fresh flavour. It is very complementary to **Mustard Baked Salmon** (page 127).

Salad:

1	large ripe tomato, sliced ½ inch (1 cm) thick	1
½	Vidalia or other sweet onion,	½
	thinly sliced and separated into rings	
1 tbsp	chopped fresh basil or 1 tsp (5 mL) dried	15 mL
2 tsp	chopped fresh chives	10 mL

Alternate tomato and onion slices on a platter. Combine basil and chives. Sprinkle over tomatoes and onion.

Vinaigrette:

2 tsp	olive oil	10 mL
2 tsp	red wine vinegar	10 mL
Pinch	each oregano and dry mustard	
1	small clove garlic, minced	1

In a bowl, whisk together oil, vinegar, oregano, mustard and garlic. Drizzle over salad and serve at room temperature.

CREAMY RANCH DRESSING

A great tasting ranch dressing that's low in fat and calories has to be a gift to healthy eaters and can be used as a dip for vegetables too. Two tablespoons of some commercial ranch-style dressings have 8 grams fat and 140 calories compared to 2 tablespoons of our Creamy Ranch Dressing, which has zero fat and 17 calories. A blender or food processor makes short work of this recipe.

1 cup	low-fat cottage cheese	250 mL
⅔ cup	low-fat plain yogurt	150 mL
2	green onions, finely chopped	2
1 tbsp	chopped fresh basil or 1 tsp (5 mL) dried	15 mL
1 tsp	Dijon mustard	5 mL
1	small clove garlic, minced	1
1 tsp	chopped fresh oregano or ¼ tsp (1 mL) dried	5 mL

In a food processor or blender, process cottage cheese and yogurt until very smooth. Remove to a bowl, stir in onions, basil, mustard, garlic and oregano.

Cover and refrigerate for up to 1 week. Stir before serving.

VARIATION

Creamy Herb Dip: For a dip, thin dressing with low-fat milk or water to desired consistency.

Dinner Menus 5, 11

Prep · 10 minutes
Yield · 1⅔ cups (400 mL)

Each serving · ¹⁄₁₆ of recipe
(2 tbsp/25 mL)
Extra

Carbohydrate 1 g
Fibre 0 g
Protein 2 g
Fat 0 g
Cholesterol 1 g
Sodium /1 mg
Calories 17

Warm Sherry Vinaigrette

Dinner Menus 7, 17

Prep · 10 minutes
Yield · about ⅔ cup (150 mL)
  dressing

Each serving · ¹⁄₁₀ of recipe
  (1 tbsp/15 mL)

Fats choice   1

Carbohydrate 1 g
  Fibre 0 g
Protein 0 g
Fat 5 g
  Saturated 1 g
Cholesterol 0 mg
Sodium 0 mg
Calories 49

Sherry vinegar is a fast-growing addition to the specialty vinegar family. This Spanish import tastes nutty and mellow compared to its more piquant cousins. Good ones are not cheap but a little goes a long way.

¼ cup	extra virgin olive oil (see Tip)	50 mL
¼ cup	sherry vinegar (see Tip)	50 mL
3 tbsp	water	45 mL
1	green onion, thinly sliced	1
¼ tsp	low-calorie sweetener	1 mL
Pinch	freshly ground pepper	

In a container with a tight-fitting lid, combine oil, vinegar, water, onion, sweetener and pepper; shake well and refrigerate for up to 2 weeks.

Warm in a microwave oven on medium (70%) for about 30 seconds just before tossing with the salad greens.

◉ *Using olive oil adds monounsaturated fat to your diet, which is a good thing.*

◉ *Today sherry vinegar is readily available in supermarkets. Red wine or cider vinegar can substitute for sherry, but the flavour will be quite different.*

Light Cranberry Sauce

It's not roast turkey or chicken without cranberry sauce. We make this very fast and easy to prepare "light" version with a very small amount of sugar plus sweetener. Orange peel adds extra zest.

2 cups	fresh or frozen cranberries (see Tip)	500 mL
½ cup	water	125 mL
1 tsp	shredded orange peel	5 mL
¼ cup	low-calorie sweetener	50 mL

Place cranberries, water and orange peel in a bowl. Cover and microwave on high (100%) for 3 minutes; stir and microwave on medium (70%) for 2 minutes or until thickened; cool slightly. Stir in sweetener to taste. Cover and refrigerate for up to 1 week.

◉ *Fresh cranberries store well—two weeks in the refrigerator and one year in the freezer. Freeze them unwashed in their bags. Then wash just the amount you need before using.*

Dinner Menus 15, 30

....

Prep · 5 minutes
Cook · about 5 minutes
Refrigerate · for up to 1 week
Yield · 2 cups (500 mL)

....

Each serving · ¹⁄₂₀ of recipe
    (2 tbsp/25 mL)
Extra

....

Carbohydrate 4 g
  Fibre 1 g
Protein 0 g
Fat 0 g
Cholesterol 0 mg
Sodium 1 mg
Calories 16

Prep · 15 minutes
Cook · 20 minutes
Yield · about 6 cups (1.5 L)

Each serving · ⅙ of recipe
(1 cup/250 mL)
Carb choice ½
Meat & Alternatives choice ½

Carbohydrate 13 g
Fibre 2 g
Protein 5 g
Fat 2 g
Saturated 0 g
Cholesterol 1 mg
Sodium 115 mg
Calories 85

MUSHROOM SQUASH BISQUE

A bisque is a very thick soup, rich in taste but not necessarily rich in fat. The low-fat ones develop their full flavour and thickness by using many puréed vegetables. This soup is an excellent example of a low-fat bisque.

1 tbsp	soft margarine or butter	15 mL
3 cups	sliced mushrooms	750 mL
2 cups	diced peeled butternut squash	500 mL
1½ cups	finely chopped carrots	375 mL
1 cup	finely chopped onions	250 mL
3 cups	*Homemade Light Chicken Broth* (page 59)	
	or salt-reduced chicken broth	750 mL
½ cup	low-fat evaporated milk	125 mL
¼ tsp	freshly ground pepper	1 mL
	sour cream or plain low-fat yogurt (optional)	

In a large saucepan, melt margarine. Add mushrooms, squash, carrots and onions. Cook over medium heat, stirring frequently, for 5 minutes. Add the broth, bring to a boil, reduce heat, cover and cook for 15 minutes or until vegetables are very tender.

Cool slightly before puréeing soup in batches in a blender or food processor until smooth. Return to the pan, add milk, season with pepper and heat to serving temperature.

Garnish with sour cream or plain low-fat yogurt, if desired

CRISPY BAKED CHICKEN

Seasoned dried bread crumbs provide a pleasantly crusty coating to succulent chicken. Take advantage of supermarket specials on chicken for this recipe.

4	small chicken thighs or drum sticks (about ½ lb/250 g)	4
⅓ cup	low-fat plain yogurt	75 mL
2 tsp	Dijon mustard	10 mL
1 tsp	minced gingerroot	5 mL
1	clove garlic, minced	1
⅓ cup	fine, dried bread crumbs	75 mL
Pinch	each freshly ground pepper, curry powder and paprika	

Remove and discard the skin and fat from chicken pieces.

In a shallow dish, stir together yogurt, mustard, gingerroot and garlic; set aside. In a second dish, combine bread crumbs, pepper, curry powder and paprika.

Dip chicken pieces into yogurt, then into bread crumbs to coat. Place on a baking pan sprayed with non-stick cooking spray. Bake in 350°F (180°C) oven for 40 minutes or until chicken is no longer pink, juices run clear and the crust is golden brown.

Dinner Menu 9

.....

Prep · 15 minutes
Cook · 40 minutes
Yield · 2 servings

.....

Each serving · ½ of recipe
    (2 pieces chicken)
Carb choice 1
Meat & Alternatives choices 3½

.....

Carbohydrate 17 g
  Fibre 1 g
Protein 28 g
Fat 8 g
  Saturated 2 g
Cholesterol 104 mg
Sodium 321 mg
Calories 261

Herbed Chicken and Vegetables

Dinner Menu 17

....

Prep · 15 minutes
Cook · about 25 minutes
Yield · 2 servings,
        2¼ cups (550 mL)

....

Each serving · ½ of recipe
        (about 1 cup/250 mL)
Carb choice   1
Meat & Alternatives choices   3

....

Carbohydrate 17 g
   Fibre 4 g
Protein 23 g
Fat 9 g
   Saturated 1 g
Cholesterol 51 mg
Sodium 129 mg
Calories 238

Onions, garlic, rosemary and marjoram pep up this colourful stove-top stew. Chock full of healthy vegetables, it is another way to use low-fat skinless chicken breasts.

1 tbsp	canola oil	15 mL
1	small onion, chopped	1
1	clove garlic, minced	1
2	small boneless, skinless chicken breast halves (250 g), cubed	2
½ tsp	each dried rosemary and marjoram	2 mL
Pinch	freshly ground pepper	
1 cup	crushed canned tomatoes	250 mL
1 cup	cubed peeled squash (see Tip)	250 mL
½	sweet green pepper, coarsely chopped	½
1 cup	halved button mushrooms	250 mL
¼ cup	salt-reduced chicken broth	50 mL

In a large non-stick skillet, heat oil over medium heat. Add onion and garlic; cook for 5 minutes or until softened.

Add chicken to skillet. Sauté for 3 minutes or until lightly browned. Sprinkle with rosemary, marjoram and pepper.

Combine tomatoes, squash, green pepper, mushrooms and broth. Pour over chicken, bring to a boil, cover, reduce heat to low. Cook for about 20 minutes or until the squash is tender and the chicken cooked. Add extra broth or water if necessary.

⊕ *Butternut squash is ideal for this recipe. It's available in the produce section of your supermarket, whole or cut up in smaller amounts.*

Roast Turkey Breast with Dressing

Make an old-fashioned meal of roast turkey with dressing with less trouble and fewer leftovers.

Whole turkey breasts (bone-in, not cut in half) are often found in the freezer section of your grocery store. Leave the skin on during cooking for maximum taste and tenderness.

| 2½ lb | whole turkey breast (see Tip on page 116) | 1.5 kg |

Dressing:

½ cup	each chopped onion and celery	125 mL
6	small mushrooms, chopped	6
1 tbsp	soft margarine or butter	15 mL
2 cups	bread crumbs (day old)	500 mL
½ cup	chopped apple	125 mL
2 tbsp	chopped pecans	25 mL
½ tsp	dried thyme	2 mL
¼ tsp	freshly ground pepper	1 mL

Clean and prepare the turkey breast for stuffing. Set aside.

In a non-stick skillet, sauté onion, celery and mushrooms in margarine on medium-high for about 5 minutes or until softened. Remove from heat and stir in the bread crumbs, apple, pecans, thyme and pepper. Set aside.

Fill turkey cavity (underside of the breast) with dressing; turn over onto a piece of foil large enough to draw edges up around the turkey breast. Punch holes in foil to allow any fat to drain.

Place the filled turkey breast on a rack in a shallow roasting pan, foil side down. Roast in 350°F (180°C) oven for 45 minutes. Pull foil away from meat to allow browning. Roast for 45 minutes longer or until a meat thermometer registers 170°F (77°C) in the thickest part.

Remove from the oven; cover loosely with foil. Let stand covered for 10 minutes before carving. Remove skin and discard. Serve dressing and sliced meat on warm serving plates.

Prep · 20 minutes
Cook · about 1½ hours
Yield · 3 cups (750 mL) dressing and enough turkey to serve 6 to 8

Each serving · ⅙ of recipe
(½ cup/125 mL dressing)

| Carb choice | ½ |
| Fats choice | 1 |

Carbohydrate 10 g
  Fibre 1 g
Protein 2 g
Fat 5 g
  Saturated 1 g
Cholesterol 0 mg
Sodium 93 mg
Calories 83

⊕ *Before roasting, pull skin back from breast and remove as much visible fat as possible. Then pull skin back over meat to keep it moist while roasting.*

⊕ ***Thaw safely by following these steps:***
  • *Never thaw at room temperature.*
  • *The safest way to thaw is in the refrigerator. Leave food in its original wrapping and place on a plate before refrigerating to prevent any juices from dripping onto other foods.*
  • *Thawing food in cold water is also safe. Leave food in its original plastic bag and submerge in cold water. Change water frequently to ensure it remains cold.*

⊕ *Any leftover turkey can be used in **Curried Turkey Salad** (page 81) or **Turkey Minestrone** (page 60).*

LIGHT TURKEY GRAVY

The most flavourful low-fat gravy is made from poultry pan drippings after all visible fat is removed.

	turkey pan juices	
	water or vegetable cooking liquid	
2 tbsp	cornstarch	25 mL
	water	
	salt and pepper to taste	

Pour pan juices through a sieve into a 2-cup (500 mL) measuring cup. Skim off the fat with a spoon or bulb baster; or drop ice cubes into the strained pan juices to chill the fat layer, then remove the hardened fat with ice.

Add enough water or vegetable cooking liquid to the pan juices to measure 1½ cups (375 mL). Return to roasting pan; bring to a boil.

Mix cornstarch with 2 tbsp (25 mL) cold water. Gradually add to boiling liquid; cook and stir for 5 minutes or until smooth and thickened. Season to taste with salt and pepper.

Dinner Menu 30
Special Occasion Menu 8

....

Prep · 10 minutes
Cook · about 8 minutes
Yield · 6 servings,
        1½ cups (375 mL)

....

Each serving · ⅙ of recipe
        (¼ cup/50 mL)
Extra

....

Carbohydrate 3 g
   Fibre 0 g
Protein 1 g
Fat 0 g
Cholesterol 0 g
Sodium 29 mg
Calories 15

Roast Cornish Hen

Prep · 10 minutes
Cook · about 1 hour
Yield · 2 servings

Each serving · ½ hen
Meat & Alternatives choices 2½

Carbohydrate 0
   Fibre 0
Protein 19 g
Fat 3 g
   Saturated 1 g
Cholesterol 86 mg
Sodium 49 mg
Calories 110

Rock Cornish hens are miniature chickens, a cross of Cornish and White Rock breeds. They can weigh up to 2½ lbs (just over 1 kg). One Cornish hen is an appropriate size for 2 people. They are best roasted or broiled and can be easily split in half once cooked.

1	Cornish hen, thawed (about 1¼ lb/625 g)	1
1	large apple, cut into pieces (see Tip)	1
	dried thyme, sage, salt and freshly ground pepper	

Rinse hen and pat dry with paper towelling. Stuff hen with apple pieces; close cavity with skewers or toothpicks.

Place hen, breast side up, on a rack in a roasting pan. Sprinkle lightly with thyme, sage, salt and pepper. Roast in 350°F (180°C) oven for about 1 hour or until juices run clear and a meat thermometer registers 165°F (74°C).

To serve, place hen on a cutting board and cut lengthwise through backbone. Discard apple and serve ½ hen on each plate.

⊕ *Apple provides extra moisture as well as flavour to the hen during cooking.*

Beef and Vegetable Meat Loaf

To most of us meat loaf says comfort food. Vegetables give moisture and extra flavour to this variation. Since it serves five, there can be leftovers for another dinner or for sandwiches.

1 lb	extra-lean ground beef	500 g
½ cup	rolled oats	125 mL
½ cup	finely chopped mushrooms	125 mL
⅓ cup	each finely chopped carrot and sweet red pepper	75 mL
3 tbsp	each finely chopped onion and parsley	45 mL
3 tbsp	tomato paste	45 mL
3 tbsp	water	45 mL
1	egg, lightly beaten	1
2 tsp	prepared mustard	10 mL
¼ tsp	each freshly ground pepper and chili powder	1 mL

Spray a 9- x 5-inch (2 L) loaf pan with non-stick cooking spray.

In a large bowl, combine beef, rolled oats, mushrooms, carrot, red pepper, onion and parsley; mix well.

In a second bowl, stir together tomato paste, water, egg, mustard, pepper and chili powder. Lightly combine with meat mixture just until mixed. Turn into the prepared pan. Bake in 375°F (190°C) oven for 50 minutes or until firm to the touch and a meat thermometer registers 160°F (71°C). Pour off the fat. Let stand for 5 minutes before cutting into 5 slices.

Dinner Menu 13

Prep · 20 minutes
Cook · 50 minutes
Yield · 5 servings

Each serving · ⅕ of recipe (1 slice)
Carb choice ½
Meat & Alternatives choices 3

Carbohydrate 12 g
  Fibre 2 g
Protein 21 g
Fat 11 g
  Saturated 4 g
Cholesterol 93 mg
Sodium 100 mg
Calories 231

Beef Strip Loin with Wine Sauce

Dinner Menu 21

....

Prep · 10 minutes
Cook · about 10 minutes
Yield · 4 servings

....

Each serving · ¼ of recipe
Meat & Alternatives choices   3

....

Carbohydrate 5 g
   Fibre 1 g
Protein 21 g
Fat 7 g
   Saturated 2 g
Cholesterol 42 mg
Sodium 330 mg
Calories 209

Entertain friends or impress your spouse with this easy-to-prepare yet elegant dish. Use the wine sauce with any steak. Most of the alcohol evaporates during cooking, leaving only a wonderful flavour.

2	strip loin grilling steaks (400 g), ½–¾ inch (1–2 cm) thick	2
4 tsp	dry red wine	20 mL
	freshly ground pepper	
2 tsp	olive oil	10 mL
2	green onions, chopped	2
2 cups	sliced mushrooms	500 mL
½ cup	dry red wine	125 mL
½ cup	salt-reduced beef broth	125 mL
1 tbsp	chopped fresh thyme or 1 tsp (5 mL) dried thyme	15 mL

Trim excess fat from the meat and discard. Brush each steak with 2 tsp (10 mL) wine and season with pepper. Broil or grill on medium 3–4 minutes per side for rare or 4–5 minutes for medium; turn once with tongs.

Meanwhile, heat oil in a non-stick skillet on medium-high heat; sauté onions and mushrooms for 5 minutes or until softened. Add ½ cup (125 mL) wine, broth and thyme. Cook for 3 minutes or until hot. Cut each steak in half, then in strips. Spoon wine sauce over and serve.

PORK CHOPS MARINARA WITH MOZZARELLA CHEESE

Delicious and made in minutes.

2	boneless (each 100 g) loin pork chops (see Tip)	2
½ cup	*Roasted Tomato Pasta Sauce* (page 75)	
	or bottled spaghetti sauce	125 mL
¼ tsp	each dried basil and oregano	1 mL
2 tbsp	shredded mozzarella cheese	25 mL
	made with skim milk	

Trim and discard fat from the chops. In a non-stick skillet, sauté chops on medium heat for 5 minutes per side or until brown.

Spoon spaghetti sauce evenly over each chop, sprinkle with basil, oregano and cheese. Cover and heat until the cheese melts and the sauce is hot.

◉ *Pork, "the other white meat," is low in fat and rich in B vitamins and minerals. It's a "heart-healthy" choice.*

Dinner Menu 8

....

Prep · 15 minutes
Cook · about 10 minutes
Yield · 2 servings

....

Each serving · ½ of recipe
   (1 chop)
Carb choice   ½
Meat & Alternatives choices 3½

....

Carbohydrate 10 g
  Fibre 1 g
Protein 26 g
Fat 7 g
  Saturated 2 g
Cholesterol 73 mg
Sodium 111 mg
Calories 192

ASIAN GRILLED PORK TENDERLOIN

Dinner Menu 1

Sesame oil and soy sauce add a touch of the Orient to pork tenderloin.

Prep · 10 minutes
Cook · about 4 minutes
Yield · 2 servings

4	slices pork tenderloin (200 g)	4
2 tsp	sesame oil	10 mL
2 tsp	fresh lime juice	10 mL
1 tsp	salt-reduced soy sauce	5 mL
	freshly ground pepper	

Each serving · ½ of recipe
Meat & Alternatives choices 3

In a non-stick skillet, heat oil on medium-high. Sauté meat on each side for 2 minutes or until golden brown and still slightly pink inside. Add lime juice and soy sauce and sprinkle with pepper. Serve immediately.

Carbohydrate 1 g
  Fibre 0
Protein 23 g
Fat 7 g
  Saturated 2 g
Cholesterol 56 mg
Sodium 122 mg
Calories 162

SAUSAGE AND SWEET POTATO CHILI

Spicy sausage, sweet potatoes and kidney beans meld together in this hearty chili. With a wealth of nutrients, particularly beta-carotene (vitamin A), sweet potatoes are sweeter than white ones, but don't have more calories or carbohydrate. Extra servings freeze well for a later meal.

¼ lb	hot or Italian low-fat sausage	125 g
½ cup	chopped onion	125 mL
1	clove garlic, minced	1
1–2 tsp	chili powder	5–10 mL
½ tsp	each dried oregano and cumin	2 mL
1	can (19 oz/540 mL) diced tomatoes without salt	1
2 cups	cubed sweet potato (see Tip)	500 mL
1 cup	canned kidney beans, drained and rinsed (see Tip)	250 mL
¼ cup	water	50 mL
Pinch	freshly ground pepper	

In a large non-stick saucepan, brown the sausage over medium heat; drain fat and discard. Cut sausage into thin slices.

Add onion, garlic, chili powder, oregano and cumin to sausage. Cook for 2 minutes, stirring frequently. Add the tomatoes, sweet potato, kidney beans and water. Bring to a boil on medium heat, cover, reduce heat and cook for 25 minutes or until the sweet potato is tender. Taste and adjust the seasonings with extra pepper, oregano and cumin, if needed. Add more water if the mixture becomes too thick.

⊕ *Sweet potatoes taste much sweeter than white ones since most of the starch changes to sugar as the sweet potatoes mature. However, due to their fibre content, they have a lower glycemic index than white potatoes.*

⊕ *Leftover beans can be saved for the **Tomato, Bean and Mozzarella Salad** (Lunch menu 4).*

HIGH FIBRE

Dinner Menu 29

....

Prep · 20 minutes
Cook · about 30 minutes
Yield · 4 servings,
    about 4 cups (1 L)

....

Each serving · ¼ of recipe
    (about 1 cup/250 mL)
Carb choices   1½
Meat & Alternatives choice   1

....

Carbohydrate 31 g
  Fibre 6 g
Protein 11 g
Fat 3 g
  Saturated 1 g
Cholesterol 21 mg
Sodium 163 mg
Calories 190

VEAL CUTLET IN TOMATO BASIL SAUCE

Dinner Menu 25

Prep • 5 minutes
Cook • about 15 minutes
Yield • 2 servings

Each serving • ½ of recipe
Meat & Alternatives choices   3

Carbohydrate 6 g
  Fibre 1 g
Protein 24 g
Fat 5 g
  Saturated 1 g
Cholesterol 113 mg
Sodium 373 mg
Calories 163

Veal is easy to overcook and dry out because of its low fat content. Cooking it in a sauce helps keeps the veal juicy and tender.

1	veal cutlet (200 g)	1
1 tsp	olive oil	5 mL
1 cup	sliced mushrooms	250 mL
½ cup	canned tomato sauce	125 mL
¼ tsp	each dried basil and oregano	1 mL

In a non-stick skillet, sauté veal in hot oil on both sides on medium-high heat until golden, being careful not to overcook. Remove and set aside.

Add mushrooms to the skillet; sauté for 5 minutes or until golden brown. Return veal to the skillet, spoon mushrooms over meat, top with tomato sauce, basil and oregano. Cook, covered, for 5 minutes or until sauce is hot. Slice cutlet into 2 servings and spoon sauce and mushrooms over each.

Calf's Liver with Onion and Herbs

People either love or hate liver. For the liver lovers, this recipe is as good as it gets.

½	small onion, chopped	½
1 tsp	canola oil	5 mL
¼ lb	calf's liver	125 g
2 tsp	all purpose flour	10 mL
Pinch	each dried thyme and freshly ground pepper	

In a non-stick skillet, cook onion in oil on medium heat for 3 minutes or until golden. Remove and set aside.

Coat liver with flour, thyme and pepper. Sauté in skillet for 2 minutes per side or just until cooked and golden brown. Top liver with cooked onions and serve.

Dinner Menu 3

....

Prep • about 10 minutes
Cook • about 8 minutes
Yield • 1 serving

....

Each serving • ½ of recipe
Carb choice   1
Meat & Alternatives choices   3

....

Carbohydrate 13 g
   Fibre 1 g
Protein 21g
Fat 10 g
   Saturated 2 g
Cholesterol 349 mg
Sodium 72 mg
Calories 226

MUSTARD BAKED SALMON

We love recipes like this one: they deliver great flavour with great ease. Remember the rule of thumb for cooking fish, 10 minutes cooking time per 1-inch (2.5 cm) thickness of fish (see page 105).

2	salmon fillets (4 oz/125 g each)	2
2 tbsp	white wine	25 mL
1 tbsp	Dijon mustard	15 mL
2 tsp	liquid honey	10 mL
½ tsp	sesame oil	2 mL
½ tsp	sesame seeds (optional)	2 mL

Spray an oblong baking pan with non-stick cooking spray. Place the salmon, skin side down, in the prepared pan.

In a bowl, combine wine, mustard, honey and oil; spoon over salmon. Sprinkle with sesame seeds (if using). Bake salmon in 425°F (220°C) oven for 10 minutes or until fish is barely opaque and flakes easily when tested with a fork. Remove skin from salmon and discard. Serve.

Prep · 10 minutes
Cook · about 10 minutes
Yield · 2 servings

Each serving · ½ of recipe (1 fillet)
Carb choice   ½
Meat & Alternatives choices   3

Carbohydrate 7 g
  Fibre 0 g
Protein 23 g
Fat 9 g
  Saturated 1 g
Cholesterol 62 mg
Sodium 133 mg
Calories 216

BAKED FISH EN PAPILLOTE WITH TOMATOES AND HERBS

Prep · 15 minutes
Cook · about 20 minutes
Yield · 2 servings

Each serving · ½ of recipe
Meat & Alternatives choices 3½

Carbohydrate 5 g
  Fibre 1 g
Protein 25 g
Fat 8 g
  Saturated 1 g
Cholesterol 75 mg
Sodium 174 mg
Calories 189

The term "en papillote" refers to food cooked in parchment paper or foil packages. No nutrients are lost in this fast and healthy style of cooking and it certainly makes things easier for the cleanup crew. Choose a fish that is fairly dense, such as salmon, arctic char, whitefish, halibut or turbot.

2	fish fillets, fresh or frozen and thawed (250 g raw) (see Tip)	2
4	drained canned plum tomatoes	4
4	medium mushrooms, sliced	4
1	clove garlic, minced	1
1 tbsp	chopped fresh basil or 1 tsp (5 mL) dried	15 mL
1 tsp	chopped fresh oregano or ¼ tsp (1 mL) dried	5 mL
Pinch	freshly ground pepper	

Cut two sheets of parchment paper (see Tip) or foil 2 inches (5 cm) larger than the fish fillets. Spray with non-stick cooking spray. Place fish in the centre of square.

In a small bowl, cut drained tomatoes into small pieces. Add mushrooms, garlic, basil, oregano and pepper; spoon evenly over the fish. Bring together long ends of paper or foil and fold over twice so fish is tightly enclosed. Lift short ends, bring together and fold twice. Place on a baking pan.

Bake fish in 400°F (200°C) oven for 20 minutes or until fish is barely opaque and flakes easily when tested with a fork. Place packages on dinner plates for each person to open at the table. Beware of steam!

◉ *It's best to use fresh fish within a day or so of purchasing. If you prefer to use frozen fish, place in refrigerator overnight to thaw, as it is much safer than thawing at room temperature.*
◉ *Parchment paper comes in rolls, much like waxed paper, and is available in grocery and specialty kitchen stores.*

KASHA AND RED PEPPER PILAF

Kasha is hulled, crushed kernels of buckwheat, a grain that digests very slowly. It has a wonderful nutty flavour, is available in whole, coarse, medium and fine grinds, and cooks much like rice.

½ cup	whole or coarse grain kasha	125 mL
1	egg, beaten	1
¾ cup	*Homemade Light Beef Broth* (page 58) (see Tip)	175 mL
¼ tsp	dried marjoram leaves	1 mL
Pinch	freshly ground black pepper	
1 tsp	olive oil	5 mL
½ cup	cubed zucchini (½ small)	125 mL
¼ cup	chopped sweet red pepper	50 mL
1	green onion, sliced	1
1	clove garlic, minced	1
1 tbsp	chopped fresh parsley	15 mL

In a large saucepan, mix kasha and egg. Let stand for 10 minutes. Cook over medium heat, stirring frequently for 4 minutes or until the kasha is dry. Add broth, marjoram and pepper. Bring to a boil, reduce heat, cover and cook for 15 minutes or until all liquid is absorbed and the kasha is tender.

Meanwhile, in a large non-stick skillet, heat oil over medium-high heat. Add the zucchini, red pepper, onion and garlic and cook for 4 minutes or until tender-crisp. Fluff kasha with a fork; stir in vegetable mixture and sprinkle with parsley.

⊕ *If you do not have our* **Homemade Light Beef Broth** *(page 58) made, a salt-reduced beef broth can replace it.*

Dinner Menu 11

....

Prep · 15 minutes
Cook · about 15 minutes
Yield · 4 servings,
     2 cups (500 mL)

....

Each serving · ¼ of recipe
     (½ cup/125 mL)
Carb choice   1
Fats choice   ½

....

Carbohydrate 17 g
   Fibre 1 g
Protein 5 g
Fat 3 g
   Saturated 1 g
Cholesterol 54 mg
Sodium 22 mg
Calories 104

Tomato and Basil Baked Eggs

Dinner Menu 12

....

Prep · 10 minutes
Cook · 20 minutes
Yield · 2 servings

....

Each serving · ½ of recipe
    (2 pieces)
Carb choices   2
Meat & Alternatives choices 2½
Fats choice   1

....

Carbohydrate 31 g
    Fibre 5 g
Protein 23 g
Fat 15 g
    Saturated 5 g
Cholesterol 438 mg
Sodium 482 mg
Calories 340

Eggs are not only for breakfast. Oven-poached in milk with a basil tomato topping and cheese garnish, eggs are just right for this easy-to-make light dinner.

4	eggs	4
¾ cup	diced tomato (1 medium)	175 mL
2 tsp	chopped fresh basil or ½ tsp (2 mL) dried	10 mL
2 tbsp	low-fat milk	25 mL
Pinch	freshly ground pepper	
¼ cup	shredded light old Cheddar cheese	50 mL
4 slices	whole wheat bread (30 g each), toasted	4

Spray a shallow casserole with non-stick cooking spray. Break the eggs, one at a time, into the casserole. Combine tomato and basil. Top each egg with some of the tomato mixture.

In a glass measure, whisk together milk and pepper; pour over tomato mixture. Sprinkle evenly with cheese. Bake eggs in 350°F (180°C) oven for 20 minutes or until eggs are set. Serve each egg on one slice of toast.

For Single Serving:

Break two eggs into a medium custard cup sprayed with non-stick cooking spray. Top with half of the tomato and milk mixture and cheese as directed in recipe. Place custard cup on small baking pan and bake as directed.

TOMATO MUSHROOM PASTA SAUCE

Red wine, mushrooms, tomatoes and other vegetables are used to make this fabulous-tasting pasta sauce. Enjoy it with your favourite pasta or polenta or over chicken or other meats. If you want to make a fast casserole dinner, see **Polenta Pie with Tomato Mushroom Pasta Sauce** (page 134).

1 tbsp	olive oil	15 mL
1	medium carrot, finely chopped	1
1	medium celery stalk, finely chopped	1
1	small onion, chopped	1
3	garlic cloves, minced	3
1½ cups	sliced small mushrooms	375 mL
2 cups	diced tomatoes (4 medium) (see Tip)	500 mL
½ cup	dry red wine or salt-reduced beef or vegetable broth	125 mL
1 tsp	granulated sugar	5 mL
Pinch	freshly ground pepper	

In a large saucepan, heat oil over medium heat. Add carrot, celery, onion and garlic; cook for 5 minutes or until vegetables are soft but not brown, stirring frequently.

Add the mushrooms; cook for 5 minutes. Add the tomatoes; cook, uncovered, for about 15 minutes or until most of the liquid has evaporated. Stir in the wine, sugar and pepper; cook for 15 minutes or until sauce has thickened.

⊕ *Fresh tomatoes may be replaced with 2 cups (500 mL) drained canned diced tomatoes without salt.*

Dinner Menu 4

....

Prep · 20 minutes
Cook · about 40 minutes
Yield · about 2½ cups (625 mL)

....

Each serving · ¾ cup (175 mL)
Carb choice   ½
Fats choice   1

Carbohydrate 12 g
   Fibre 3 g
Protein 2 g
Fat 4 g
   Saturated 0 g
Cholesterol 0 mg
Sodium 28 mg
Calories 85

Cheese and Spinach Lasagne Roll-Ups

Rolling each lasagne noodle around a filling is an easy way to create individual same-sized serving portions. Since this recipe makes 8 servings, you can freeze or store the leftovers individually or in portions that work best for your family.

8	whole wheat lasagne noodles	8
1 cup	low-fat cottage cheese	250 mL
2 cups	shredded mozzarella cheese made with skim milk, divided	500 mL
¼ cup	freshly grated Parmesan cheese	50 mL
1	egg, lightly beaten	1
1	pkg (300 g) frozen chopped spinach, thawed and well drained	1
¼ cup	finely chopped onion	50 mL
Pinch	each ground nutmeg and pepper	
2½ cups	*Tomato Mushroom Pasta Sauce* (page 131) or bottled spaguetti sauce	625 mL

In a large pot of boiling water, cook lasagne noodles according to package directions or until al dente (tender but firm). Drain well and set aside.

In a bowl, combine cottage cheese, 1 cup (250 mL) of the mozzarella cheese and all of the Parmesan cheese; add egg, drained spinach, onion, nutmeg and pepper.

Spray a 13- x 9-inch (3.5L) baking dish or two 8-inch (2 L) square baking pans with non-stick cooking spray (see Tip). Spread ⅓ of pasta sauce in bottom of pan.

Pat lasagne noodles dry with paper towel. Spread the cheese mixture evenly along the length of each lasagne noodle, roll up and place in baking pan seam-side down. Complete until all cheese filling has been used. Pour remaining sauce over the noodles. Top with extra mozzarella cheese. Bake, covered, in 350°F (180°C) oven for 25 minutes. Uncover and bake for 5 minutes longer or until cheese bubbles. Let stand for 5 minutes before serving.

⊕ *If you make two pans, securely cover the second one and freeze for later use. Cooking time will be reduced with a smaller pan size.*

HIGH FIBRE

Dinner Menu 24

....

Prep · 30 minutes
Cook · about 30 minutes
Yield · 8 servings

....

Each serving · ⅛ of recipe (1 filled lasagne noodle with sauce)
Carb choices   1½
Meat & Alternatives choice   1
Fats choice   1

....

Carbohydrate 28 g
  Fibre 5 g
Protein 14 g
Fat 8 g
  Saturated 4 g
Cholesterol 45 mg
Sodium 219 mg
Calories 231

Polenta Pie with Tomato Mushroom Pasta Sauce

Polenta, the staple of northern Italy, is made from cornmeal. You can use a ready prepared product available in the deli department of many supermarkets. This very simple one dish vegetarian meal is hearty without being heavy. Perfect for a busy day dinner. There should be leftovers for the next day unless you decide to invite guests.

1	roll (1 lb/500 g) ready-made polenta	1
2 tbsp	chopped fresh basil or 2 tsp (5 mL) dried	25 mL
2½ cups	*Tomato Mushroom Pasta Sauce* (page 131), divided	625 mL
1½ cups	coarsely shredded mozzarella cheese made with skim milk, divided	375 mL

Spray a deep 9-inch (23 cm) pie plate with non-stick cooking spray.

Cut polenta roll crosswise into ¼-inch (6 mm) slices. Line pie plate with half of the slices, overlapping to completely cover bottom of plate.

Stir basil into pasta sauce. Spread half the sauce over polenta. Sprinkle with half of the mozzarella. Repeat layers. Bake in 450°F (230°C) oven for about 20 minutes or until bubbling and golden. Remove pie from oven, let stand for 5 minutes before cutting into 4 servings.

Dinner Menu 20

....

Prep · 15 minutes, if sauce is made
Cook · about 20 minutes
Yield · 4 servings

....

Each serving · ¼ of recipe
Carb choices 2
Meat & Alternatives choices 1½
Fats choices 1½

....

Carbohydrate 33 g
 Fibre 4 g
Protein 14 g
Fat 11 g
 Saturated 5 g
Cholesterol 24 mg
Sodium 571 mg
Calories 279

PASTA WITH CHICKPEA GARLIC SAUCE

Using puréed chickpeas to make a hearty pasta sauce is rustic Italian cooking at its finest. To make this a vegetarian meal, replace chicken broth with vegetable broth. If less heat is desired, just omit the red pepper flakes.

1 tbsp	olive oil	15 mL
¼ cup	chopped onion	50 mL
2	garlic cloves, crushed	2
1	can (19 oz/540 mL) chickpeas, drained and rinsed (about 2 cups)	1
1½ cups	*Homemade Light Chicken Broth* (page 59) or salt-reduced chicken broth	375 mL
¼ tsp	crushed red pepper flakes or cayenne (optional)	1 mL
2¼ cups	dry whole wheat pasta (160 g) (see Tip)	625 mL
¾ cup	halved cherry tomatoes (about 12)	175 mL
2	cloves garlic, minced	2
2 tbsp	minced fresh parsley	25 mL
1 tbsp	fresh lemon juice	15 mL

In a medium saucepan, heat oil over medium heat. Add onion and crushed garlic; sauté for 1 minute. Add chickpeas, broth and red pepper flakes (if using). Bring to a boil, cover, reduce heat and cook slowly for 15 minutes. Remove chickpea mixture to a food processor and process until smooth.

Meanwhile, cook pasta in a large amount of boiling unsalted water according to package directions or until al dente; drain well. Combine the chickpea sauce with pasta, cherry tomatoes, minced garlic, parsley and lemon juice; toss well. Serve immediately.

⊕ *Whole wheat pasta is high in fibre and readily available in different shapes—bows, rotini, fusilli as well as macaroni and spaghetti. Your choice. We have given weights since that is more accurate than measure. One Carb choice is 20 g dry pasta.*

VERY HIGH FIBRE

Dinner Menu 28

Prep · 25 minutes
Cook · about 20 minutes
Yield · 4 servings ,
6½ cups (1.625 L)

Each serving · ¼ of recipe
(1⅔ cups, 400 mL)
Carb choices · 2½
Meat & Alternatives choice · ½
Fats choice · ½

Carbohydrate 51 g
Fibre 10 g
Protein 13 g
Fat 6 g
Saturated 1 g
Cholesterol 10 mg
Sodium 294 mg
Calories 309

Dinner Menu 9

....

Prep · 10 minutes
Cook · about 3 minutes
Yield · 2 servings

....

Each serving · ½ of recipe
    (¾ cup/175 mL)
Carb choice   ½
Meat & Alternatives choice ½

....

Carbohydrate 16 g
   Fibre 5 g
Protein 6 g
Fat 3 g
   Saturated 0 g
Cholesterol 0 mg
Sodium 148 mg
Calories 107

FRENCH-STYLE GREEN PEAS WITH LETTUCE

Lettuce supplies the moisture to gently steam the peas—it makes frozen taste like fresh.

1 tsp	soft margarine or butter	5 mL
¾ cup	thinly sliced iceberg lettuce	175 mL
1½ cups	frozen peas	375 mL
1	chopped green onion	1
Pinch	each freshly ground pepper & dried marjoram	

In a saucepan, melt margarine over medium heat. Add lettuce. Top with frozen peas and onion. Sprinkle with pepper and marjoram. Cover and cook for 3 minutes or until peas are just cooked, stirring occasionally. Serve immediately.

Roasted Sweet Peppers with Parsley

Peppers can be roasted on the barbecue or under the broiler. Whatever the method, the result is a lovely combination of intense smoky-sweet pepper flavours. If you have never done it, roasting peppers is not difficult and the results are well worth the effort. While you're at it, why not roast several as they can be frozen for another use?

2	whole sweet red, orange or yellow peppers (see Tips)	2
2 tbsp	chopped fresh parsley	25 mL
	freshly ground pepper	

Place peppers on a barbecue grill or under a broiler, about 2 inches (5 cm) from heat. Grill for about 20 minutes, turning often, until skin is charred all over. Remove from grill and place in paper or plastic bag until cool (see Tip).

Peel away blackened skin and discard. Cut in half, remove seeds and core, slice into thin strips, toss with parsley and pepper and serve at room temperature or reheat.

◉ *Placing grilled peppers in a paper or plastic bag keeps them moist as they cool. This makes it easier to remove the charred outer skin, leaving only the wonderful roasted sweet pepper flesh.*

◉ *One serving is an excellent source of vitamins A and C as well as a source of folic acid and B$_6$.*

Prep · 5 minutes
Cook · about 20 minutes
Yield · 4 servings

Each serving · ¼ of recipe
Extra

Carbohydrate 5 g
  Fibre 1 g
Protein 1 g
Fat 0 g
Cholesterol 0 mg
Sodium 3 mg
Calories 23

Dinner Menu 15

....

Prep · 15 minutes
Cook · about 40 minutes
Yield · 2 servings,
about 2 cups (500 mL)

....

Each serving · ½ of recipe
(about 1 cup/250 mL)

Carb choices	2
Fats choice	1

....

Carbohydrate 36 g
Fibre 4 g
Protein 4 g
Fat 4 g
Saturated 1 g
Cholesterol 0 mg
Sodium 158 mg
Calories 192

SCALLOPED SWEET AND WHITE POTATOES

Add sweet potatoes to white ones for a dynamite variation to traditional scalloped potatoes. Both varieties are a source of fibre and full of great nutrients. We use broth instead of milk for flavour.

1 cup	thinly sliced white potatoes (2 small)	250 mL
1 cup	thinly sliced sweet potato (½ small)	250 mL
½	small onion, thinly sliced, divided	½
Pinch	freshly ground pepper	
⅓ cup	salt-reduced chicken or vegetable broth	75 mL
2 tsp	soft margarine or butter	10 mL
¼ tsp	ground nutmeg	1 mL

Lightly spray two small baking pans (see Tip) or casseroles with non-stick cooking spray.

In a medium bowl, combine white and sweet potato slices. Place ¼ of the potatoes in each prepared pan. Top with ¼ of the onion and sprinkle with ½ of the pepper. Repeat layers.

Heat broth and margarine to boiling; pour over potatoes. Sprinkle with nutmeg. Cover each pan with foil. Bake in 350°F (180°C) oven for 25 minutes. Uncover and bake for about 15 minutes longer or until the potatoes are tender and golden brown.

◉ *We find the small foil pans very useful for this type of recipe. However, one medium loaf pan is a good alternative.*

Baked Layered Tomato and Potato Slices

A delicious way to add colour, nutrition and extra vegetables to dinner.

2 tsp	olive oil	10 mL
1 tsp	dried thyme leaves	5 mL
1	clove garlic, minced	1
¼ tsp	freshly ground pepper	1 mL
1	medium potato, peeled and thinly sliced	1
1	medium tomato, thinly sliced	1
	thyme sprigs (optional)	

Spray a shallow casserole with non-stick cooking spray.

In a bowl, stir together oil, thyme, garlic and pepper. Add potato slices; toss to coat.

Arrange potatoes in the prepared dish by overlapping slices. Add tomatoes to the bowl and toss with remaining oil to coat. Place tomato slices over potatoes. Bake in 400°F (200°C) oven for 20 minutes or until the vegetables are tender and edges are beginning to brown. Garnish with thyme sprigs (if using).

Dinner Menu 19

....

Prep · 15 minutes
Cook · about 20 minutes
Yield · 2 servings

....

Each serving · ½ of recipe
Carb choice	1
Fats choice	1

....

Carbohydrate 19 g
  Fibre 2 g
Protein 3 g
Fat 5 g
  Saturated 1 g
Cholesterol 0 mg
Sodium 11 mg
Calories 125

PROVENÇAL GARLIC POTATOES

....

Prep · 10 minutes
Cook · about 25 minutes
Yield · 4 servings,
      3 cups (750 mL)

....

Each serving · ¼ of recipe
      (¾ cup/175 mL)
Carb choice   1
Fats choice   ½

....

Carbohydrate 20 g
  Fibre 2 g
Protein 3 g
Fat 2 g
  Saturated 0 g
Cholesterol 0 mg
Sodium 64 mg
Calories 107

Cooking with fresh garlic is typical of French Provençal cooking. But if you find the garlic "hit" a bit much, just reduce the number of cloves.

1 tbsp	olive oil	15 mL
4	large cloves garlic, thinly sliced	4
3 cups	cubed unpeeled potatoes (3 medium)	750 mL
Pinch	each salt and freshly ground black pepper	

In a medium non-stick skillet, heat oil on medium-high heat; add garlic and cook for 30 seconds. Add potatoes and cook for 15 minutes, turning frequently or until golden on all sides. Sprinkle lightly with salt and pepper. Reduce heat to low, cover and cook for 10 minutes or until the potatoes are tender; stir occasionally.

BAKED RICE

We really enjoy making rice by this easy baking method. It can be prepared ahead of time and popped in the oven about 40 minutes before sitting down at the table.

½	small onion, thinly sliced	½
1	clove garlic, chopped	1
1 tsp	olive oil	5 mL
⅓ cup	basmati or parboiled rice	75 mL
⅔ cup	salt-reduced beef broth (see Tip)	150 mL
1 tbsp	chopped fresh parsley	15 mL
1 tsp	chopped fresh thyme or	5 mL
	¼ tsp (1 mL) dried thyme	
¼ tsp	freshly ground pepper	1 mL
1 tbsp	chopped fresh parsley	15 mL

In a medium saucepan, sauté onion and garlic in oil over medium heat for about 5 minutes (do not brown).

Rinse rice well under cold running water. Add rice to onion, cook and stir until translucent. Add broth, parsley, thyme and pepper. Bring to a boil. Transfer to a covered baking dish and bake in 350°F oven for 40 minutes or until all liquid is absorbed. Add chopped parsley, stir and serve.

◉ *Homemade Light Beef Broth* (page 58) could replace salt-reduced beef broth.

Dinner Menu 22

....

Prep · 10 minutes
Cook · 40 minutes
Yield · 2 servings,
 ⅔ cup (150 mL)

....

Each serving · ½ of recipe
 (⅓ cup/75 mL)
Carb choices 1½
Fats choice ½

....

Carbohydrate 27 g
 Fibre 1 g
Protein 3 g
Fat 2 g
 Saturated 0 g
Cholesterol 0 mg
Sodium 191 mg
Calories 137

MINTED CARROTS AND SNOW PEAS

Dinner Menu 22

....

Prep · 10 minutes
Cook · 10 minutes
Yield · 2 servings

....

Each serving · ½ of recipe
Carb choice   1
Fats choice   1

....

Carbohydrate 16 g
   Fibre 4 g
Protein 4 g
Fat 4 g
   Saturated 1 g
Cholesterol 0 mg
Sodium 80 mg
Calories 111

Chopped fresh mint provides a distinctive taste and aroma to this vegetable dish.

1 cup	thinly sliced carrots (3 medium)	250 mL
2 cups	trimmed snow peas	500 mL
2 tsp	soft margarine or butter	10 mL
2 tsp	fresh lemon juice	10 mL
2 tsp	chopped fresh mint leaves or	
	1 tsp (5 mL) dried	10 mL

Cook carrots in a small amount of boiling water for about 5 minutes; add peas and continue to cook for 5 more minutes or until carrots are tender (do not overcook). Drain well. Stir in margarine, lemon juice and mint.

Roasted Lemon Potatoes

The flavour of lemon makes these potatoes a marvellous accompaniment to grilled fish, lamb, steak or chicken.

1	medium potato, unpeeled (190 g) (see Tip)	1
1 tsp	olive oil	5 mL
1	clove garlic, minced	1
Pinch	each paprika and freshly ground pepper	
1 tsp	grated lemon peel	5 mL
1 tsp	fresh lemon juice	5 mL

Cut potato in half lengthwise; deeply score cut surfaces.

Combine oil, garlic, paprika, pepper, lemon peel and juice. Brush cut side of potato halves with mixture. Place potato halves, cut side up, in baking pan. Bake in 350°F (180°C) oven for 40 minutes or until potato is tender, turning once.

- *Yukon Gold or red-skinned potatoes are good choices for this recipe.*
- *If possible, choose individual potatoes from a bulk display to get the size you want.*
- *Rather than roasting, potato halves may be micro-baked on high (100%) for 4–5 minutes.*
- *Nutritionally speaking, the less you do to a potato, the better. Since skin is an excellent form of fibre, leave it on.*

Dinner Menu 23

....

Prep • 5 minutes
Cook • 40 minutes
Yield • 2 servings

....

Each serving • ½ of recipe
    (½ potato)

Carb choice	1
Fats choice	½

....

Carbohydrate 17 g
  Fibre 2 g
Protein 2 g
Fat 2 g
  Saturated 0 g
Cholesterol 0 mg
Sodium 7 mg
Calories 94

Dinner Menu 25

....

Prep · 10 minutes
Cook · about 15 minutes
Yield · 2 servings,
       3 cups (750 mL)

....

Each serving · ½ of recipe
       (1½ cups/375 mL)
Carb choices   2
Fats choice   1

....

Carbohydrate 33 g
   Fibre 6 g
Protein 6 g
Fat 6 g
   Saturated 1 g
Cholesterol 0 mg
Sodium 10 mg
Calories 185

CORN AND ZUCCHINI SAUTÉ

Margaret enjoyed this dish in Mexico and thought it so appropriate for a Canadian cookbook that emphasizes eating a variety of many vegetables. Replace basil with chili powder for a more Mexican flavour.

2 tsp	canola oil	10 mL
1 cup	thinly sliced onion	250 mL
2	cloves garlic, minced	2
2½ cups	diced zucchini (2 large)	625 mL
1½ cups	corn kernels, fresh or frozen	375 mL
1 tbsp	fresh chopped basil or 1 tsp (5 mL) dried	15 mL
¼ tsp	freshly ground pepper	1 mL

In a large non-stick skillet, heat oil over medium heat. Add onion, cook for 3 minutes; add garlic and cook, stirring frequently, for 1 minute or until onion and garlic are tender and golden. Add zucchini, corn, basil and pepper. Cover and cook on medium-low for 10 minutes or until vegetables are tender.

Cauliflower Potato Mash

The combination of these two vegetables cooked and eaten as one is an example of the whole being even better than the individual parts. It's a great accompaniment to a roast beef dinner.

4 cups	cauliflower florets (½ medium head)	1 L
3½ cups	cubed peeled baking potatoes	825 mL
¼ cup	chopped onion	50 mL
¼ cup	hot low-fat milk	50 mL
1 tbsp	soft margarine or butter	15 mL
¼ tsp	each freshly ground pepper and ground nutmeg	1 mL

In a large saucepan, cook cauliflower, potatoes and onion in boiling water for 15 minutes or until tender. Drain and set aside.

Place cooked vegetables, milk, margarine, pepper and nutmeg in a food processor. Process, using on/off motion, just until mixture is smooth. Be careful not to over process. Serve at once or place in a microwave-safe dish and reheat when ready to serve.

Dinner Menu 26

....

Prep • 20 minutes
Cook • about 15 minutes
Yield • 6 servings, 4 cups (1 L)

....

Each serving • ⅙ of recipe
    (⅔ cup/150 mL)
Carb choice   1
Fats choice   ½

....

Carbohydrate 20 g
  Fibre 3 g
Protein 4 g
Fat 2 g
  Saturated 0 g
Cholesterol 0 mg
Sodium 56 mg
Calories 110

CARDAMOM-SCENTED RUTABAGA

Dinner Menu 30

Prep · 10 minutes
Cook · about 20 minutes
Yield · 2 servings,
      1 cup (250 mL)

Each serving · ½ of recipe
      (½ cup/125 mL)
Carb choice   ½
Fats choice   ½

Carbohydrate 12 g
   Fibre 2 g
Protein 2 g
Fat 2 g
   Saturated 0 g
Cholesterol 1 mg
Sodium 114 mg
Calories 71

Cardamom, a very aromatic spice with a warm, sweet flavour, is a member of the ginger family and goes especially well with winter vegetables such as rutabaga. Be frugal when using cardamom as a little goes a long way.

2 cups	cubed rutabaga (see Tips)	500 mL
2 tbsp	low-fat milk	25 mL
1 tsp	soft margarine or butter	5 mL
1 tsp	liquid honey	5 mL
Pinch	ground cardamom	

Cook rutabaga in boiling water for about 20 minutes or until tender, drain and dry. Transfer to a food processor or blender and purée until smooth.

Heat milk, margarine, honey and cardamom until milk is hot. Gradually add to rutabaga while processor is running. Process until light and creamy. Serve at once or place in a microwave-safe dish and reheat when ready to serve.

⊕ *Rutabagas are confused with turnips. Turnips are the size of a baseball with white flesh and very few nutrients. Rutabagas are larger, have a sweeter, yellow flesh and are richer in vitamin C and beta-carotene than turnips.*

⊕ *How do you cut a rutabaga? It's a question often asked. Microwave the whole rutabaga wrapped in paper towel for 2 to 3 minutes. Slicing, cubing or dicing will be a lot easier.*

⊕ *If you want to cook a whole rutabaga, wrap it in paper towels and microwave on high (100%) for about 20 minutes for a 2 lb (1 kg) rutabaga. Then cover with foil and let stand for 10 minutes.*

WARM CRANBERRY FALL FRUIT COMPOTE

Fall fruit flavours predominate in this warm dessert. The cranberries require less sweetening when cooked with the sweeter apples and pears. Served with a simple cookie, or topped with plain or vanilla low-fat yogurt, this is a superb dessert.

1	medium apple, unpeeled and cut in eighths	1
1	medium pear, unpeeled and cut in eighths	1
½ cup	fresh or frozen cranberries (see Tip)	125 mL
1 tbsp	brown sugar	15 mL
¼ cup	water	50 mL
1 tsp	fresh lemon juice	5 mL
½ tsp	grated lemon peel	2 mL
¼ tsp	ground nutmeg	1 mL
	low-calorie sweetener to taste	

In a medium saucepan, combine apple, pear, cranberries, brown sugar and water. Cover and cook on medium heat for 8 minutes or until the fruit is softened (see Tip). Stir in lemon juice and peel and nutmeg. Taste and adjust sweetness, if desired (see Tip). Delicious when served warm.

- *Cranberries alone need to be sweetened, but too much detracts from their refreshingly tart natural flavour.*
- *This recipe can also be microwaved on medium (70%) for about 5 minutes or until fruit is tender.*

Dinner Menu 5

....

Prep · 10 minutes
Cook · about 8 minutes
Yield · 3 servings,
about 1½ cups (375 mL)

....

Each serving · ⅓ of recipe
(about ½ cup/125 mL)
Carb choice 1

....

Carbohydrate 22 g
Fibre 3 g
Protein 0 g
Fat 0 g
Cholesterol 0 mg
Sodium 3 mg
Calories 87

BAKED SLICED APPLES

Dinner Menu 9

....

Prep • 10 minutes
Cook • about 6 minutes
Yield • 2 servings

....

Each serving • ½ of recipe
Carb choice   1

....

Carbohydrate 19 g
   Fibre 2 g
Protein 1 g
Fat 1 g
   Saturated 1 g
Cholesterol 0 mg
Sodium 8 mg

Calories 88

Apples are such a Canadian favourite. Plentiful in many interesting varieties, flavourful, nutritious and economical, they are a great dessert choice. Cortland, Spy and Ida Red varieties are excellent all-purpose apples. Their mellow goodness cooked with cinnamon and served with sour cream is evident in this dessert.

2 cups	sliced unpeeled apples (2 medium) (see Tip)	500 mL
2 tbsp	granular brown low-calorie sweetener	25 mL
1 tsp	vanilla extract	5 mL
¼ tsp	cinnamon	1 mL
2 tbsp	low-fat sour cream	25 mL

Place apples in a shallow microwave-safe casserole. Sprinkle with sweetener, vanilla and cinnamon. Cover and microwave on medium (70%) for 5 minutes or until apples are tender. Spoon sour cream around edges; cook for 1 minute. Serve warm.

⊕ *A medium apple has about 70 calories and is a good source of vitamin A (providing you eat the skin), fibre and potassium. Over 80% of the fibre in apples is soluble fibre in the form of pectin. Studies have shown that pectin and other soluble fibres help lower cholesterol levels and slow the digestion of carbohydrate into glucose.*

CITRUS YOGURT JELLY

Yogurt's delightfully tart, subtle flavour turns this easy dessert into something quite marvellous. Its creamy texture makes yogurt the perfect replacement for higher fat whipped cream. If you are not serving the entire jelly, the dessert can be poured into 4 individual dishes.

1	pkg (7 g) unflavoured gelatin	1
¼ cup	cold water	50 mL
2 cups	low-fat plain yogurt (see Tip)	500 mL
2 tsp	grated lemon rind	10 mL
⅓ cup	fresh lemon juice	75 mL
2 tbsp	low-calorie sweetener	25 mL
2 tbsp	granulated sugar	25 mL
	fresh mint leaves and extra lemon rind	
	for garnish	

In a small saucepan, combine gelatin and water. Let stand for 2 minutes. Heat until gelatin has dissolved. Cool for 5 minutes.

In a bowl, whisk together yogurt, lemon rind, juice, sweetener and sugar. Whisk in gelatin mixture. Pour into a 3-cup (750 mL) bowl; refrigerate for 2 hours or until set. Unmold onto serving plate, garnish with mint and extra lemon rind.

⊕ *According to the Dairy Bureau of Canada, newly identified "good for you" microorganisms in yogurt called probiotic bacteria may offer health benefits beyond yogurt's well-known nutritional strengths.*

Dinner Menu 10

....

Prep · 15 minutes
Refrigerate · 2 hours
Yield · 4 servings,
    about 2½ cups (625 mL)

....

Each serving · ¼ of recipe
    (about ⅔ cup/150 mL)
Carb choice   1
Meat & Alternatives choice   ½

....

Carbohydrate 18 g
  Fibre 0 g
Protein 8 g
Fat 0 g
Cholesterol 2 mg
Sodium 92 mg

Calories 101

PEACH COBBLER

Cobbler is the name given to a baked deep-dish fruit dessert, which is topped with a thick biscuit crust. Any fresh fruit, especially peaches, makes a wonderful cobbler.

2 cups	sliced fresh peaches (see Tip)	500 mL
2 tbsp	granulated sugar	25 mL
2 tbsp	granular low-calorie sweetener with sucralose	25 mL
2 tsp	fresh lemon juice	10 mL
½ cup	all purpose flour	125 mL
1 tsp	baking powder	5 mL
Pinch	ground nutmeg	
1 tbsp	soft margarine or butter	15 mL
2 tbsp	low-fat milk	25 mL
1	egg	1
½ tsp	vanilla extract	2 ml

In a bowl, combine peaches, sugar, sweetener and lemon juice. Transfer to a shallow 8-inch (20 cm) square baking dish (see Tip) sprayed with non-stick cooking spray. Set aside.

In a second bowl, combine flour, baking powder and nutmeg. Cut in the margarine until the mixture resembles fine crumbs.

In a small bowl, whisk together milk, egg and vanilla. Stir into flour mixture to make a stiff batter. Spoon the batter evenly over peaches. Bake in 425°F (210°C) oven for 18 minutes or until the crust is golden and peach juice bubbles around the edges. Serve warm.

- *For 2 cups (500 mL) fresh peaches, you will need about 7 peaches. If you decide to use sliced canned peaches, 1 cup (250 mL) will replace the fresh.*
- *Four small individual baking dishes make for easier serving of equal amounts.*

Dinner Menu 11

....

Prep · 20 minutes
Cook · about 18 minutes
Yield · 4 servings

....

Each serving · ¼ of recipe
Carb choices   2
Fats choice   1

....

Carbohydrate 30 g
  Fibre 2 g
Protein 4 g
Fat 4 g
  Saturated 1 g
Cholesterol 54 mg
Sodium 142 mg
Calories 173

Dinner Menu 12

....

Prep · 10 minutes
Yield · 2 servings

....

Each serving · ½ of recipe
Carb choices   2

....

Carbohydrate 31 g
   Fibre 4 g
Protein 6 g
Fat 0 g
Cholesterol 0 mg
Sodium 55 mg
Calories 143

ORANGES IN YOGURT CREAM

How easy can you get. This quick-to-make light and healthy dessert really delivers.

1 cup	low-fat vanilla yogurt sweetened with aspartame	250 mL
2 tbsp	frozen orange juice concentrate, thawed	25 mL
2	medium oranges, peeled and sliced crosswise ground cinnamon	2

In a bowl, whisk together yogurt and orange juice concentrate. Spoon evenly over 4 dessert plates. Arrange orange slices on top of yogurt. Sprinkle lightly with cinnamon and serve.

NUTTY MANGO CRISP

The tangy-sweet taste and velvety texture of mangoes are a nice contrast to the crisp's crunchy nut topping. Bottled, canned or frozen mango may be substituted for fresh.

TOPPING:

¼ cup	whole wheat flour	50 mL
¼ cup	large-flake rolled oats	50 mL
2 tbsp	granular low-calorie sweetener with sucralose	25 mL
2 tbsp	packed brown sugar	25 mL
½ tsp	ground ginger	2 mL
2 tbsp	soft margarine or butter	25 mL
2 tbsp	chopped walnuts	25 mL

In a medium bowl, combine flour, rolled oats, sweetener, sugar and ginger; stir well. Cut in margarine until mixture resembles coarse meal. Stir in nuts. Set aside.

FILLING:

2 cups	chopped peeled fresh mango (about 3 mangoes)	500 mL
1 tbsp	granular low-calorie sweetener with sucralose	15 mL
½ tsp	grated lime peel	2 mL
2 tbsp	fresh lime juice	25 mL

In another bowl, combine mango, sweetener, lime peel and juice, toss well. Divide mixture into four individual ramekins sprayed with non-stick cooking spray.

Sprinkle about ¼ cup (50 mL) topping evenly over each fruit ramekin. Bake in 375°F (190°C) oven for 15 minutes or until topping is browned and fruit is tender.

VARIATION

Mixed Berry Crisp: Today there is greater availability of frozen fruits, including many tropical and mixed berry ones. We substituted 2 cups (500 mL/400 g) unsweetened frozen mixed berries for the chopped fresh mango and followed the above recipe to make this interesting variation.

Dinner Menu 14

Prep • 20 minutes
Cook • 15 minutes
Yield • 4 servings

Each serving • ¼ of recipe

Carb choices	2
Fats choices	1½

Carbohydrate 33 g
  Fibre 3 g
Protein 3 g
Fat 8 g
  Saturated 1 g
Cholesterol 0 mg
Sodium 78 mg
Calories 207

....

**Variation HIGH FIBRE
Dinner Menu 27**

Prep • 20 minutes
Cook • 15 minutes
Yield • 4 servings

Each serving • ¼ of recipe

Carb choice	1
Fats choices	1½

Carbohydrate 25 g
  Fibre 5 g
Protein 3 g
Fat 8 g
  Saturated 1 g
Cholesterol 0 mg
Sodium 77 mg
Calories 177

Dinner Menu 15

Prep · 15 minutes
Cook · about 5 minutes
Yield · 1½ cups (375 mL)

Each serving · ½ of recipe
Carb choice   1
Fats choice   ½

Carbohydrate 22 g
   Fibre 3 g
Protein 1 g
Fat 2 g
   Saturated 0 g
Cholesterol 0 mg
Sodium 27 mg
Calories 112

SAUTÉED SPICED FRUITS

Peach and pineapple become succulent when quickly cooked with white wine and a teaspoon of brown sugar. Blueberries add colour for this simple and elegant way to end dinner.

1	large peach, peeled and sliced (see Tip)	1
1 cup	diced fresh pineapple	250 mL
1 tsp	soft margarine or butter	5 mL
1 tsp	brown sugar	5 mL
2 tbsp	dry white wine	25 mL
¼ cup	fresh blueberries	50 mL
¼ tsp	ground nutmeg	1 mL

Prepare the peach and pineapple and set aside.

In a non-stick skillet, melt margarine and brown sugar over medium heat. When bubbly, add peaches, pineapple and wine. Cook for 5 minutes or until the fruit starts to soften. Add blueberries; cook for 2 minutes. Sprinkle with nutmeg, remove from heat and serve.

◉ *When fresh fruit is not available, replace with ½ cup (125 mL) each sliced canned peaches in light syrup and pineapple chunks. Frozen blueberries can replace fresh.*

CRANBERRY ALMOND CRUMBLE

The tartness of cranberries combined with ground almonds adds an interesting note to this comfort food.

2 cups	fresh or frozen cranberries	500 mL
⅓ cup	granular low-calorie sweetener with sucralose, divided	75 mL
1	egg	1
¼ cup	low-fat milk	50 mL
½ tsp	each vanilla and almond extract	2 mL
¼ cup	ground almonds	50 mL
¼ cup	dried bread crumbs	50 mL

Spray four 1-cup (250 mL) ramekins with non-stick cooking spray. Divide the cranberries into each dish. Sprinkle cranberries with 1 tbsp (15 mL) sweetener per dish.

In a bowl, beat egg with remaining sweetener, milk, vanilla and almond extracts. Stir in almonds and bread crumbs. Pour evenly over cranberries. Bake in 400°F (200°C) oven for 18 minutes or until golden brown and fruit is tender. Serve warm.

Dinner Menu 16

....

Prep · 15 minutes
Cook · 30 minutes
Yield · 4 servings

....

Each serving · ¼ of recipe
Carb choice   1
Fats choice   ½

....

Carbohydrate 17 g
   Fibre 3 g
Protein 5 g
Fat 3 g
   Saturated 1 g
Cholesterol 55 mg
Sodium 79 mg
Calories 113

RASPBERRY BAVARIAN

Dinner Menu 17

Prep · 10 minutes
Refrigerate · for about 1 hour
Yield · 3 servings

Each serving · ⅓ of recipe
Carb choice   ½
Meat & Alternatives choice ½

Carbohydrate 13 g
   Fibre 2 g
Protein 5 g
Fat 1 g
   Saturated 0 g
Cholesterol 2 mg
Sodium 46 mg
Calories 74

Our "Bavarian" is a low-fat version of the traditional cold dessert of custard, fruit purée and gelatin. This version and its strawberry variation (see below) are a wonderful way to use these succulent fruits in season.

1 cup	fresh or frozen raspberries	250 mL
2 tsp	unflavoured gelatin	10 mL
½ cup	low-fat milk	125 mL
⅔ cup	low-fat French vanilla yogurt sweetened with aspartame	150 mL
2 tsp	granulated sugar	10 mL
	whole raspberries (optional) (see Tip)	

In a blender or food processor, purée raspberries until almost smooth; remove to a bowl and set aside.

In a small saucepan or a microwave-safe dish, sprinkle gelatin over milk. Heat until gelatin is completely dissolved. Stir into puréed fruit; add yogurt and sugar and stir to blend. Pour into three dessert dishes; refrigerate for about 1 hour, or until set (see Tip). To serve, garnish with extra whole raspberries (if using).

VARIATION

Strawberry Bavarian, Dinner Menu 22: Replace raspberries with 1 cup (250 mL) halved strawberries. To serve, garnish with whole strawberries (if using).

⊕ *Raspberries are very fragile and should be used within a day or two of purchase.*

⊕ *For faster chilling, set dishes in freezer section of refrigerator.*

⊕ *Strawberries contain more vitamin C than any other berry and a ½ cup (125 mL) provides more fibre than a slice of whole wheat bread.*

Balsamic Strawberries

You may well wonder about serving strawberries in balsamic vinegar. But when you try it, you will marvel at the magic this mellow, slightly sweet flavoured vinegar brings to a strawberry or a peach.

3 cups	sliced strawberries	750 mL
1 tbsp	balsamic vinegar	15 mL
2 tsp	brown sugar	10 mL
1 tsp	low-calorie sweetener	5 mL
	fresh mint leaves (optional)	

Place fruit in a shallow bowl. Sprinkle with vinegar, sugar and sweetener; toss to coat well. Leave at room temperature for up to 30 minutes. Garnish with mint (if using).

VARIATION

Balsamic Peaches, Dinner Menu 26: Replace strawberries with 1 cup (250 ml) sliced fresh peaches.

HIGH FIBRE

Dinner Menu 18

....

Prep · 10 minutes
Stand time · 30 minutes
Yield · 2 servings,
2 cups (500 mL)

....

Each serving · ½ of recipe
Carb choice   1

....

Carbohydrate 23 g
Fibre 6 g
Protein 2 g
Fat 1 g
Saturated 0 g
Cholesterol 0 mg
Sodium 4 mg
Calories 94

HIGH FIBRE

Dinner Menu 19

....

Prep · 15 minutes
Cook · about 6 minutes
Yield · 2 servings

....

Each serving · 2 pear halves
    with juice
Carb choices   1½

....

Carbohydrate 30 g
   Fibre 5 g
Protein 1 g
Fat 1 g
   Saturated 0 g
Cholesterol 0 mg
Sodium 3 mg
Calories 134

ROSY POACHED PEARS

We like this light, simply prepared and elegant ending to a meal. Truly attractive when served on a glass plate.

2	medium pears, peeled, halved and cored (with a melon baller)	2
¼ cup	each dry red wine and water	50 mL
2	thin lemon slices, quartered	2
1 tsp	granulated sugar	5 mL
¼ tsp	ground cinnamon	1 mL

Place pears, cut side down, in shallow microwave-safe dish. Combine wine, water, lemon slices, sugar and cinnamon. Pour over pears, spooning some over each half.

Cover and microwave on high (100%) for 6 minutes or until pears are tender. Cool, occasionally spooning juice over pears. Serve two pear halves with extra syrup and lemon slices on two glass plates.

PEARS WITH RASPBERRY SAUCE

Pears, gently cooked, bring out a whole new level of concentrated fruit flavour. Adding a raspberry sauce makes this dessert quite fabulous.

2	medium pears, peeled, halved and cored (with a melon baller)	2
½ cup	water	125 mL
½	cinnamon stick	½
1	whole clove	1
½ cup	part-skim ricotta cheese	125 mL
2 tsp	fresh lemon juice	10 mL
1 tbsp	liquid honey	15 mL
1 cup	fresh or frozen unsweetened raspberries, thawed	250 mL
2 tbsp	sliced almonds, toasted	25 mL

In a large skillet, bring pears, water, cinnamon stick and clove to a boil over medium heat. Cover, reduce heat and simmer for 10 minutes or until tender. Drain pears, discard liquid (see Tip).

In a small bowl, combine cheese, lemon juice and honey. Evenly spoon the mixture into each pear half.

Purée the raspberries. Strain to remove seeds (see Tip). Place 2 tbsp (25 mL) sauce on each of 4 individual serving plates. Place one pear half on sauce, sprinkle with almonds and serve.

⊕ *Rather than discard the liquid, it can be used when making applesauce, instead of water.*

⊕ *If you decide to not remove the raspberry seeds, you will be that much further ahead, as much of the dietary fibre from raspberries comes from the seeds.*

HIGH FIBRE

Dinner Menu 21

....

Prep · 25 minutes
Cook · about 10 minutes
Yield · 4 servings

....

Each serving · ¼ of recipe
Carb choice   1
Meat & Alternatives choice   ½
Fats choice   ½

....

Carbohydrate 24 g
  Fibre 5 g
Protein 5 g
Fat 5 g
  Saturated 2 g
Cholesterol 9 mg
Sodium 38 mg
Calories 152

Fresh Fruit Jelly

Dinner Menu 23

Fresh, light and full of flavour, this dessert provides a fine finish to Dinner Menu 23.

Prep · 15 minutes
Refrigerate · for several hours
Yield · 4 servings

1 cup	sliced strawberries	250 mL
½ cup	fresh or frozen blueberries	125 mL
½ cup	drained canned pineapple tidbits in juice	125 mL
1	pkg (9.1 g) light fruit-flavoured gelatin (see Tip)	1
1 cup	boiling water	250 mL
½ cup	pineapple juice	125 mL
½ cup	cold water	125 mL

Each serving · ¼ of recipe
Carb choice   1

Prepare strawberries and blueberries. Drain pineapple and reserve pineapple juice.

Meanwhile, stir fruit gelatin with boiling water until dissolved. Add pineapple juice and cold water. Fold in prepared fruit and turn into an attractive serving dish. Cover and refrigerate for several hours or until set.

Carbohydrate 16 g
  Fibre 2 g
Protein 1 g
Fat 0 g
Cholesterol 0 mg
Sodium 17 mg

Calories 63

◉ *Any light fruit-flavoured gelatin will be fine with these fresh fruits.*

Gingered Fruit Parfait

This combination of fruits and candied ginger offers a stunning variety of colours, textures and flavours. If you wish, you can use ground ginger rather than candied ginger.

½ cup	plain low-fat yogurt	125 mL
1 tbsp	minced candied ginger or	15 mL
	½ tsp (2 mL) ground ginger	
½ cup	bite-size pieces honeydew melon	125 mL
½ cup	quartered strawberries	125 mL
1	kiwi fruit, peeled and sliced	1
	fresh mint leaves	

In a small bowl, blend yogurt and ginger. Cover and refrigerate for up to 2 hours so flavours will blend.

In a bowl, combine prepared melon, strawberries and kiwi fruit.

In two parfait or wine glasses, layer fruit, yogurt sauce and repeat layers. Garnish with fresh mint.

Dinner Menu 30

....

Prep · 15 minutes
Refrigerate · up to 2 hours
Yield · 2 servings,
       1½ cups (350 mL)

....

Each serving · ½ of recipe
       (¾ cup/175 mL)
Carb choice   1

....

Carbohydrate 22 g
  Fibre 3 g
Protein 4 g
Fat 0 g
Cholesterol 1 mg
Sodium 53 mg
Calories 100

SNACKS

Recipes	Carbs	Page
Fresh Cucumber Salsa	Extra	168
Frozen Melon Smoothie	1½	169
Minted Limeade	Extra	170
Curried Lentil Dip	1	171
Salsa Cheese Spread	0	172
Herbed Cornbread	1½	173
Oatmeal Date Muffins	1	174
Orange Date and Bran Muffins, Rhubarb Bran Muffins	1	175
Chocolate Chip Oatmeal Cookies	½	176
Peanut Butter Granola Cookies	½	177

HEALTHY SNACKING

WHY DO WE SNACK?

Perhaps because we're hungry, bored, anxious or just need a boost in energy? But if you have diabetes, there's an even better reason. Studies have shown that spreading the food you need over several small meals a day improves diabetes control by smoothing out blood glucose highs and lows. And healthy snacking is a great way to manage your hunger and help you resist unplanned high-fat, high-calorie snacks between meals, making it easier to control your weight. A planned snack can keep you satisfied between meals and discourage overeating at the next meal.

ARE SNACKS A GOOD IDEA?

Most people need more food energy and nutrients than three meals can provide. Choosing any three menus of breakfast, lunch and dinner from *Choice Menus: Cooking for One or Two* gives you about 1,300 calories of food energy per day. This is a significant weight loss path for most people, and you may need more calories than this. How many more? Your dietitian can recommend an energy intake based on your age, activity level and weight goal (see "How to Use This Book," page 17). You then plan whatever snacks are required to make up any difference between the basic 1,300 calories and your prescribed calorie intake.

The snack menus in the split-page section come in three different sizes: 75 calories, when you want just a bite; 150 calories, for mid-morning, mid-afternoon or bedtime; and 300 calories (really small meals) for active days or for shift-workers. If you're counting carbohydrate, each snack menu is marked with the number of Carbs it contains. Our motto is "a planned snack is better than an unplanned snack."

WHEN SHOULD YOU SNACK?

Eating a snack when you have a long stretch between meals, usually more than four hours, keeps your appetite under control, at the same time making sure your blood glucose doesn't dip uncomfortably low before your next meal. This may mean planning to have mid-morning, mid-afternoon or bedtime snacks that fit within the total calories of your meal plan. Those people taking insulin or pills for their diabetes may find that a mid-afternoon snack or a bedtime

Opposite: Chocolate Chip Oatmeal Cookies (page 176)

snack helps protect against hypoglycemia (low blood sugar). Doing blood glucose tests can help you and your health professional decide whether to add a snack or to reduce medication.

Our snacks are planned to be suitable for the usual snacking times. A refreshing snack on a warm day might be **Minted Limeade** (page 170) or a **Frozen Melon Smoothie** (page 169). A snack to go with tea or coffee or a glass of milk, or to carry with you when you're away from home, could be **Peanut Butter Granola Cookies** (page 177) or an **Oatmeal Date Muffin** (page 174). A delayed meal, perhaps on a social occasion, is another time for a planned snack. **Curried Lentil Dip** (page 171) with assorted raw vegetables or whole wheat pita bread, or crackers with **Salsa Cheese Spread** (page 172) are all healthy choices that both you and your guests will enjoy.

What Foods Make Healthy Snack Choices?
Fresh fruits and vegetables are always healthy choices rich in vitamins and fibre and you'll find them in many of our Snack menus. Whole grain crackers and cereals provide fibre as well as B vitamins. And snacks are a great time to work in more calcium-rich milk, whether it be a refreshing glass of cold milk or a warming latte or café au lait or a cup of light hot chocolate. To make it easier to reach for a healthy snack, keep the makings handy in your refrigerator or cupboard, or your desk drawer or lunch box if away from home.

Now that all food products require nutritional information on their labels, it's easier to make an informed choice among packaged snack foods as well. The key words to look for are *whole grain*, *low fat*, *low saturated fat* and *zero trans fat*. Then check Nutrition Facts for size of serving and available carbohydrate (total carbohydrate minus fibre) to see how it might fit into your meal plan. See pages 24–25 for more advice on how to read labels.

FRESH CUCUMBER SALSA

Dinner Menu 14
Snack Menu 1

Prep · 10 minutes
Refrigerate · for several hours
Yield · about 1⅓ cups (325 mL)

Each serving · ¼ of recipe
(⅓ cup/75 mL)
Extra

Carbohydrate 3 g
Fibre 1 g
Protein 1 g
Fat 0 g
Cholesterol 0 mg
Sodium 8 mg
Calories 13

Enjoy this salsa with broiled or grilled fish, as well as cold meats. Tossed with crisp lettuce, it makes a refreshing side salad that can be added to any meal as a low carbohydrate Extra.

1 cup	finely chopped cucumber	250 mL
½ cup	chopped radish	125 mL
2 tbsp	minced fresh coriander or parsley	25 mL
1 tbsp	white wine vinegar	15 mL
1 tsp	low-calorie sweetener	5 mL
Pinch	freshly ground pepper	

In a bowl, combine cucumber, radish, coriander, vinegar and sweetener. Stir in pepper to taste. Cover and refrigerate for several hours or until ready to serve.

FROZEN MELON SMOOTHIE

Enjoy the sweet fruity flavour of cantaloupe in this elegant and healthy fruit drink. Of all the melons, cantaloupe is the highest in beta-carotene, potassium and vitamin C. Garnish each serving with a lime slice or fresh mint sprig.

½ cup	low-fat evaporated milk	125 mL
1½ cups	cubed ripe cantaloupe (see Tips)	375 mL
2 tsp	low-calorie sweetener	10 mL
½ cup	light vanilla ice cream	125 mL
4	ice cubes	4
	lime slice or fresh mint sprigs	

Freeze the milk in a shallow metal bowl for about 2 hours. Remove from freezer and transfer to a blender container or food processor. Add cantaloupe, sweetener, ice cream and ice cubes. Blend on high speed until slushy. Pour into two glasses and serve with lime or mint.

⦾ *Bright orange and red fruits and vegetables, such as cantaloupe, mangoes, oranges, carrots, red pepper and squash, are bursting with the antioxidants vitamin C and beta-carotene, which the body converts to vitamin A.*

⦾ *Since melons will not ripen further once they have been picked, be sure to choose a ripe one. A fruity fragrance as well as a slight indentation in the stem end may be a clue to maturity.*

Snack Menus 4, 13

....

Prep • 20 minutes
Freeze • about 2 hours
Yield • 3 cups (750 mL)

....

Each serving • ⅓ of recipe
        (1½ cups/375 mL)
Carb choices   1½
Meat & Alternatives choice   ½

....

Carbohydrate 26 g
  Fibre 1 g
Protein 8 g
Fat 3 g
  Saturated 2 g
Cholesterol 5 mg
Sodium 112 mg
Calories 154

Minted Limeade

Snack Menus 3, 7

Prep · 5 minutes
Yield · 1 cup (250 mL)

Each serving · 1 cup (250 mL)
Extra

Carbohydrate 5 g
  Fibre 0 g
Protein 0 g
Fat 0 g
Cholesterol 0 mg
Sodium 11 mg
Calories 16

Beverage coolers are simple to make and so very refreshing.

2 tbsp	fresh lime juice	25 mL
1 tbsp	low-calorie sweetener	15 mL
2	fresh mint sprigs	2
4	ice cubes	4
½ cup	diet ginger ale	125 mL
1	lime slice	1
	fresh mint sprigs	

In a blender, process lime juice, sweetener and mint until smooth. With the blender running, add ice cubes, one at a time. Process until smooth and slushy. Add ginger ale, stir and serve over ice, garnished with lime slice and extra mint.

Curried Lentil Dip

Much like hummus, this new take on a vegetable dip is sufficiently different that it makes a nice alternative to hummus.

1 cup	dried red lentils, rinsed and drained	250 mL
3 cups	water	750 mL
3–4	cloves garlic, sliced	3–4
1 tbsp	olive oil	15 mL
2 tsp	white wine vinegar	10 mL
1 tsp	curry powder	5 mL
½ tsp	dry mustard	2 mL
Pinch	cayenne pepper	

In a saucepan, combine lentils, water and garlic. Bring to a boil, reduce heat to low and cook, covered, for 10 minutes or until the lentils are tender (do not overcook). Drain immediately.

In a food processor or blender, process drained lentils, garlic, oil, vinegar, curry powder, mustard and cayenne until mixture is smooth. Move to covered container and refrigerate for up to 1 week or freeze for longer storage

Snack Menus 1, 29

Prep · 10 minutes
Cook · 10 minutes
Refrigerate · for up to 1 week
Yield · 1¾ cups (425 mL)

Each serving · ⅐ of recipe
(¼ cup/50 mL)
Carb choice   1
Meat & Alternatives choice   ½

Carbohydrate 16 g
   Fibre 3 g
Protein 8 g
Fat 2 g
   Saturated 0 g
Cholesterol 0 mg
Sodium 6 mg
Calories 114

Salsa Cheese Spread

Lunch Menu 27
Snack Menus 1, 7, 17

....

Prep · 15 minutes
Refrigerate · up to 1 week
Yield · about 2 cups (500 mL)

....

Each serving · ⅛ of recipe
      (¼ cup/50 mL)
Meat & Alternatives choice   1

....

Carbohydrate 3 g
  Fibre 0 g
Protein 6 g
Fat 2 g
  Saturated 1 g
Cholesterol 5 mg
Sodium 206 mg

Calories 52

A commercial salsa adds zesty flavour and moisture to this high-protein cheese spread. And the addition of carrot makes it an excellent source of vitamin A. Served with raw veggies or crackers, it becomes a great party appetizer.

1 cup	light cottage cheese	250 mL
½ cup	shredded light Cheddar cheese	125 mL
¼ cup	mild or medium salsa	50 mL
1 tbsp	light mayonnaise	15 mL
2 tsp	Dijon mustard	10 mL
1	medium carrot, grated (½ cup/125 mL)	1
1	green onion, chopped	1
1 tbsp	chopped chives or fresh parsley	15 mL

In a blender or food processor, combine cottage cheese, Cheddar cheese, salsa, mayonnaise and mustard. Pulse until smooth. Remove the mixture to a bowl; stir in carrot, onion and chives.

Cover and refrigerate for at least 1 hour to allow flavours to develop. Keep for up to 1 week in the refrigerator or freeze for longer storage.

Herbed Cornbread

This herbed version of a traditional cornmeal muffin can also be baked in 12 paper-lined medium muffin cups for 18 minutes. Both freeze well.

1 cup	low-fat milk	250 mL
¾ cup	fine cornmeal	175 mL
½ cup	light sour cream or plain low-fat yogurt	125 mL
Pinch	baking soda	
¼ cup	canola oil or melted soft margarine	50 mL
1	egg, beaten, or 2 egg whites	1
1¼ cups	all purpose flour	300 mL
3 tbsp	granulated sugar	45 mL
2 tsp	baking powder	10 mL
2	green onions, chopped	2
1 tsp	dried thyme or 1 tbsp (15 mL) fresh, chopped	5 mL

In a medium bowl, combine milk and cornmeal; let stand for 5 minutes.

In a measuring cup, stir together sour cream and baking soda. Let stand for 5 minutes, then stir into the cornmeal mixture. Stir in oil and egg.

Meanwhile, in a large bowl, combine flour, sugar, baking powder, onions and thyme. Stir the cornmeal mixture into flour just until combined.

Spoon batter into a lightly greased 8-inch (20 cm) square baking pan. Bake in 375°F (190°C) oven for 25 minutes or until top springs back when lightly touched. Cool slightly before cutting into 12 pieces.

Lunch Menu 10
Snack Menu 14

Prep · 15 minutes
Cook · about 25 minutes
Yield · 12 servings

Each serving · ¹/₁₂ of recipe
(1 piece or 1 muffin)
Carb choices	1½
Fats choice	1

Carbohydrate 23 g
  Fibre 1 g
Protein 4 g
Fat 6 g
  Saturated 1 g
Cholesterol 19 mg
Sodium 93 mg
Calories 162

Oatmeal Date Muffins

These muffins are especially tasty and freeze well for a quick start to the day or when a "snack attack" hits. One muffin is a source of dietary fibre.

Snack Menu 6

Prep · 15 minutes
Cook · 18 minutes
Yield · 12 medium muffins

Each serving · ¹⁄₁₂ of recipe
    (1 muffin)
Carb choice   1
Fats choice   1

Carbohydrate 20 g
    Fibre 2 g
Protein 4 g
Fat 5 g
    Saturated 1 g
Cholesterol 19 mg
Sodium 195 mg
Calories 135

1½ cups	buttermilk	375 mL
1 cup	large-flake rolled oats	250 mL
3 tbsp	canola oil	45 mL
1	egg, slightly beaten	1
½ tsp	each ground nutmeg and vanilla extract	2 mL
1 cup	whole wheat flour	250 mL
2 tsp	baking powder	10 mL
1 tsp	baking soda	5 mL
¼ cup	firmly packed brown sugar	50 mL
¼ cup	granular low-calorie sweetener with sucralose	50 mL
¼ cup	finely diced dates (see Tip)	50 mL

In a bowl, stir buttermilk into rolled oats; let stand for 30 minutes. Stir in oil, egg, nutmeg and vanilla.

In a large bowl, combine flour, baking powder, baking soda, sugar, sweetener and dates. Add buttermilk mixture; stir just until combined (see Tip).

Divide the batter evenly among 12 non-stick or paper-lined medium muffin cups, filling ¾ full. Bake in 400°F (200°C) oven for 18 minutes or until tops are lightly browned and firm to the touch.

- *Be careful when measuring dates and brown sugar. They are both high in simple sugar.*
- *Muffin baking is easy—just follow a couple of these tips for success. First measure dry ingredients using graduated dry measures. Make a "well" in the centre into which all the wet ingredients are added and stir just until moistened. Over-stirring produces muffins filled with tunnels and peaked tops. Then bake on the middle rack in a preheated oven.*

ORANGE DATE AND BRAN MUFFINS

These muffins have an intense orange flavour that shouts "let me have one." They freeze well and a fast 15-second warming in the microwave will refresh them.

1¼ cups	whole wheat flour	300 mL
1 cup	natural bran	250 mL
¼ cup	granulated sugar	50 mL
¼ cup	granular low-calorie sweetener with sucralose	50 mL
2 tsp	ground cinnamon	10 mL
2 tsp	baking powder	10 mL
1 tsp	baking soda	5 mL
1	medium orange, unpeeled	1
¼ cup	water	50 mL
1	egg or 2 egg whites, lightly beaten	1
½ cup	buttermilk	125 mL
¼ cup	canola oil	50 mL
¼ cup	finely chopped dates	50 mL

In a large bowl, combine flour, bran, sugar, sweetener, cinnamon, baking powder and baking soda. Set aside.

Cut orange into pieces and remove seeds. In a food processor or blender, finely chop orange with ¼ cup (50 mL) water. Remove to a small bowl; stir in egg, buttermilk, oil and dates. Stir into flour mixture just until combined.

Divide the batter evenly among 12 non-stick or paper-lined medium muffin cups, filling ¾ full. Bake in 400°F (200°C) oven for 18 minutes or until tops are lightly brown and firm to the touch.

VARIATION

Rhubarb Bran Muffins, Snack Menu 22: Replace 1 medium orange and ¼ cup (50 mL) water with 1 cup (250 mL) ***Orange Stewed Rhubarb*** (page 89) and omit dates.

HIGH FIBRE

Snack Menu 10

....

Prep • 10 minutes
Cook • about 18 minutes
Yield • 12 medium muffins

....

Each serving • ¹⁄₁₂ of recipe
        (1 muffin)

Carb choice	1
Fats choice	1

....

Carbohydrate 22 g
  Fibre 4 g
Protein 4 g
Fat 6 g
  Saturated 1 g
Cholesterol 18 mg
Sodium 173 mg
Calories 138

CHOCOLATE CHIP OATMEAL COOKIES

Snack Menus 4, 9

Prep · 20 minutes
Cook · about 10 minutes
Yield · 3 dozen

Each serving · ¹⁄₁₈ of recipe
 (2 cookies)
Carb choice   ½
Fats choice   1

Carbohydrate 12 g
 Fibre 1 g
Protein 2 g
Fat 6 g
 Saturated 1 g
Cholesterol 12 mg
Sodium 103 mg
Calories 107

Making oatmeal cookies from scratch is a snap. They also taste better and are generally healthier for you than commercial ones. Store or freeze them in a tightly closed container.

1 cup	large-flake rolled oats	250 mL
½ cup	whole wheat flour	125 mL
½ tsp	baking soda	2 mL
½ cup	soft margarine or butter	125 mL
½ cup	lightly packed brown sugar	125 mL
¼ cup	granular low-calorie sweetener with sucralose	50 mL
1	egg	1
1 tsp	finely grated orange peel	5 mL
½ tsp	vanilla extract	2 mL
¼ cup	chocolate chips	50 mL

In a bowl, combine rolled oats, flour and baking soda. Set aside.

In a large bowl, cream together margarine, sugar, sweetener, egg, orange peel and vanilla until well blended. Add flour mixture and stir until well mixed. Stir in chocolate chips.

Spray 2 baking sheets with non-stick cooking spray or line with parchment paper. Drop dough by teaspoonfuls onto pan and flatten with a fork. Bake in 350°F (180°C) oven for 10 minutes or until edges are browned. Transfer to rack to cool.

Peanut Butter Granola Cookies

Power Granola (page 31) and peanut butter make these snack cookies healthy and hearty.

½ cup	crunchy peanut butter	125 mL
2	eggs or 4 egg whites	2
1 tbsp	liquid honey	15 mL
2 tsp	vanilla extract	10 mL
2½ cups	*Power Granola* (page 31)	625 mL

In a bowl, combine peanut butter, eggs, honey and vanilla. Stir in granola. Shape mixture into 1-inch (2.5 cm) balls.

Spray a baking sheet with non-stick cooking spray. Place cookie balls on sheet, flatten with a fork. Bake in 350°F (180°C) oven for 8 minutes or until golden brown and cookie is set. Remove from pan to wire rack to cool.

Snack Menus 12, 24

Prep • 10 minutes if *Power Granola* is made
Cook • about 8 minutes
Yield • 28 cookies

Each serving • ¹⁄₁₄ of recipe (2 cookies)

Carb choice	½
Fats choice	1

Carbohydrate 13 g
  Fibre 2 g
Protein 5 g
Fat 6 g
  Saturated 1 g
Cholesterol 0 mg
Sodium 18 mg
Calories 120

SPECIAL MEALS FOR SPECIAL OCCASIONS

RECIPES	CARBS	PAGE
MENU 1 • A BIRTHDAY CELEBRATION (SERVES 4 OR MORE)		
Rhubarb Punch	½	184
Poached Chicken Breasts	0	185
Cranberry Citrus Coulis	½	186
Orange Vinaigrette	0	187
Ice Cream Birthday Cake	2½	188
Light Whipped Topping	½	189
MENU 2 • DINNER WITH FRIENDS (SERVES 4)		
Thai Peppered Shrimp with Leeks	½	190
Stir-Fried Vegetables	½	191
Fragrant Rice	1½	192
Mango Mint Sorbet	1	193
MENU 3 • GOURMET BUFFET DINNER (SERVES 6)		
Beef Burgundy	2	194
Mocha Soufflé Dessert	1	195
MENU 4 • A SPRING BRUNCH (SERVES 4)		
Three Cheese Mushroom Risotto	2	196

Recipes	Carbs	Page
Menu 5 · A Spanish Lunch (serves 4)		
Gazpacho	½	198
Tortilla Española	2	199
Lemon Flan	1	200
Menu 6 · A Romantic Dinner (serves 2)		
Golden Harvest Soup	1	201
Roast Cornish Hen with Wild Rice Dressing	½	202
Raspberry Fool	1	203
Menu 7 · Passover Seder (serves 6)		
Chicken and Matzo Ball Soup	1	204
Spinach and Orange Salad	½	205
Spiced Beef Brisket	½	206
Oven-Roasted Asparagus	0	207
Potato Kugel	½	208
Lemon Passover Cake	1	209
Menu 8 · Harvest Thanksgiving (serves 6)		
Vegetable Bread Stuffing	1	210
Fresh Cranberry Chutney	½	212
Turnip Potato Purée	½	213
Spicy Pumpkin Pie	1	214

SPECIAL MEALS FOR SPECIAL OCCASIONS
. . . .

Although this book is aimed at cooking for just one or two, meals for special occasions—birthdays, holidays, entertaining—usually involve guests and special meals, so we have designed the recipes in this chapter to serve four or more people. All recipes can be doubled if you're serving more guests.

Our birthday dinner naturally includes an **Ice Cream Birthday Cake** (page 188), as well as a refreshing **Rhubarb Punch** (page 184), and **Poached Chicken** (page 185) with **Cranberry Citrus Coulis** (pages 185 and 186). All quite luscious! And you won't need to go out to a Thai restaurant when you can prepare a Thai meal for friends at home. **Thai Peppered Shrimp with Leeks** (page 190) is the main course along with **Fragrant Rice** (page 192) and **Stir-Fried Vegetables** (page 191). The meal ends with a refreshing **Mango Mint Sorbet** (page 193).

Brunch and lunch recipes for a weekend include **Three Cheese Mushroom Risotto** (page 196), and a Spanish lunch with **Gazpacho** (page 198), **Tortilla Española** (page 199) and **Lemon Flan** (page 200).

And for Valentine's Day—or any time you choose—A Romantic Dinner menu serves two with ease and simplicity. **Golden Harvest Soup** (page 201), **Cornish Hen with Wild Rice Dressing** (page 202) and **Raspberry Fool** (page 203) all make it happen.

Thanksgiving and Passover are always times when families get together, and traditional menus are provided for these occasions. We know the **Spicy Pumpkin Pie** (page 214) and **Lemon Passover Cake** (page 209) will become family favourites.

Naturally these meals require more preparation time than our regular day-to-day menus, but they are, after all, for special occasions. All but two of the menus are based on the dinner meal plan (page 97). The Spring Brunch and the Spanish Lunch are both based on the lunch meal plan (page 51). Some menus are a bit higher in fat and calories than the usual ones, but the carbohydrate content remains the same, with each menu equal to 4 Carb choices. All menus meet healthy eating goals and provide suggested serving sizes for people watching portions.

We hope you enjoy preparing and savoring these special meals, all of which fit into a diabetes meal plan. Bon appétit!

Opposite: Ice Cream Birthday Cake (page 188)

EATING OUT

You may be invited to someone's home for dinner. Not being in control of the menu doesn't have to be a challenge for the person with diabetes. Just stay with your usual portions and leave food that doesn't fit your meal plan. Dining out at a restaurant? Not a problem! You can make choices from the menu and request smaller portions or share with a friend. "All-you-can-eat" buffets can be a real temptation to overeat. Be sure to circle the buffet once or twice, mentally making choices using the Plate Method (page 11), before starting to fill your dish—and only go through the buffet line once. (See "Celebrations" in the *Beyond the Basics* meal planning resource for more information.)

BEVERAGES AND SPECIAL OCCASIONS

Special occasions often include an alcoholic drink before or with a meal. As a general rule there is no need to avoid alcohol because you have diabetes. Current guidelines for everyone, not just those with diabetes, advise "moderation," meaning no more than one drink per day for women, two per day for men. If you have other problems such as elevated cholesterol or triglycerides, hypertension, or are taking insulin or diabetes pills or other medications, discuss the use of alcoholic beverages with your diabetes health care team first.

Of course, substituting a low-calorie non-alcoholic beverage is another solution. Some choices are water, mineral or soda water with lime, tea or coffee or a diet soft drink.

Tips to remember when drinking alcoholic beverages.
• Always eat carbohydrate foods when drinking alcohol. Never drink on an empty stomach. Do not take extra insulin to offset the carbohydrate content of alcoholic drinks.

- If you are on insulin or certain diabetes medications, alcohol can cause hypoglycemia or low blood sugar (see Appendix IV, page 227). Learn how to recognize symptoms (cold, sweating, shaking, very hungry), how to treat it (glucose tablets or juice) and, better still, how to prevent it (don't skip your usual meals and snacks during the day to make up for the meal out, and have an extra snack if your meal is going to be much later than usual).
- When going out, take your glucose meter and wear diabetes identification.
- Be aware of the amount of alcohol in the beverage you are drinking. Pour your own drinks whenever possible and drink slowly.
- Drink less alcohol and stretch your drinks with sugar-free mixes.
- If you are watching your weight, remember that alcohol adds extra calories.

BEVERAGE	STANDARD SERVING SIZE	CARBOHYDRATE CONTENT (g)	ENERGY VALUE (CALORIES)
Beer			
regular	360 mL (12 fl oz)	10	140
light	360 mL (12 fl oz)	5	100
non-alcoholic	360 mL (12 fl oz)	11–15	50–75
low carb	360 mL (12 fl oz)	2.5	90–97
Wine			
red or white	150 mL (5 oz)	1–2.5	102–108
dessert	150 mL (5 oz)	17–21	231–243
non-alcoholic	150 mL (5 oz)	2	9
Spirits/hard liquor	45 mL (1.5 fl oz)	0	98
Liqueurs and cordials	45 mL (1.5 fl oz)	17–21	163–190
Mixes			
Sugar-free pop	240 mL (8 fl oz)	0.2	2
Regular pop	240 mL (8 fl oz)	22–31	84–120
Club soda	240 mL (8 fl oz)	0	0
Tonic water	240 mL (8 fl oz)	22	84
Tomato juice	240 mL (8 fl oz)	9	41
Clamato juice	240 mL (8 fl oz)	26	116
Orange juice	240 mL (8 fl oz)	25	110

Source: *Alcohol + Diabetes* (2006), published by the Canadian Diabetes Association. Used with permission.

Special Occasion Menu 1

....

Prep · 20 minutes
Cook · about 10 minutes
Yield · 6 cups (1.5 L)
        punch concentrate

....

Each serving · ¹⁄₁₈ of recipe
        (⅓ cup/75 mL)
Carb choice   ½

....

Carbohydrate 8 g
   Fibre 1 g
Protein 1 g
Fat 0 g
Cholesterol 0 mg
Sodium 4 mg
Calories 32

RHUBARB PUNCH

Tangy rhubarb makes a thirst-quenching beverage. You can prepare the concentrate in large amounts when spring rhubarb is available, and freeze in small amounts for use throughout the year.

4	oranges	4
2	lemons	2
8 cups	sliced fresh or frozen rhubarb	2 L
4 cups	water	1 L
1 cup	low-calorie sweetener	250 mL

Remove the peel from the oranges and lemons. Squeeze juice and reserve.

In a large saucepan, combine rhubarb, water, orange and lemon peel. Cover and cook over medium heat for 10 minutes or until the rhubarb is tender. Remove from heat, stir in lemon and orange juice. Cool.

Press through a sieve to remove rhubarb pulp; discard pulp. Add sweetener to strained juice. Pour into sterilized bottles and seal. Keep in refrigerator for up to 2 weeks, or freeze for longer storage.

TO SERVE:

Combine ⅓ cup (75 mL) punch concentrate with ⅔ cup (150 mL) soda or mineral water and ice cubes.

Poached Chicken Breasts

Poached chicken breasts take on an entirely new persona with the addition of a tart **Cranberry Citrus Coulis** (page 186).

2 cups	water	500 mL
1	bay leaf	1
2 tbsp	chopped onion	25 mL
2 tbsp	chopped celery leaves	25 mL
Pinch	freshly ground pepper	
4	boneless, skinless chicken breast halves (100 g each)	4

In a skillet, bring water, bay leaf, onion, celery and pepper to a boil. Add chicken; cover, reduce heat to medium-low and cook for 15 minutes or until chicken is no longer pink inside. Remove chicken from liquid; reserve liquid (see Tip).

Chicken Broth: Pour liquid through a sieve; discard the cooked vegetables. Freeze and use when chicken broth is called for in a recipe.

⊕ *Handle with care: Salmonella is one of the bacteria that thrives in raw chicken. Each year many cases of food poisoning and deaths occur because of it. Contamination can occur at the farm or at any stage from processing to packaging. To prevent salmonella poisoning, always cook poultry thoroughly, never allow raw poultry juices to contaminate other foods, wash all surfaces and utensils that come in contact with raw poultry with soap and warm water, and wash your hands thoroughly after handling.*

A Birthday Celebration

Special Occasion Menu 1

....

Prep · 10 minutes
Cook · about 15 minutes
Yield · 4 servings

....

Each serving · ¼ of recipe
　　　(1 chicken breast half)
Meat & Alternatives choices　3

....

Carbohydrate 0 g
　Fibre 0 g
Protein 23 g
Fat 2 g
　Saturated 0 g
Cholesterol 58 mg
Sodium 54 mg
Calories 113

Special Occasion Menu 1

....

Prep · 10 minutes
Cook · 8 minutes
Yield · 1½ cups (375 mL)

....

Each serving · ⅛ of recipe
    (3 tbsp/45 mL)
Carb choice   ½

....

Carbohydrate 6 g
  Fibre 0 g
Protein 0 g
Fat 0 g
Cholesterol 0 mg
Sodium 1 mg
Calories 24

CRANBERRY CITRUS COULIS

Coulis means a thick sauce. Serve this with **Poached Chicken Breasts** (page 185) and chicken will become gourmet. Any extra coulis will keep well for another occasion.

2 cups	fresh or frozen cranberries (see Tip)	500 mL
1 cup	water	250 mL
4 tsp	fresh lemon juice	20 mL
2 tsp	granulated sugar	10 mL
1	orange, juiced, peel reserved	1
2 tbsp	granular low-calorie sweetener with sucralose	25 mL

In a saucepan, over medium-low heat, combine cranberries, water, lemon juice, sugar, orange peel and juice and cook for 8 minutes or until cranberries pop. Remove to a sieve or food mill and press through. Discard the pulp, stir sweetener into sieved mixture and refrigerate.

◉ *Make this sauce when fresh cranberries are available in the fall. It can be frozen to serve later.*

Orange Vinaigrette

Use this dressing to add extra sparkle to fresh spinach as well as to tossed greens. Fresh and simply delicious, this dressing is also ideal for cooked vegetables such as asparagus.

¼ cup	frozen orange juice concentrate, thawed	50 mL
¼ cup	water	50 mL
3 tbsp	red wine vinegar	45 mL
2 tbsp	fresh lemon juice	25 mL
1	clove garlic, crushed	1
½ tsp	low-calorie sweetener	2 ml
¼ tsp	each dry mustard and ground ginger	1 mL
¼ cup	olive oil	50 mL

In a container with a tight-fitting lid, combine orange juice concentrate, water, vinegar, lemon juice, garlic, sweetener, mustard and ginger; shake well. Add oil and shake again. Refrigerate for up to 2 weeks. Shake before using.

Special Occasion Menu 1

....

Prep · 10 minutes
Refrigerate · up to 2 weeks
Yield · 1 cup (250 mL)

....

Each serving · 1 tbsp (15 mL)
Fats choice   ½

....

Carbohydrate 2 g
    Fibre 0 g
Protein 0 g
Fat 3 g
    Saturated 0 g
Cholesterol 0 mg
Sodium 0 mg
Calories 38

....

Prep · 30 minutes
Cook cake · about 35 minutes
Freeze cake · until 15 minutes
    before serving
Yield · 8 servings

....

Each serving · ⅛ of Ice Cream
    Birthday Cake

Carb choices	2½
Fats choice	1

....

Carbohydrate 39 g
    Fibre 1 g
Protein 6 g
Fat 7 g
    Saturated 3 g
Cholesterol 56 mg
Sodium 84 mg

Calories 247

ICE CREAM BIRTHDAY CAKE

No birthday dinner is complete without a cake. This one combines cake and ice cream, frosts it with a light whipped topping and garnishes it with ruby red raspberries and mint leaves. Celebrate—it will fit into a diabetes meal plan!

CAKE:

1¼ cups	cake and pastry flour	300 mL
½ cup	granular low-calorie sweetener with sucralose	125 mL
1 tbsp	baking powder	15 mL
2	eggs	2
1 tsp	vanilla extract	5 mL
⅓ cup	granulated sugar	75 mL
½ cup	low-fat milk	125 mL
2 tbsp	canola oil	25 mL

Line an 8-inch (20 cm) round cake pan with waxed or parchment paper. Set aside.

In a bowl, combine flour, sweetener and baking powder.

In a second bowl, beat eggs and vanilla until light and fluffy. Gradually add sugar and beat for 3 minutes or until thickened and light in colour.

In a glass measure, combine milk and oil. Alternately beat flour mixture and milk into egg mixture making three of dry and two of milk; beat well after each addition. Scrape into prepared pan.

Bake in 350°F (180°C) oven for 35 minutes or until a cake tester inserted in centre comes out clean. Cool on rack for 10 minutes before removing from pan.

LIGHT WHIPPED TOPPING:

1 tsp	cold water	5 mL
½ tsp	unflavoured gelatin	2 mL
¾ cup	low-fat evaporated milk	175 mL
1 tbsp	granulated sugar	15 mL
Dash	vanilla extract	

In a bowl, combine water and gelatin; let stand for 2 minutes to soften.

In a glass measure, heat milk in microwave oven until steaming. Stir some hot milk into softened gelatin until gelatin is dissolved. When dissolved, stir into remaining hot milk. Chill in deep bowl in freezer along with beaters for 20 minutes or until mixture begins to thicken.

Beat chilled mixture at high speed with chilled beaters for 1 minute. Gradually beat in sugar and vanilla until soft peaks form. Use immediately or refrigerate for 3 to 4 hours.

Makes about 2½ cups (625 mL).

FILLING:

2 cups	light chocolate ice cream	500 mL

GARNISH:

1 cup	whole raspberries	250 mL
	mint leaves	

CAKE ASSEMBLY:

Cut cake layer horizontally in half. Spoon slightly softened ice cream over bottom half. Press top layer over ice cream.

Spread **Light Whipped Topping** over top and sides of cake. Cover and place in freezer until 15 minutes before serving. Garnish with raspberries and mint leaves and cut into 8 slices to serve.

⊕ *The **Light Whipped Topping** also can be used alone as a delicious dip for fresh fruit. You may want to add ½ tsp (2 mL) almond, peppermint or rum extract instead of vanilla for added flavour.*

TOPPING ONLY (SEE TIP)

Each serving · ⅕ of recipe
  (½ cup/125 mL)
Carb choice   ½

....

Carbohydrate 7 g
  Fibre 0 g
Protein 3 g
Fat 1 g
  Saturated 0 g
Cholesterol 3 mg
Sodium 43 mg
Calories 47

Special Occasion Menu 2

. . . .

Prep · 15 minutes
Cook · about 10 minutes
Yield · 4 servings

. . . .

Each serving · ¼ of recipe
Carb choice   ½
Meat & Alternatives choices   3

. . . .

Carbohydrate 12 g
   Fibre 2 g
Protein 25 g
Fat 6 g
   Saturated 1 g
Cholesterol 172 mg
Sodium 324 mg
Calories 199

THAI PEPPERED SHRIMP WITH LEEKS

The most commonly used flavours in Thai cuisine are fish sauce, fresh ginger, pepper, limes and garlic. All are readily found in supermarkets, although you may have to go to the Asian section for fish sauce.

1 lb	uncooked fresh or frozen jumbo shrimp (see Tip)	500 g
2	large leeks	2
1 tbsp	canola oil	15 mL
1	clove garlic, crushed	1
2 tbsp	fresh lime juice	25 mL
1 tbsp	sodium-reduced soy sauce (see Tip)	15 mL
1 tsp	brown sugar	5 mL
½–1 tsp	freshly ground pepper	2–5 mL
1 tbsp	chopped fresh coriander	15 mL

Thaw shrimp (if frozen)(see Tip). Peel main part of shell from shrimp and discard. (You may leave the tail in place if you want to serve shrimp that way.) Set shrimp aside.

Cut leeks in half lengthwise, then into 1-inch (2.5 cm) pieces. Wash thoroughly. Bring a saucepan of water to a boil and add leeks. Cook for 5 minutes, or until just tender; drain and keep warm.

Meanwhile, heat oil on medium-high in a wok or large non-stick skillet. Add garlic; stir-fry for 30 seconds being careful it does not brown. Add shrimp; cook for 3 minutes, turning over until shrimp are coral-coloured and cooked. Stir in lime juice, soy sauce, sugar and pepper.

Serve shrimp over cooked leeks, adding any shrimp liquid. Sprinkle with coriander and serve.

⊚ *We use uncooked frozen jumbo tiger shrimp in the shell and find them to be the most flavourful as well as an ideal size.*

⊚ *To thaw shrimp quickly, place them in a bowl of cold water for about 10 minutes.*

⊚ *Light or sodium-reduced soy sauce averages 608 mg of sodium per tablespoon, while regular soy sauce averages 1019 mg of sodium; fish sauce is even higher at 1408 mg of sodium per tablespoon. Use regular soy sauce or fish sauce in moderation and only on special occasions.*

STIR-FRIED VEGETABLES

Nothing has as much appeal as a skillet full of fresh vegetables flavoured with ginger and garlic. Asparagus, lightly cooked but still somewhat crisp, in combination with snow peas and red pepper, makes a very colourful addition to this Thai meal.

2 tsp	sesame or canola oil (see Tip)	10 mL
4 tsp	grated fresh gingerroot (see Tip)	20 mL
2	large cloves garlic, sliced	2
12	stalks asparagus, trimmed and cut into 2-inch (5 cm) pieces	12
2 cups	snow peas, strings removed	500 mL
1	medium sweet red pepper, seeded and thinly sliced	1
4	green onions, cut into 1-inch (2.5 cm) pieces freshly ground pepper	4

In a non-stick skillet, heat oil over medium-high heat until hot. Cook gingerroot and garlic for 30 seconds. Add asparagus, snow peas and red pepper. Stir-fry for 3 minutes.

Add green onion, pepper and ¼ cup (50 mL) water. Cover and steam for 4 minutes.

- ◉ *Sesame oil, used often in Asian cooking, has equal amounts of mononunsaturated and polyunsaturated fats—and is low in saturated fat.*
- ◉ *A carpenter's rasp is ideal for grating gingerroot as well as citrus peel, whole nutmeg or garlic cloves.*

Special Occasion Menu 2

....

Prep · 15 minutes
Cook · about 8 minutes
Yield · 4 servings, 4 cups (1 L)

....

Each serving · ¼ of recipe
        (1 cup/250 mL)
Carb choice   ½
Fats choice   ¼

....

Carbohydrate 9 g
  Fibre 2 g
Protein 3 g
Fat 3 g
  Saturated 0 g
Cholesterol 0 mg
Sodium 6 mg
Calories 64

Special Occasion Menu 2

Prep • 5 minutes
Cook • about 15 minutes
Yield • 4 servings, 2 cups
(500 mL)

Each serving • ¼ of recipe
(½ cup/125 mL)
Carb choices   1½
Fats choice   ½

Carbohydrate 25 g
  Fibre 0 g
Protein 2 g
Fat 2 g
  Saturated 2 g
Cholesterol 0 mg
Sodium 19 mg
Calories 134

FRAGRANT RICE

Fragrant is indeed descriptive of the jasmine rice used in Thai cuisine. When cooked in coconut milk, the rice has a soft, sticky consistency and an authentic Thai flavour.

⅔ cup	jasmine rice (see Tip)	150 mL
1¼ cups	water	300 mL
¾ cup	light coconut milk (see Tip)	175 mL

Stove top: In a saucepan, bring rice, water and coconut milk to a boil on high. Reduce heat to medium-low, cover and cook for 15 minutes or until all liquid is absorbed. Remove from heat; let stand, covered, for 5 minutes before serving.

Microwave: In a microwave-safe casserole combine rice, water and coconut milk. Cover and microwave on high (100%) for 5 minutes; reduce to medium (70%) for about 15 minutes. Let stand, covered, for 5 minutes, or until liquid is absorbed. Fluff rice with a fork before serving.

⊛ *Jasmine rice has a wonderful, delicate flavour. Look for it in bulk food stores and some supermarkets. Rice should be rinsed before cooking.*

⊛ *Unsweetened coconut milk is easily found in larger supermarkets in the Asian section. It comes in three forms—dry mix, full fat and light. Since coconut milk is quite high in fat, you can use the canned "light" variety with great-tasting results.*

Mango Mint Sorbet

Mangoes, those golden-orange, juicy-fleshed fruits, are outstanding in a sorbet. With the refreshing flavours of mint and lime, this sorbet is the perfect end to a Thai dinner. Sorbets differ from sherbet by never containing milk and often having a softer consistency (see Tip).

1 cup	water	250 mL
2 tbsp	chopped fresh mint	25 mL
⅓ cup	granulated sugar	75 mL
1 cup	mango chunks (1–2 medium mangoes)(see Tip)	250 mL
1 tbsp	granulated sugar	15 mL
½ tsp	finely shredded lime peel	2 mL
¼ cup	fresh lime juice	50 ml
1 tbsp	orange liqueur (optional)	15 ml
	fresh mint leaves	

In a small saucepan, combine water and mint. Bring to a boil; remove from heat. Cover to steep for 10 minutes. Strain through a lined sieve, discarding mint.

Return mint liquid to saucepan; add ⅓ cup (75 mL) sugar. Bring to a boil, stirring until sugar is dissolved. Remove from heat and cool.

Process cool liquid, mango chunks, 1 tbsp (15 mL) sugar, lime peel and juice in a blender or food processor until very smooth. Remove, stir in liqueur (if using).

Freeze in a metal pan for 1 hour or until frozen around the outside. Process in a food processor or beat with electric mixer until smooth. Return to pan and freeze until firm or freeze in an ice cream maker according to manufacturer's directions. Serve with mint leaves.

Move frozen sorbet from the freezer to the refrigerator for about 1 hour before serving to allow softening.

Sorbet is especially easy to make in an ice cream maker, but still quite manageable without.

- *Although lower in fat than ice cream, commercial sorbets and sherbets are higher in carbohydrate.*
- *Mangoes, although high in natural sugar, are packed with beta-carotene, fibre and vitamin C.*

Special Occasion Menu 2

....

Prep • about 20 minutes
Freeze • 30 minutes in ice cream maker, longer in freezer
Yield • 6 servings, 2¼ cups (550 mL)

....

Each serving • ⅙ of recipe (about ⅓ cup/75 mL)
Carb choice   1

....

Carbohydrate 21 g
  Fibre 1 g
Protein 0 g
Fat 0 g
Cholesterol 0 mg
Sodium 2 mg
Calories 82

BEEF BURGUNDY

Special Occasion Menu 3

....

Prep · 20 minutes
Cook · about 3 hours
Yield · 6 servings

....

Each serving · ⅙ of recipe
Carb choices   2
Meat & Alternatives choices 2½
Fats choices   2

....

Carbohydrate 29 g
   Fibre 2 g
Protein 24 g
Fat 17 g
   Saturated 3 g
Cholesterol 49 mg
Sodium 415 mg
Calories 371

Beef Burgundy is cooked in red wine by first braising the meat in the wine, then adding the mushrooms and onions. The meat is topped with pastry and baked. The result—beef full of robust wine and onion flavours. The best part is this recipe can be prepared ahead of time and makes a great buffet dinner dish. Bon appétit.

3 tbsp	cornstarch	45 mL
1¾ cups	*Homemade Light Beef Broth* (page 58)	
	or salt-reduced beef broth	425 mL
½	pkg (40 g) dry onion soup mix	½
¼ cup	red wine or beef broth	50 mL
1	bay leaf	1
1½ lb	lean stewing beef, cubed	750 g
18	baby carrots	18
6	small onions, halved, or 12 pearl onions	6
24	small mushrooms, trimmed and halved	24
½	pkg (397 g) frozen puff pastry	½
	chopped fresh parsley	

In an 11- x 7-inch (2 L) rectangular casserole, combine cornstarch, broth, soup mix, wine and bay leaf. Add beef and mix well. Cover and bake in 300°F (150°C) oven, stirring occasionally, for about 2½ hours or until meat is tender.

Arrange the carrots, onions and mushrooms over meat. Cover and return to oven; bake for 30 minutes, or until vegetables are almost tender. Remove bay leaf and discard.

Follow package directions for defrosting the pastry. Roll pastry on a lightly floured surface into a rectangle slightly larger than the pan. Cover casserole with pastry, fluting the edges. Cut steam holes and bake in 400°F (200°C) oven for 30 minutes or until pastry is golden and filling is bubbly. Sprinkle with parsley and serve.

Mocha Soufflé Dessert

Made with low-fat cottage cheese and eggs, this vanilla soufflé cake with a molten chocolate centre provides an elegant ending to dinner—with a chocolate surprise!

2	squares bittersweet chocolate, chopped	2
2 tbsp	water	25 mL
1 tsp	soft margarine or butter	5 mL
1 cup	low-fat cottage cheese	250 mL
3	eggs, separated	3
½ cup	all purpose flour	125 mL
1 tsp	vanilla extract	5 mL
3 tbsp	granular low-calorie sweetener with sucralose	45 mL
2 tbsp	granulated sugar	25 mL

Spray eight ½ cup/125 mL ramekins with non-stick cooking spray.

In a bowl, melt chocolate, water and margarine over boiling water, stirring frequently, until chocolate is smooth. When chocolate is cool, use a teaspoon to form into 8 balls, placing them on waxed paper to harden. Set aside.

In a food processor, beat cottage cheese until it is perfectly smooth. Add egg yolks, flour and vanilla. Process mixture until well blended. Remove to a bowl.

In a second bowl, beat egg whites with an electric mixer on medium-high speed until soft peaks form. Add sweetener and sugar gradually and beat until stiff and glossy. Fold half of beaten egg whites into cheese mixture, then fold in remaining whites. Spoon batter into prepared cups. Chill until ready to bake (see Tip).

Just before baking, place a chocolate ball in the centre of each cup. Bake in 400°F (200°C) oven for 13 minutes or until soufflé cakes are puffed and golden brown on top. Remove from oven and serve at once.

◉ *There will be two extra desserts—wrap well and freeze for later.*

Special Occasion Menu 3

Prep · 20 minutes
Cook · 13 minutes
Yield · 8 servings

Each serving · ⅛ of recipe
Carb choice   1
Meat & Alternatives choice   ½
Fats choice   1

Carbohydrate 13 g
  Fibre 1 g
Protein 8 g
Fat 6 g
  Saturated 3 g
Cholesterol 82 mg
Sodium 136 mg
Calories 130

Three Cheese Mushroom Risotto

Special Occasion Menu 4

....

Prep · 15 minutes
Cook · about 25 minutes
Yield · 4 servings, 4 cups (1 L)

....

Each serving · ¼ of recipe
         (1 cup/250 mL)
Carb choices   2
Meat & Alternatives choice   1
Fats choices   1½

....

Carbohydrate 35 g
   Fibre 2 g
Protein 15 g
Fat 10 g
   Saturated 5 g
Cholesterol 21 mg
Sodium 455 mg
Calories 298

Arborio is Italian short- to medium-grain rice that can absorb great quantities of flavourful broth. Simmering the rice slowly with constant stirring produces a marvellous and creamy risotto. Risotto, like pasta, can be "dressed up" by adding almost anything you want. In this recipe we have three great Italian cheeses to dress it up. This is truly one of the world's great comfort foods.

1 tsp	olive oil	5 mL
⅓ cup	finely chopped onion	75 mL
¾ cup	Arborio rice	175 mL
⅓ cup	white wine (or salt-reduced chicken broth)	75 mL
2¾ cups	*Homemade Light Chicken Broth* (page 59) or salt-reduced chicken broth, heated to boiling	675 mL
1⅓ cups	sliced mushrooms (see Tip)	325 mL
1 cup	sliced sweet red pepper	250 mL
½ cup	shredded Asiago cheese (50 g) (see Tip)	125 mL
½ cup	shredded provolone cheese (50 g) (see Tip)	125 mL
3 tbsp	grated Parmesan cheese (see Tip)	45 mL
¼ tsp	each freshly ground pepper and ground nutmeg	1 mL

In a heavy medium saucepan, heat oil over medium heat. Cook onion for 5 minutes or until soft. Stir in rice; cook for 2 minutes (do not allow rice to brown). Add wine; cook, stirring, until wine is absorbed.

Stir in ½ cup (125 mL) of the broth, stirring often. Before adding more both, wait until almost all liquid is absorbed, then add next ½ cup (125 mL) broth. Continue adding broth, stirring frequently, until all broth has been used and rice is tender and creamy. (The cooking process will take about 20 minutes and is necessary to achieve creaminess).

Meanwhile in a non-stick skillet, sauté mushrooms and red pepper for 5 minutes or until soft (you may need a little water).

Stir cheeses into rice until they are melted. Stir mushroom mixture into rice. Add pepper and nutmeg.

- *Portobello and porcini mushrooms, both more expensive than white, add a richer mushroom flavour, but any kind of mushroom will still do the job.*
- *Asiago cheese is a semi-firm cheese with a rich, nutty flavour. Provolone, another Italian cheese, has a firmer texture with a mild smoky flavour and is an excellent cooking cheese. The better-known Parmesan, Parmigiano-Reggiano, is a hard cheese with a rich, sharp flavour and granular texture that makes it ideal for grating.*

Special Occasion Menu 5

· ·

Prep · 15 minutes
Refrigerate · several hours
Yield · 4 servings,
4½ cups (1.25 L)

· ·

Each serving · ¼ of recipe
(about 1 cup/250 mL)
Carb choice ½

· ·

Carbohydrate 15 g
Fibre 4 g
Protein 3 g
Fat 1 g
Saturated 0 g
Cholesterol 0 mg
Sodium 97 mg
Calories 75

GAZPACHO

This refreshing cold summer soup hails from the Andalusia region of southern Spain. It is a wonderful blend of fresh tomatoes, cucumbers, green pepper, onion, olive oil and red wine vinegar.

1 cup	finely chopped cucumber, divided	250 mL
1 cup	finely chopped tomato, divided	250 mL
½ cup	finely chopped sweet green pepper, divided	125 mL
¼ cup	minced onion	50 mL
1–2	cloves garlic, minced	1–2
3 cups	salt-reduced vegetable juice cocktail	750 mL
1 tsp	each olive oil and red wine vinegar	5 mL
	freshly ground pepper	

Reserve ¼ cup (50 mL) cucumber and tomato and 2 tbsp (25 mL) green pepper; cover and refrigerate.

In a medium bowl, combine remaining cucumber, tomato, green pepper, onion, garlic and vegetable juice cocktail. Stir in oil, vinegar and pepper. Process in a food processor or blender until smooth. Remove to a bowl, cover and refrigerate for several hours or until soup is cold (see Tips).

To serve, ladle into four chilled soup bowls. Sprinkle each with ¼ of reserved vegetables.

◉ *This soup will keep for several days in the refrigerator. However, it is best the day it is made.*

◉ *Flavours blend best when cold soups are made several hours before serving.*

Tortilla Española

In Spain "tortilla" refers to a thin omelette, not the corn or wheat flour pancake common to Mexico. This tortilla is a potato omelette with a Spanish flavour and an abundance of vitamins and minerals.

1 tbsp	olive oil, divided	15 mL
1	medium onion, thinly sliced	1
2	cloves garlic, minced	2
2½ cups	thinly sliced potatoes (3 medium)(see Tip)	625 mL
4	eggs	4
¼ tsp	freshly ground pepper	1 mL
	Fresh Tomato Salsa (page 74)	

In a large non-stick skillet, heat 1 tsp (5 mL) of the oil over medium-high. Add onion and cook for 5 minutes. Reduce heat to low, cook for 10 minutes, stirring occasionally or until onion is soft and golden brown. Add garlic and cook for 1 minute. Remove onion and garlic to a bowl and reserve.

Heat 1 tsp (5 mL) of the oil in a skillet over medium and add potato slices. Lower heat to medium-low, cook for 20 minutes, stirring occasionally, or until tender, but not browned. Remove potatoes and reserve.

In a bowl, beat eggs and pepper. Stir into onions; mix well. Add potatoes and toss to coat slices well with egg mixture.

Heat a non-stick skillet on medium heat with remaining oil. Add potato and egg mixture, cover and reduce heat to low allowing mixture to cook for 8 minutes or until almost set. When bottom is set and not sticking to pan, invert tortilla onto large flat plate, then slide back into skillet, bottom side up. Cook, covered, over low heat for 5 minutes or until golden and egg is set (see Tip).

Slide tortilla onto a serving plate, cut into 4 wedges and serve with *Fresh Tomato Salsa*.

⊕ *Round red potatoes were our choice for this recipe as they remain firm-textured when cooked.*

⊕ *Use moderate heat when cooking eggs. Cooking at too high a temperature, or for too long at too low a temperature, causes both egg whites and egg yolks to become tough.*

Special Occasion Menu 5

....

Prep · 15 minutes
Cook · about 40 minutes
Yield · 4 servings

....

Each serving · ¼ of recipe
Carb choices 2
Meat & Alternatives choice ½
Fats choices 1½

....

Carbohydrate 32 g
Fibre 3 g
Protein 10 g
Fat 9 g
Saturated 2 g
Cholesterol 216 mg
Sodium 70 mg
Calories 241

Special Occasion Menu 5

Prep · 20 minutes
Cook · about 60 minutes
Yield · 4 servings

Each serving · ¼ of recipe

Carb choice	1
Meat & Alternatives choice	½
Fats choice	1

Carbohydrate 14 g
   Fibre 0 g
Protein 8 g
Fat 6 g
   Saturated 2 g
Cholesterol 220 mg
Sodium 78 mg
Calories 145

Lemon Flan

This is a very light flan made with low-fat milk, sweetened with a low-calorie sweetener and a little sugar. The essence of lemon peel provides extra sparkle. It can be baked in either individual ramekins or a mold. It keeps for several days in the refrigerator.

2 cups	low-fat milk	500 mL
2	strips lemon peel	2
3	egg yolks	3
1	whole egg	1
¼ cup	granular low-calorie sweetener with sucralose	50 mL
2 tbsp	granulated sugar	25 mL

In a saucepan, bring milk and lemon peel to a boil over high heat. Immediately reduce heat to low and simmer for 10 minutes. This allows the milk to be infused with the lemon. Remove from heat; cool.

In a bowl, whisk together egg yolks, whole egg, sweetener and sugar until foamy. Pour cooled milk through a fine-meshed sieve held over the egg mixture; whisk until well blended. Discard peel.

Divide mixture between four small baking dishes. Place in a baking pan, fill pan with boiling water halfway up the sides of dishes.

Bake in 300°F (150°C) oven for about 1 hour or until flan is set when a knife inserted in the centre comes out clean. Carefully remove from oven, remove from water bath and allow flans to cool completely. Cover and chill, or serve at room temperature.

GOLDEN HARVEST SOUP

This very mellow soup is perfect for fall and winter dinners and will provide extra for another meal. And it freezes well!

1 tbsp	soft margarine or butter	15 mL
1 cup	chopped onion (1 medium)	250 mL
2	leeks, chopped (white part only)	2
1½ cups	cubed potato (1 large)	375 mL
2 cups	cubed squash	500 mL
1 cup	thinly sliced carrot (2 medium)	250 mL
3 cups	*Homemade Light Chicken Broth* (page 59) or salt-reduced chicken broth	750 mL
1½ cups	low-fat milk	375 mL
¼ cup	dry white wine or chicken broth	50 mL
	freshly ground pepper to taste	
	chopped chives or green onions	

In a saucepan, melt margarine over low heat. Add onion and leeks and cook for 10 minutes, stirring occasionally. Add potato, squash, carrot and chicken broth. Cover and cook on medium heat for 20 minutes or until vegetables are tender. Cool slightly before placing in a food processor or blender; purée until smooth.

Return to saucepan; add milk, wine and pepper. Heat to serving temperature on low heat. To serve, sprinkle with chives or green onions.

⊕ *Extra soup may be frozen in 1 cup (250 mL) amounts.*

A ROMANTIC DINNER

Special Occasion Menu 6

....

Prep · 20 minutes
Cook · about 30 minutes
Yield · 8 cups (2 L)

....

Each serving · ⅛ of recipe (1 cup/250 mL)

Carb choice	1
Fats choice	½

....

Carbohydrate 17 g
  Fibre 2 g
Protein 4 g
Fat 2 g
  Saturated 1 g
Cholesterol 2 mg
Sodium 94 mg
Calories 105

·····································

Prep · 20 minutes providing
    wild rice is cooked
Cook · about 1 hour
Yield · 2 servings,
    1 stuffed Cornish hen

·····································

Each serving · ½ hen with
    ½ cup (125 mL) dressing
Carb choice   ½
Meat & Alternatives choices   3

·····································

Carbohydrate 13 g
  Fibre 2 g
Protein 22 g
Fat 5 g
  Saturated 1 g
Cholesterol 86 mg
Sodium 164 mg
Calories 187

ROAST CORNISH HEN WITH WILD RICE DRESSING

If you decide to invite guests to enjoy this dinner, then you will probably use all of the dressing, which will fill three hens. The dressing can also be used for roast turkey.

| 1 | Cornish hen, thawed (about 1¼ lb/625 g) | 1 |

DRESSING:

1 tbsp	soft margarine or butter	15 mL
½ cup	chopped celery	125 mL
¼ cup	chopped onion	50 mL
¼ cup	chopped fresh parsley	50 mL
1 cup	soft bread crumbs	250 mL
¾ cup	cooked wild rice (¼ cup/50 mL uncooked)	175 mL
½	medium unpeeled tart apple, chopped	½
2 tbsp	chopped pecans	25 mL
¼ tsp	each dried thyme and dried sage	1 mL
Pinch	freshly ground pepper	

Rinse hen and pat dry with paper towelling. Set aside.

In a non-stick skillet, melt margarine over medium heat. Add celery, onion and parsley and cook for 5 minutes.

In a bowl, combine celery mixture, bread crumbs, wild rice, apple, pecans, thyme, sage and pepper. Stuff hen with 1 cup (250 mL) dressing (see Tip); close cavity with skewers or toothpicks. Place hen, breast side up, on a rack in a roasting pan.

Roast in 350°F (180°C) oven for about 1 hour or until juices run clear and meat thermometer registers 165°F (74°C).

To serve, place hen on a cutting board and cut lengthwise through backbone. Serve one-half hen, stuffing side down, on each plate.

⊕ *Extra dressing freezes well.*

Raspberry Fool

Light and luscious is a good way to describe this dessert, which is so right after a hearty main course. Usually this dessert is made with heavy whipping cream., but we make it with light ricotta cheese.

1 cup	light ricotta cheese	250 mL
	(about half of a 475 g package)	
2 tbsp	sifted icing sugar	25 mL
2 tbsp	granular low-calorie sweetener	25 mL
	with sucralose, divided	
2 cups	fresh or frozen raspberries, divided (see Tip)	500 mL
½ tsp	finely grated orange peel	2 mL
2 tbsp	fresh orange juice	25 mL
	mint leaves	

In a food processor or blender, process ricotta cheese, sugar and 1 tbsp (25 mL) of the sweetener until smooth. Add ¾ cup (175 mL) of the raspberries, orange peel and juice. Process with on/off motion just until raspberries begin to combine with the creamed mixture. Do not overmix. Stir remaining sweetener into remaining raspberries.

In parfait glasses, layer about ¼ cup (50 mL) cheese mixture alternately with ⅓ of raspberry mixture. Repeat layers once. Garnish with mint leaves.

⊕ *Whole strawberries, hulled and sliced, may replace raspberries. Store strawberries, unwashed, with hulls intact, in the refrigerator, loosely covered with paper towels. Hull strawberries after washing, as they will absorb water without their caps.*

Prep · 15 minutes
Refrigerate · at least 30 minutes
Yield · 3 servings

Each serving · ⅓ of recipe

Carb choice	1
Meat & Alternatives choice	1
Fats choice	1

Carbohydrate 20 g
  Fibre 4 g
Protein 10 g
Fat 7 g
  Saturated 4 g
Cholesterol 25 mg
Sodium 102 mg
Calories 181

Special Occasion Menu 7

....

Prep • about 45 minutes if
         soup is made
Cook • 45 minutes
Yield • 6 cups (1.5L) and
         12 matzo balls

....

Each serving • ⅙ of recipe
         (1 cup/250 mL soup
         and 2 matzo balls)
Carb choice   1
Meat & Alternatives choice   ½

....

Carbohydrate 13 g
   Fibre 2 g
Protein 8 g
Fat 3 g
   Saturated 1 g
Cholesterol 108 mg
Sodium 143 mg
Calories 107

CHICKEN AND MATZO BALL SOUP

Chicken soup is a universal remedy for anything from a cure for colds to a broken heart. With matzo balls added, it becomes a meal—and a part of a traditional Jewish Passover Seder.

MATZO BALLS:

3	eggs, beaten	3
3 tbsp	*Homemade Light Chicken Broth* (page 59)	45 mL
¾ cup	whole wheat matzo meal	175 mL
2 tbsp	grated onion	25 mL
2 tbsp	finely chopped fresh parsley	25 mL

CHICKEN BROTH:

6 cups	*Homemade Light Chicken Broth* (page 59)	1.5 L
	freshly ground pepper	
	chopped fresh dill, optional	

In a bowl, beat eggs and chicken broth until light and fluffy. Stir in matzo meal, onion and parsley. Mix well. Cover and refrigerate for about 30 minutes.

Wet hands and roll matzo mixture in your palms into 12 small oval-shaped balls (see Tip).

Meanwhile, bring a large saucepan of water to a boil. Drop matzo balls into water, one at a time. Reduce heat , cover and simmer for 45 minutes. Drain, remove to a plate, cover until ready to use.

In a large saucepan, heat broth until serving temperature. Season to taste with pepper. Drop balls into broth to reheat before serving.

To serve, ladle 1 cup (250 mL) soup into each bowl. Add 2 matzo balls and sprinkle with dill (if using).

◉ *Shaped matzo balls may be refrigerated overnight or frozen for longer storage.*

Spinach and Orange Salad

A perfect salad that can be prepared ahead of time for a last-minute toss with the dressing.

Salad:

3 cups	fresh spinach	750 mL
2	medium oranges, peeled and sectioned or 1½ cups (375 mL) canned mandarin sections, drained	2
¼	small red onion, sliced	¼

Dressing:

3 tbsp	red wine vinegar or raspberry vinegar (see Tip)	45 mL
2 tbsp	canola oil	25 mL
1 tsp	low-calorie sweetener	5 ml
	freshly ground pepper	

In a salad spinner, wash and dry spinach. Remove stems and tear leaves into bite-size pieces.

In a salad bowl, combine spinach, oranges and red onion. Cover with damp paper towel and refrigerate until ready to serve.

In a container with a tight-fitting lid, combine vinegar, oil, sweetener and pepper. Shake well and refrigerate until ready to serve. Pour dressing over salad and toss lightly just before serving.

⊕ *If you wish to make your own raspberry vinegar, add 3 cups (750 mL) fresh or frozen raspberries to 1½ cups (375 mL) white wine vinegar. Allow to stand at room temperature for several days. Strain and pour into clean sealed bottles. Makes about 2 cups (500 mL) vinegar.*

Passover Seder

Special Occasion Menu 7

....

Prep · 15 minutes
Refrigerate · 30 minutes
   or longer
Yield · 6 servings, 6 cups (1.5 L)

....

Each serving · 1 cup (250 mL)
   salad with dressing
Carb choice   ½
Fats choice   1

....

Carbohydrate 8 g
   Fibre 2 g
Protein 1 g
Fat 5 g
   Saturated 0 g
Cholesterol 0 mg
Sodium 23 mg
Calories 73

....

Prep · 10 minutes
Refrigerate · overnight
Cook · about 3 hours
Yield · 8 servings

....

Each serving · ⅛ of recipe
    (3 slices/90 g)
Carb choice   ½
Meat & Alternatives choices 3

....

Carbohydrate 7 g
   Fibre 1 g
Protein 19 g
Fat 7 g
   Saturated 2 g
Cholesterol 43 mg
Sodium 139 mg
Calories 175

SPICED BEEF BRISKET

Traditional in many Jewish households, beef brisket varies only in the seasonings used. Best of all, leftovers are absolutely delicious.

2 lbs	lean beef brisket, rolled and tied with string (see Tip)	1 kg
2	large cloves garlic, minced	2
1 tsp	canola oil	5 mL
1 tbsp	chopped fresh thyme (optional)	15 mL
½ tsp	paprika	2 mL
¼ tsp	freshly ground pepper	1 mL
2	medium onions, sliced	2
1	large carrot, sliced	1
6	cloves garlic, peeled and halved	6
⅔ cup	tomato juice	150 mL
⅓ cup	each red wine and water	75 mL
2 tsp	liquid honey	10 mL

Pat brisket dry with paper towels.

Combine garlic, oil, fresh thyme (if using), paprika and pepper to make a paste. Press paste over surface of beef, cover and refrigerate overnight.

In the bottom of a roasting pan, place onions, carrot and garlic. Top the vegetables with meat.

In a bowl, whisk together tomato juice, wine, water and honey. Pour over beef, cover pan tightly and cook in 325°F (160°C) oven for 2½ hours or until meat is fork tender (see Tip). Uncover and bake for 30 minutes longer.

Transfer beef to a cutting board. Skim fat from juices. Carve roast against the grain into thin slices and serve with juices.

⊕ *When buying beef brisket, ask for a "single" brisket, as the more traditional "double" brisket is higher in fat.*
⊕ *Check every 45 minutes to ensure there is still plenty of liquid surrounding the beef (you may add water if needed).*
⊕ *The meat is best sliced across the grain at serving time.*

Oven-Roasted Asparagus

You can use this oven roasting method for many vegetables, not just asparagus. Try sweet red, green or yellow peppers, zucchini, mushrooms, red onions—in the oven or on the barbecue grill.

¼ tsp	freshly grated lemon peel	1 mL
2 tbsp	fresh lemon juice or wine vinegar	25 mL
1 tbsp	canola oil	15 mL
Pinch	freshly ground pepper and salt	
3 lbs	asparagus spears	1.3 kg

Line a baking sheet with foil. Arrange asparagus on pan (allow 6–8 spears per person). Set aside.

In a bowl, whisk together lemon peel and juice, oil, pepper and salt. Brush mixture over each spear. Bake asparagus in 425°F (220°C) oven for 10 minutes or until asparagus is tender.

Special Occasion Menu 7

....

Prep · 10 minutes
Cook · about 10 minutes
Yield · 6 servings

....

Each serving · ⅙ of recipe
(6 asparagus spears)
Fats choice   ½

....

Carbohydrate 6 g
Fibre 2 g
Protein 2 g
Fat 3 g
Saturated 0 g
Cholesterol 0 mg
Sodium 2 mg
Calories 49

Special Occasion Menu 7

....

Prep · 20 minutes
Cook · about 35 minutes
Yield · 12 kugels

....

Each serving · ¹⁄₁₂ of recipe,
        1 kugel
Carb choice   ½

....

Carbohydrate 9 g
    Fibre 1 g
Protein 2 g
Fat 1 g
    Saturated 0 g
Cholesterol 36 mg
Sodium 15 mg
Calories 53

POTATO KUGEL

Absolutely a fabulous potato recipe and no need to serve only at a Passover Seder. When serving, pour some of the **Spiced Beef Brisket** (page 206) juices over each kugel.

2	large potatoes	2
1	small onion	1
1	medium carrot	1
2	eggs, beaten	2
3 tbsp	whole wheat matzo meal	45 mL
1 tsp	fresh lemon juice	5 mL
¼ tsp	freshly ground pepper	1 mL

Spray large muffin pans with non-stick cooking spray.

Cut potatoes, onion and carrot into pieces and press through the grater attachment on a food processor or grate on a hand grater. Transfer to a bowl.

In a second bowl, combine beaten eggs, matzo meal, lemon juice and pepper. Stir into vegetable mixture.

Divide vegetable mixture evenly between the prepared muffin pans. Bake in 350°F (180°C) oven for 35 minutes or until crisp and brown.

LEMON PASSOVER CAKE

This light chiffon-like cake looks so very attractive served with fresh fruit. It is best served the day it is made; however, leftovers can be frozen.

6	eggs, separated	6
½ cup	granulated sugar, divided	125 mL
½ cup	granular low-calorie sweetener with sucralose	125 mL
2 tsp	grated lemon peel	10 mL
3 tbsp	fresh lemon juice	45 mL
⅓ cup	Passover cake meal (see Tip)	75 mL
⅓ cup	potato starch	75 mL

Line the bottom of a 9-inch (23 cm) tube pan with parchment paper.

In a bowl, beat egg whites until fluffy. Add ¼ cup (50 mL) sugar and beat until stiff but not dry. In a second bowl, beat egg yolks with remaining sugar until thickened and pale coloured. Beat in sweetener, peel and juice.

Sift cake meal and potato starch over yolk mixture. Using a rubber spatula, fold in gently. Fold in egg whites mixture. Transfer the batter to the prepared pan.

Bake in 325°F (160°C) oven for 40 minutes or until cake is golden brown and springs back when gently touched. Remove from oven, invert tube pan and cool completely. When cool, run knife around edges to loosen. Invert onto a serving plate.

Cut cake into 12 slices and serve.

◉ *Passover cake meal can be made by grinding matzo meal until very fine, using either whole wheat or regular.*

Special Occasion Menu 7

Prep · about 30 minutes
Cook · about 40 minutes
Yield · 12 slices

Each serving · ¹⁄₁₂ of recipe
          (1 slice)

Carb choice	1
Fats choice	½

Carbohydrate 18 g
   Fibre 0 g
Protein 4 g
Fat 3 g
   Saturated 1g
Cholesterol 108 mg
Sodium 33 mg
Calories 108

....

Prep • 25 minutes
Cook • 10 minutes for vegetables
Yield • 16 servings, 8 cups (2 L)

....

Each serving • ¹⁄₁₆ of recipe
            (½ cup/125 mL stuffing)
Carb choice   1
Fats choice   1

....

Carbohydrate 14 g
    Fibre 1 g
Protein 3 g
Fat 4 g
    Saturated 1 g
Cholesterol 0 mg
Sodium 131 mg
Calories 100

VEGETABLE BREAD STUFFING

This moist dressing is so full of vegetables—mushrooms, carrots, celery, onions and fresh parsley—that much less margarine or butter is required without sacrificing flavour. The recipe is sufficient to stuff one 12–14 lb (6–7 kg) turkey or two 5 lb (2.4 kg) chickens. For 1 chicken, prepare one-half of the stuffing recipe (see turkey information below stuffing recipe).

¼ cup	unsalted soft margarine or butter	50 mL
3 cups	thinly sliced mushrooms (12 medium)	750 mL
1¼ cups	chopped onion (2 small)	300 mL
1 cup	shredded carrot	250 mL
1 cup	finely chopped celery	250 mL
¼ cup	chopped fresh parsley	50 mL
1½ tsp	dried thyme leaves	7 mL
1 tsp	each dried rosemary and granulated sugar	5 mL
½ tsp	each pepper and summer savory	2 mL
8 cups	soft bread crumbs (see Tip)	2 L

In a non-stick skillet, melt margarine over medium heat. Add mushrooms, onion, carrot and celery and cook for 10 minutes or until vegetables are tender. Remove from heat; cool. Stir in parsley, thyme, rosemary, sugar, pepper and summer savory.

In a bowl, combine bread crumbs and vegetable mixture. Set aside while preparing turkey.

TO STUFF AND ROAST POULTRY:

Do not stuff the bird until just before putting it in the oven. Rinse and dry well with paper towelling. Stuff the cavity with prepared dressing. Close opening by trussing with a large needle and string or insert skewers and criss-cross the string. Cross legs over tail and tie with string so legs are close to body. Turn wings back, tuck under the bird and secure with skewers or string.

Place poultry on the rack of an open roasting pan, breast side up, with a meat thermometer inserted in thigh. Roast in 325°F (160°C) oven until thermometer reaches 185°F (85°C) and juices run clear. If breast starts to brown too much, cover loosely with foil.

- *The bread used for stuffing should be slightly stale, about 2 or 3 days old, before making into crumbs. The food processor makes short work of this.*
- *Jazz up the bird with this baste: combine 1 tbsp (15 mL) each dried rosemary and finely grated orange peel with ¼ cup (50 mL) fat-free drippings (drippings that are chilled until all fat has been solidified and removed). Brush baste on skin during last hour of roasting time.*
- *Be safe: Do not defrost frozen poultry at room temperature because of the danger of bacteria development. Instead, defrost in the refrigerator allowing 1 day for each 5 lb (2 kg). If time is short, defrost by submerging in cold water. This takes about 10 hours for 20 lb (9 kg).*

Special Occasion Menu 8

. . . .

Prep · 10 minutes
Cook · 10 minutes
Yield · 1¾ cups (425 mL)

. . . .

Each serving · ¹⁄₁₄ of recipe
            (2 tbsp/25 mL)
Carb choice   ½

. . . .

Carbohydrate 6 g
    Fibre 1 g
Protein 0 g
Fat 0 g
Cholesterol 0 mg
Sodium 1 mg
Calories 23

FRESH CRANBERRY CHUTNEY

Chutneys are sophisticated condiments. Generally, they contain fruit, vinegar, sugar and spices. We love curry flavour, but if you don't, use less than we suggest.

1½ cups	chopped fresh or frozen cranberries	375 mL
1 cup	chopped unpeeled apple (2 small)	250 mL
½ cup	chopped red onion	125 mL
½ cup	red wine vinegar	125 mL
¼ cup	water	50 mL
2 tbsp	packed brown sugar	25 mL
2 tbsp	granular low-calorie sweetener with sucralose	25 mL
2	large cloves garlic, minced	2
1 tbsp	minced fresh gingerroot	15 mL
½ tsp	curry powder	2 mL

In a saucepan, combine cranberries, apple, onion, vinegar, water, sugar, sweetener, garlic, gingerroot and curry powder. Bring to a boil; reduce heat and cook, uncovered, for 10 minutes or until mixture thickens, stirring often.

Remove from heat; let cool. Cover and store in the refrigerator for up to 1 week or freeze for longer storage. Serve at room temperature.

Turnip Potato Purée

Many people think that turnip and rutabaga are the same vegetable. However, rutabaga comes from the Swedish *rotabagge*, and is sometimes called a *Swede* or Swedish turnip. It has yellow flesh while turnips are smaller and have white flesh, with white skin and a purple-fringed top.

1 lb	rutabaga, peeled and cut into small chunks (see Tip)	500 g
½ lb	potatoes, peeled and cut into large chunks	250 g
2	cloves garlic, minced	2
¼ cup	light sour cream	50 mL
Pinch	each ground nutmeg and freshly ground pepper	

In a saucepan, cook rutabaga on medium heat for 10 minutes in a small amount of boiling water. Add potatoes and garlic; cook for 20 minutes or until vegetables are tender. Remove from heat, drain and leave in pan several minutes to dry.

With a potato masher or hand mixer, mash vegetables. Add sour cream, nutmeg and pepper. Serve at once or place in a microwave-safe casserole, cover and refrigerate until ready to reheat on high (100%) for 6 minutes or until serving temperature.

⊕ *Rutabagas are waxed to prevent exposure to air, thereby extending storage time. To remove wax easily, wrap rutabaga in paper towel, place in a microwaveable baking dish; heat on high (100%) for several minutes. Remove from microwave and discard paper towel along with wax.*

Special Occasion Menu 8

Prep · 20 minutes
Cook · about 30 minutes
Yield · 6 servings,
3 cups (750 mL)

Each serving · ⅙ of recipe
(½ cup/125 mL)
Carb choice   ½

Carbohydrate 13 g
Fibre 2 g
Protein 2 g
Fat 1 g
Saturated 1 g
Cholesterol 4 mg
Sodium 61 mg
Calories 67

Special Occasion Menu 8

....

Prep · 15 minutes
Cook · 50 minutes
Yield · 8 servings

....

Each serving · ⅛ of pie
Carb choice   1
Fats choices   1½

....

Carbohydrate 18 g
    Fibre 1 g
Protein 4 g
Fat 7 g
    Saturated 2 g
Cholesterol 55 mg
Sodium 130 mg
Calories 145

SPICY PUMPKIN PIE

There are at least as many versions of pumpkin pie as there are provinces in Canada. We found this one to have a nice balance of spice to sweetness.

1	9-inch (23 cm) frozen pastry shell	1
1½ cups	canned unsweetened pumpkin purée	375 mL
2	eggs, beaten	2
1 cup	low-fat milk	250 mL
3 tbsp	granular low-calorie sweetener with sucralose	45 mL
2 tbsp	packed brown sugar	25 mL
1 tsp	ground cinnamon	5 mL
½ tsp	ground nutmeg	2 mL
½ tsp	ground ginger	2 mL
Pinch	ground cloves	

Prick the pastry shell with a fork. Bake in 450°F (230°C) oven for 8 minutes.

In a bowl, combine pumpkin, eggs, milk, sweetener, sugar, cinnamon, nutmeg, ginger and cloves. Pour into partially baked pie shell. Bake in 350°F (180°C) oven for 50 minutes or until centre is almost set. Cool slightly and then refrigerate until serving time.

To serve, cut into 8 wedges.

APPENDICES

....

I	Beyond the Basics: Meal Planning for Healthy Eating	216
II	Breakfast Cereals of Your Choice	223
III	Fruits of Your Choice	224
IV	The ABCs of Nutrition and Diabetes	225
V	Food Definitions and Procedures	229
VI	Common Herbs and Spices	231
VII	The Well-Stocked Diabetes Kitchen	232
VIII	Recommended Storage Times for Refrigerator and Freezer Food	233
IX	Nutrient Analysis of Recipes and Menus	237

1 · BEYOND THE BASICS: MEAL PLANNING FOR HEALTHY EATING

Beyond the Basics: Meal Planning for Healthy Eating, Diabetes Prevention and Management (published by the Canadian Diabetes Association, 2006) has replaced the earlier *Good Health Eating Guide* system of meal planning used by many people with diabetes. As before, it is based on *Canada's Food Guide*, with some changes to meet the needs of people with diabetes. The goal of *Beyond the Basics* is to make it easy for you to include a variety of foods in meals and, at the same time, keep carbohydrate intake consistent, thus promoting good diabetes management.

Foods are divided into two categories, based on whether they contain carbohydrate or not. The food groups that contain carbohydrate and raise blood glucose are GRAINS & STARCHES, FRUITS, MILK & ALTERNATIVES and OTHER CHOICES. Any choice from any of these groups contains 15 grams of available carbohydrate and is called a Carbohydrate Choice or Carb Choice. Groups containing little or no carbohydrate are the VEGETABLES, MEAT & ALTERNATIVES, FATS and EXTRAS groups.

Within each of these eight groups, foods are divided into two categories: foods to "choose more often" and foods to "choose less often." Although all foods may be enjoyed in moderation, the foods in the first group are considered healthier since they are higher in fibre, higher in vitamins and minerals, or lower in fat.

A serving of a food is described as a "Choice," since it is your choice. By following a meal plan and choosing a variety of foods from each group, you're sure to get all the nutrients you need, as well as having a consistent amount of carbohydrate at each meal.

CARBOHYDRATE-CONTAINING FOODS

Grains & Starches

This group includes all types of breads and cereals, as well as rice, corn, pasta and potatoes. These foods contain the carbohydrate you need for energy and are also the ones that have the greatest impact on blood glucose. Most are low in fat and often high in fibre, especially whole grains, but the amount you eat at any one meal matters. The amount of any food described as 1 GRAINS & STARCHES CHOICE (or 1 CARB CHOICE) contains 15 grams of available carbohydrate (total carbohydrate minus fibre).

Breads and rolls: You can choose any bread you like—they all fit into your meal plan. The trick is to know how much. One ounce (or 30 grams) of any fresh bread item is equal to 1 CARB CHOICE. Packaged breads, bagels, pita breads and so on clearly state the weight of one slice or one piece on the label. If your favourite bread or roll comes unpackaged, a small kitchen scale makes it easy to determine the weight (see page 25).

Crackers and breadsticks: There are many healthy high-fibre, whole grain, low-fat, lower-salt varieties out there. Read labels. Look to see how many crackers the label says are in a serving, then compare the fat and fibre content (and sodium, if you're watching your salt intake). Because Melba toasts, breadsticks and crackers contain less moisture than breads, 20 grams of crackers is usually equal to 1 CARB CHOICE.

Breakfast cereals: When reading Nutrition Facts on labels, subtract fibre from total carbohydrate and get the actual amount of available carbohydrate. To make this simpler, we've included a list of popular ready to eat breakfast cereals in Appendix II (page 223), showing the amount of each that's equal to 1 CARB CHOICE.

Rice, pasta and legumes: A good rule of thumb is that ½ cup (125 mL) cooked pasta or ⅓ cup (75 mL) cooked rice is equal to 1 GRAINS & STARCHES or 1 CARB CHOICE. Use a ½-cup (125 mL) or ⅓-cup (75 mL) measure when serving these foods. With meat alternatives such as dried peas, beans or lentils, 1 cup (250 mL) cooked would count as 1 CARB CHOICE plus 1 MEAT & ALTERNATIVES CHOICE.

Starchy vegetables: Potatoes and corn are classed as GRAINS & STARCHES (even though we may think of them as vegetables), and ½ cup (125 mL) of either one is 1 CARB CHOICE.

Fruits

We have used a wide variety of fruits in our menus and recipes. Each choice from this group contains 15 grams available carbohydrate and counts as 1 FRUITS CHOICE (or 1 CARB CHOICE). This could describe an orange or a small apple, half a medium mango or 2 cups (500 mL) strawberries. You'll find that the more moisture and fibre a fruit contains, the larger the serving. Each of these choices contains a variety of vitamins and minerals, as well as fibre.

For your convenience, we have included a list of the fruits we've used in menus, so if you don't have the one named, you can replace it with another and still get the same amount of carbohydrate (Appendix III, page 224).

Milk & Alternatives

Milk and yogurt: Low-fat or non-fat milk and yogurt are excellent sources of calcium and protein and good sources of riboflavin, phosphorus and vitamin B_{12}. Our menus and recipes call for low-fat milk, which could be non-fat skim or 1%; we leave the choice up to you. The amount of milk sugar is the same; the only difference is in fat and calories. A cup (250 mL) of non-fat skim has 80 calories; the same amount of 1% has 100 calories. Both contain 8 grams of protein and 15 grams of carbohydrate. And both would be called 1 MILK & ALTERNATIVES or 1 CARB CHOICE. You may prefer to do as we do—drink skim and use it in cooking, and have 1% on hand to use on cereal and in tea or coffee.

Lactose intolerance: Some people have difficulty digesting the lactose (milk sugar) in regular milk because they lack the necessary digestive enzyme. However, low-fat lactose-reduced milk is available in the dairy section of most supermarkets. It has the same nutrients and the same amount of carbohydrate and protein as regular milk, so 1 cup (250 mL) still counts as 1 MILK & ALTERNATIVES or 1 CARB CHOICE.

Soy beverage: Some prefer a milk made from soybeans, and if unsweetened and enriched with calcium, 1 cup (250 mL) soy beverage counts as 1 MILK & ALTERNATIVES or 1 CARB CHOICE. If sweetened or fruit flavoured, the serving would be ½ cup (125 mL). Read labels for fat and sugar content.

Cheese: Usually cheese is included in discussions of milk products. However, since cheese lacks the carbohydrate of milk but contains protein and fat, it is found in the MEAT & ALTERNATIVES group.

Other Choices

This group includes a wide variety of snacks and sweet foods that add variety but tend to lack nutrients and are high in calories. However, used occasionally and in moderation, they will not upset diabetes control. The key is *how much* and *when*. Sugars should be spread throughout the day as part of slowly digested meals. The trick is to work it into a meal, not just add it on. Each choice from the OTHER CHOICES group contains 15 grams carbohydrate, so it could take the place of a CARB CHOICE in a regular meal or snack. We have included cookies and ice cream on occasion as part of our planned menus. For more details, see *Beyond the Basics.*

FOODS THAT CONTAIN LITTLE OR NO CARBOHYDRATE

Vegetables

The majority of vegetables are low in carbohydrate, calories and fat. They are also an excellent source of vitamins, minerals and fibre. *Beyond the Basics* recommends eating these vegetables freely. A few of the sweeter vegetables count as a CARB CHOICE only when more than one cup (250 mL) is eaten at a meal (see pages 98–102 for lots more about vegetables).

Meat & Alternatives

This group contains meat, poultry, fish, eggs and cheese. 1 CHOICE is equal to 1 ounce or 30 grams of cooked meat or cheese, or one egg. Each choice contains about 7 grams of protein and 3 grams of fat, although some choices may have more (or less) fat than this.

Meat: Meat is a good source of protein but can contain too much saturated fat for heart health. Choose smaller portions, leaner cuts and trim well. Since most of the fat in poultry is in or under the skin, remove it either before or after cooking.

Fish and shellfish: These are also excellent sources of protein and are relatively low in calories and fat, especially saturated fat. Eating even one or two servings of fish a week is associated with a lower risk of heart disease. And the higher the fat content of the fish, the greater the "heart-healthy" benefits since fatty fish have the most omega-3 fatty acids (see Appendix IV, pages 225–227). Fish with a moderate to high fat content include bass, catfish, halibut, herring, mackerel, ocean perch, orange roughy, rainbow trout, salmon, sardines and smelt. Whitefish, cod, haddock and shellfish are very low in total fat.

Eggs: Since they are an inexpensive source of quality protein as well as vitamins B_{12} and E, eggs are listed as "choose more often." Eggs have been given an undeserved bad reputation as being high in fat and high in cholesterol. First of all, one egg yolk contains only 2 grams of saturated fat and 5 grams total fat. And second, it is the saturated and trans fats in food that are the main villain when it comes to increasing risk of heart disease, not the cholesterol in food. Egg whites contain no fat or cholesterol; two whites can replace one egg in many recipes.

Cheese: Like all dairy products, cheese is high in protein and calcium. It also tends to be high in saturated fat and sodium. However, some types of cheese are already low or moderate in fat (part-skim mozzarella, ricotta, low-fat cottage cheese, light cheeses). All cheese is marked with its fat content, so read labels and choose those with less fat (17% or less) as often as possible. Check the Nutrition Facts on cheese for sodium content as well, and compare. Whenever we use cheese in a menu or recipe, we specify the weight in grams. Usually 30 grams of cheese equals 1 MEAT & ALTERNATIVES CHOICE.

Meat alternatives: Dried beans, peas and lentils are also excellent sources of protein as well as carbohydrate.

Fats
Fats have little or no carbohydrate and therefore little effect on blood glucose. They are found in butter, margarine, oils, nuts and seeds, as well as in baked products and snack foods. We do need some fat

in our diet to store energy, provide insulation and build hormones, but it is easy to go overboard. Choosing the right type and amount of dietary fat is important for people with diabetes, as some fats are more heart healthy than others (see page 14 and Appendix IV, pages 225–226).

Since fat has twice the calories of carbohydrate or protein, how much fat you eat is an important factor in weight control. Each FATS CHOICE (such as 1 tsp/5 mL margarine or butter or oil) contains 5 grams fat and has 45 calories. This group also contains foods such as nuts and seeds that are high in hidden fat. In a healthy diet, fats and oils should be used sparingly.

Margarine: A healthy margarine is soft, non-hydrogenated, trans fat–free, low in saturated fat, and made from vegetable oils rich in monounsaturated fat (such as canola or olive oil). Light or diet margarine has been diluted with water to reduce calories, so it's not recommended for cooking or baking.

Butter: Butter contains the same amount of calories and fat as margarine, so we give it as an alternative in our menus. If your diet is already low in fat, a little butter now and then won't hurt you.

Vegetable oils: Olive, canola and corn oils are all heart-healthy choices. The highest in monounsaturated oils are canola and olive (see page 15), so choose those often.

EXTRAS

Last but not least are the things that add flavour to food. The term EXTRAS means that one serving of any item in this group contains less than 5 grams carbohydrate and no more than 20 calories per serving. This group includes "Extras" that can be used without limit: beverages such as herbal teas, coffee, mineral water and diet pop; and seasonings and flavours such as herbs and spices, lemon and lime juice, and non-nutritive sweeteners (see below).

Also in this group are condiments that contain more carbohydrate and are "extra" in *measured amounts* only. Examples are ketchup, reduced sugar fruit spreads (see page 26), barbecue sauce and so on. See the *Beyond the Basics* resource for more information.

Non-nutritive sweeteners

There are different kinds and forms of sweeteners with different tastes and different uses. Some come in packets as tabletop sweeteners, others in tablets, others as liquids. Health Canada has approved all the sweeteners listed below as safe for all Canadians. However, only Ace-K, aspartame and sucralose are permitted in packaged foods and beverages. Stevia has not been approved by Health Canada as a sweetener. Generic names are listed first, followed by brand names.

acesulfame potassium (Ace-K): added to foods but not available as sweetener

aspartame (Equal, Nutrasweet): available in packets, tablets, granulated

cyclamate (Sucaryl, Sugar Twin, Sweet 'N Low): available in packets, tablets, liquid and granulated

saccharin (Hermesetas): available in tablets

sucralose (Splenda): available in packets or granulated

We have used a variety of sweeteners in our recipes and menus. Some sweeteners may lose sweetness or develop a bitter taste at high temperatures. However, in all recipes that are cooked or baked, we have used sucralose with excellent results. In recipes where cooking is not required, use the sweetener of your choice.

The *Beyond the Basics* resource contains more about sweeteners, reading labels, dining out, travel, and managing meals when you're feeling sick. It can be ordered at **www.diabetes.ca.**

II · BREAKFAST CEREALS OF YOUR CHOICE

Most ready-to-eat cold cereals are sweetened, but remember that it is total carbohydrate that counts. *Beyond the Basics* defines the amount of cereal equal to 1 GRAINS & STARCHES CHOICE (or 1 CARB CHOICE) as the amount that contains 15 grams of carbohydrate (not including fibre). The Nutrition Facts panel sometimes describes a serving that is larger than this. To avoid guesswork, refer to the list below when you want to exchange one cereal in our menus for another. All are healthy choices but the ones highest in fibre are listed first.

HIGH FIBRE CHOICES:

1/2 cup (125 mL)	All Bran Buds	15 grams fibre
1/2 cup (125 mL)	Fibre 1 (with sucralose)	14 grams fibre
1/2 cup (125 mL)	Fibre First	13 grams fibre
1/2 cup (125 mL)	All Bran	12 grams fibre
1/2 cup (125 mL)	100 % Bran	10 grams fibre

OTHER CHOICES:

3 tbsp (45 mL) Grape-Nuts
1/4 cup (50 mL) granola (5 grams fat)
1/3 cup (75 mL) Oatmeal Squares
1/3 cup (75 mL) wheat germ (5 grams fat)
1/2 cup (125 mL) bran flakes
1/2 cup (125 mL) Flax Plus
1/2 cup (125 mL) Shreddies
1/2 cup (125 mL) shredded wheat, spoon-size
2/3 cup (150 mL) Cheerios
2/3 cup (150 mL) Life, original
3/4 cup (175 mL) Life, multigrain
1 ½ cups (375 mL) puffed wheat
1 shredded wheat biscuit

III · FRUITS OF YOUR CHOICE

We have used a wide variety of fruits in our menus. Each choice from this group contains 15 grams carbohydrate and is called 1 FRUITS or 1 CARB CHOICE.

For your convenience, we have included a list of the fruits we've used so that if you don't have the one named in the menu, you can replace it with another and still get the same amount of carbohydrate.

Each of the following is 1 FRUITS CHOICE (or 1 CARB CHOICE).

1	medium apple, with skin	(150 g)
½ cup (125 mL)	applesauce	
4	apricots	(140 g)
1	small banana, without peel	(100 g)
1 cup (250 mL)	blueberries	(150 g)
1 cup (250 mL)	cubed cantaloupe	(160 g)
15	cherries with pits	(100 g)
2	clementine or mandarin oranges	(150 g)
1	small grapefruit	(240 g)
15	red or green grapes	(80 g)
1 cup (250 mL)	cubed honeydew melon	(170 g)
2	medium kiwi fruit	(150 g)
½ cup (125 mL)	cubed mango	(85 g)
1	medium orange with rind	(130 g)
1	large nectarine	(138 g)
1 cup (250 mL)	cubed papaya	(150 g)
1	large peach	(170 g)
1	medium pear, with skin and core	(165 g)
2	slices fresh pineapple	(120 g)
2	rings canned pineapple in juice	(100 g)
2	medium plums	(130 g)
2	stewed prunes in juice	(65 g)
2 cups (500 mL)	raspberries	(245 g)
2 cups (500 mL)	strawberries	(290 g)
2	medium tangerines	(168 g)
1	wedge watermelon, with rind	(310 g)
½ cup (125 mL)	canned fruit in light syrup or juice	
½ cup (125 mL)	orange, grapefruit or cranberry juice	
1 cup (250 mL)	tomato juice or vegetable juice cocktail	

From *Beyond the Basics,* published by the Canadian Diabetes Association (2006)

IV · THE ABCS OF NUTRITION AND DIABETES

A1C (glycosolated hemoglobin) is a measure of your average blood glucose level over the past two to three months. The goal is an A1C of less than 7%.

Antioxidants are substances in food that repair cell damage and protect the body against disease. Vitamins A, C and E act as antioxidants.

Beta-carotene comes from dark green and yellow vegetables and fruits and is converted into vitamin A in the body. It is thought to act as an antioxidant.

Carbohydrate provides energy for the body in the form of glucose. It comes mainly from sugar (found naturally in fruits and vegetables or added to food) and starch (found in grains and legumes). Carbohydrate breaks down into glucose during digestion and raises blood glucose.

Cholesterol is a waxy substance found naturally in the bloodstream and body cells. It is needed by the body to build cells and certain hormones. Most is manufactured in the liver after eating saturated fat from animal products, as well as trans fats from baked goods and fried foods. Plant foods do not contain cholesterol. Too much cholesterol in the blood is linked to increased risk of heart disease.

Diabetes is a lifelong condition in which the body either cannot produce insulin or cannot use the insulin it produces effectively (see *Insulin, Type 1* and *Type 2 diabetes*).

Fatty acids are the building blocks that make up fats and oils. There are four different types of fatty acids: *saturated, monounsaturated, polyunsaturated* and *trans*. All fats in food are combinations of both *saturated* and *unsaturated* fatty acids.

- *Saturated fatty acids* are loaded (or saturated) with all the hydrogen they can carry. Fats containing a lot of saturated fat are usually solid at room temperature. Most come from animal fats, but both palm oil and coconut oil contain saturated fat. A diet high in saturated fat can raise LDL cholesterol levels and increase the risk of heart disease or stroke.

- *Unsaturated fatty acids* still have room for more hydrogen and are either monounsaturated or polyunsaturated. Fats containing these fatty acids are usually liquid at room temperature and come from plants and fish.

- *Monounsaturated* fatty acids are highest in olive oil and canola oil.

- *Polyunsaturated* fats, made up of omega-3 and omega-6 fatty acids, are essential to good health. Omega-3 fatty acids are found in fish oils as well as canola and soybean oils. Omega-6 is highest in corn, sunflower and soybean oils.

- *Trans fatty acids* are formed when hydrogen is added to the liquid vegetable oils used in the making of shortening and margarine. This *hydrogenation* makes them harder and more stable. These fats are used in many commercial bakery products and fried foods. They are even more harmful than saturated fats since they not only raise the "bad" LDL cholesterol but also lower the "good" HDL cholesterol that protects against heart disease.

Fibre comes in two forms: *soluble* (found in oat bran, barley, legumes and pectin-rich fruit) and *insoluble* (found in wheat bran, whole grains and seeds, and fruit and vegetable skins). Both types of fibre are important (see page 14).

Glucose is the simplest form of sugar, found in fruits and vegetables, and is the end result of starch digestion. Glucose circulates in the blood as the body's main source of energy. When too much glucose is present in the blood, as in uncontrolled diabetes, the condition is called *hyperglycemia.*

Glucose monitors or meters are small hand-held electronic devices that can estimate one's blood glucose level from a drop of blood placed on a sensor pad. The blood is obtained by pricking one's finger. Glucose monitoring at regular intervals makes improved diabetes control possible.

Glycemic index (GI) is a way of measuring how quickly a food is digested. This is influenced by many factors, such as amount of fibre and degree of processing. It compares the rise in blood glucose that occurs after different carbohydrate-containing foods are eaten with the rise in blood glucose that occurs when the same person eats the same amount of carbohydrate as white bread only. Slowly digested foods have a low glycemic index, while more rapidly digested foods have a higher glycemic index, closer to that of white bread. Foods with a low GI can help you manage your diabetes.

Glycogen is a form of starchy carbohydrate stored in our muscles and liver. Glycogen serves as a reserve of glucose energy that can be used during periods of fasting or increased exercise.

Hypoglycemia occurs when blood glucose levels are lower than usual, usually below 3.5 millimoles per litre of blood. Normal blood glucose values are between 4 and 6 mmol/L. Usually only those using insulin or certain diabetes pills are at risk. Symptoms of hypoglycemia may include sweating, trembling, hunger, dizziness, change of mood, confusion, blurred vision and nausea.

Insulin is a hormone produced by the beta cells of the pancreas in response to a rise in blood glucose. Insulin is the "key" that allows glucose to enter your body cells.

Monounsaturated fatty acids (see *Fatty acids*).

Omega-3 fatty acids are a type of polyunsaturated fatty acid found in cold-water fatty fish. They not only help lower blood triglyceride but also make blood platelets less "sticky" or likely to clot, thus reducing the risk of heart attack and stroke (see *Fatty acids*).

Polyunsaturated fatty acids (see *Fatty acids*).

Protein, the basic material of life, exists in many forms and is not intended to be an energy source (although an excess may end up as excess calories). Muscles, organs, antibodies, some hormones and all enzymes are mostly protein. Proteins consist of chains of 22 assorted amino acids in different combinations. Some of these amino acids (the 10 *essential* ones) can only be obtained from food. The rest can be manufactured in the body (so are *non-essential* in our diet).

Proteinuria is the abnormal loss of protein into the urine and is considered a measure of kidney function.

Saturated fatty acids (see *Fatty acids*).

Sodium is most familiar as part of sodium chloride, which we know as table salt. However, many processed foods may have other kinds of sodium added to preserve or flavour them, such as sodium citrate or nitrite. Baked goods often contain sodium bicarbonate as baking soda or baking powder. People with high blood pressure or hypertension find it easier to control their blood pressure if they restrict their salt and sodium intake.

Sorbitol is an alcohol form of sugar often used to sweeten dietetic candies and chocolate. It is more slowly digested than sugar but can end up as glucose in the blood. These foods are often high in fat and calories as well. Too much at one time can cause cramping and diarrhea.

Trans fatty acids (see *Fatty acids*).

Triglyceride is a kind of fat found in the blood, often measured at the same time as cholesterol. Too much (hypertriglyceridemia) is also considered a risk factor for heart disease, especially in diabetes.

Type 1 diabetes is the less common form of diabetes, usually but not always diagnosed before age 40. The pancreas either does not produce insulin or produces very, very little, making a person with type 1 diabetes dependent on daily injections of insulin for life.

Type 2 diabetes is the type affecting 90 per cent of those with diabetes. In this type, the pancreas can still make insulin, but the body doesn't use the insulin effectively. Type 2 diabetes can sometimes be treated with diet and physical activity alone, or in combination with diabetes pills and/or insulin injections.

V · FOOD DEFINITIONS AND PROCEDURES

Balsamic vinegar: A dark, rich-flavoured, slightly sweet vinegar from Italy. Widely available in grocery stores.

Blanch: To plunge food (usually vegetables and fruit) into boiling water briefly, then into cold water to stop the cooking process.

Braise: A cooking method by which food (usually meat or vegetables) is first browned in a non-stick or heavy pan, then cooked, tightly covered, in a small amount of liquid at low heat for a lengthy period of time, thus tenderizing the foods.

Bran: The outer layer of grains (including bran from wheat and oats) that is removed during milling. Wheat and oat bran are both excellent sources of fibre. They are found in cereals and baked goods and can be purchased at health-food stores and supermarkets.

Broil: Food, generally meat, is cooked directly under the electric or gas heat source in an oven, or on a barbecue grill, either directly over charcoal or another heat source. Any fat in the meat drains away during cooking.

Cruciferous vegetables: This is the scientific name for a group of vegetables that may provide protection against certain cancers. Included in this group are broccoli, Brussels sprouts, cabbage, cauliflower, kale and turnip.

Flaxseed: These tiny seeds contain several essential nutrients, including calcium, iron, phosphorus and vitamin E, and are a source of omega-3 fatty acids. Flaxseed has a mild, nutty flavour. Since it has a high fat content, it is best stored in the refrigerator, where it will keep for up to six months (see Tip 3 on page 29 for ground flax).

Parboil: To partially cook food by boiling it briefly in water.

Rye flakes: These resemble rolled oats and are made by the same process. They can be used in much the same way as oats.

Sauté: To cook food quickly in a small amount of oil or broth in a skillet over direct heat, thus creating intensely flavoured meats and sauces.

Steaming: A method of cooking vegetables, whereby they are placed in a steamer basket over a small amount of boiling water and covered, then cooked for a short time until tender-crisp. It is the preferred stove-top method for retaining flavour, shape, texture, and vitamin and mineral content.

Stir-frying: Food is cooked at a very high heat for a very short time. This cooking technique requires a minimum amount of fat and results in fresh-tasting, tender-crisp food.

Tortillas: Mexico's everyday bread, the tortilla resembles a flat pancake and can be made from corn or wheat flour. Both corn and wheat tortillas are sold pre-packaged in most supermarkets.

Wheat flakes: These are whole wheat berries that have been flattened between rollers and resemble rolled oats. They can be used in much the same way as rolled oats and rye flakes.

VI · COMMON HERBS AND SPICES

WHERE DO WE USE HERBS?

Basil: meats, poultry, eggs and cheese, vegetables and soups, stews and sauces

Dill: fish, eggs and cheese, vegetables, salad dressings and soups, stews and sauces

Mint: vegetables, salads and dressings, fruit, meats (especially lamb)

Oregano: fish, meats, poultry, vegetables, salad dressing, soups, stews and sauces

Parsley: fish, meats, poultry, eggs and cheese, vegetables, salad dressings, soups, stews and sauces

Rosemary: fish, meats, poultry, vegetables, salad dressings

Sage: meats, poultry, eggs and cheese

Tarragon: fish, poultry, eggs and cheese, vegetables, salad dressing, soups, stews and sauces

Thyme: fish, meats, eggs and cheese, vegetables, poultry, soups, stews and sauces

FRESH VS DRIED

Nothing quite beats using fresh herbs, and today they are widely available in stores. Grow your favourites in the garden or keep a pot in the house on the windowsill. If using dried herbs, be sure they are stored in tightly closed containers in a dark cupboard away from heat, light and moisture. Replace them once a year.

WHERE DO WE USE SPICES?

Allspice: soups, stews and sauces, fish, meats, poultry, pastry, cookies and desserts

Cinnamon: soups, stews and sauces, meats, vegetables, pastry, cookies and desserts

Cloves: soups, stews and sauces, meats, poultry, pastry, cookies and desserts

Cumin: fish, meats, poultry, eggs and cheese

Ginger: soups, stews and sauces, fish, meats, poultry, vegetables, salad dressing, pastry, cookies and desserts

Nutmeg: vegetables, soups, stews and sauces, pastry, cookies and desserts

Pepper: soups, stews and sauces, fish, meats, poultry, eggs and cheese, vegetables, salad dressings

VII · THE WELL-STOCKED DIABETES KITCHEN

Preparing quick and healthy meals is always easier when you have the basics on hand, whether you're cooking for one or two or you have unexpected guests. Stock up on these essentials and you'll be prepared for anything.

See Appendix VIII (pages 233–236) for Recommended Storage Times for Refrigerator and Freezer Food.

Cupboard

Assorted dry pastas and
rice (preferably whole grain)
Baked snacks
Calorie-reduced gelatin
Canned soups
Canned tomatoes
Canned tuna, salmon, crab
or shrimp
Canola and olive oils
Dried fruits
Fruit packed in juice
Low salt baked beans in tomato sauce
Mustard
Pasta sauces
Peanut butter
Powdered skim milk
Rolled oats
Salsa
Salt-reduced broths
Vinegar

Refrigerator

Assorted cheeses
Eggs
Fresh fruit
Fresh vegetables
Light sour cream
Low-fat dips and spreads
Low-fat milk
Low-fat salad dressings
Salad greens
Soft margarine or butter
Yogurt

Freezer

Chicken breasts
Fish fillets
Frozen unsweetened fruit
Frozen vegetables
Ground beef or chicken
Homemade broths
Lasagne
Light ice cream
Small lean steaks
Whole wheat bread

VIII · RECOMMENDED STORAGE TIMES FOR REFRIGERATOR AND FREEZER FOOD

The following is a list of extra ingredients to help make cooking more creative and certainly more fun. Keep on hand certain staples, like low-fat milk, all purpose flour, eggs, margarine or butter, salt, canned low-fat milk, sweeteners and sugar. Then look over our list of ingredients below, make your own list based on the menus you've chosen and then order or go shopping. In this way, you will be able to prepare a variety of the recipes in this book. We have indicated the "best refrigerator and freezer storage" life for the following.

Note: These short but safe time limits will help keep refrigerated foods from spoiling or becoming dangerous to eat. Because freezing keeps food safe indefinitely, recommended storage times are for quality only. Storage times are from date of purchase unless specified on chart. It is not important if a date expires after food is frozen.

Sources:
USDA, Food Safety and Inspection Service
The Food Keeper, The Food Marketing Institute

And here are several more websites to assist you in finding additional information:

Health Canada
http://www.inspection.gc.ca/english/fssa/concen/tipcon/storagee.shtml

Canadian Partnership for Consumer Food Safety Education
http://www.canfightbac.org/cpcfse/en/cookwell/

National Center for Home Food Preservation
http://www.uga.edu/nchfp/

Product	Refrigerator (4°C/40°F)	Freezer (-18°C/0°F)
Eggs		
Fresh, in shell	3 to 5 weeks, use-by date	Don't freeze
Raw yolks, whites	2 to 4 days	1 year
Hard cooked	1 week	Don't freeze well
Liquid pasteurized eggs, egg substitutes, opened	3 days	Don't freeze well
Unopened	10 days, use-by date	1 year
Mayonnaise		
Commercial, refrigerate after opening	2 months	Doesn't freeze
Deli and Vacuum-Packed Products		
Store-prepared (or homemade) egg, chicken, ham, tuna, macaroni salads	3 to 5 days, use-by date	Don't freeze well
Hotdogs and Luncheon Meats		
Hot dogs, opened	1 week	1 to 2 months
Unopened	2 weeks, use-by date	1 to 2 months
Luncheon meats, opened	3 to 5 days	1 to 2 months
Unopened	2 weeks, use-by date	1 to 2 months
Bacon and Sausage		
Bacon	7 days	1 month
Unopened	use-by date	1 month
Sausage, raw from chicken, turkey, pork, beef	1 to 2 days	1 to 2 months
Unopened	use-by date	1 to 2 months
Smoked breakfast links, patties	7 days	1 to 2 months
Hard sausage—pepperoni, jerky sticks	2 to 3 weeks	1 to 2 months
Summer sausage—labelled "Keep Refrigerated," opened	3 weeks	1 to 2 months
Unopened	3 months, use-by date	1 to 2 months
Ham, Corned Beef		
Corned beef, in pouch with pickling juices	5 to 7 days	Drained, 1 month
Unopened	use-by date	-
Ham, canned—labelled "Keep Refrigerated," opened	3 to 5 days	1 to 2 months
Unopened	6 to 9 months	Doesn't freeze
Ham, fully cooked, vacuum sealed at plant, undated, unopened	2 weeks	1 to 2 months
Ham, fully cooked, vacuum sealed at plant, dated, unopened	use-by date on package	1 to 2 months
Ham, fully cooked, whole	7 days	1 to 2 months
Ham, fully cooked, half	3 to 5 days	1 to 2 months
Ham, fully cooked, slices	3 to 4 days	1 to 2 months
Hamburger, Ground, and Stew Meat		
Hamburger and stew meat	1 to 2 days, use-by date	3 to 4 months
Ground turkey, veal, pork, lamb and mixtures of them	1 to 2 days, use-by date	3 to 4 months

Product	Refrigerator (4°C/40°F)	Freezer (-18°C/0°F)
Fresh Beef, Veal, Lamb, Pork		
Steaks	3 to 5 days, use-by date	6 to 12 months
Chops	3 to 5 days, use-by date	4 to 6 months
Roasts	3 to 5 days, use-by date	4 to 12 months
Variety meats—tongue, liver, heart, kidneys, chitterlings	1 to 2 days, use-by date	3 to 4 months
Pre-stuffed, uncooked pork chops, lamb chops, or chicken breast stuffed with dressing	1 day	Don't freeze well
Soup and Stews		
Vegetable or meat added	3 to 4 days	2 to 3 months
Meat Leftovers		
Cooked meat and meat casseroles	3 to 4 days	2 to 3 months
Gravy and meat broth	1 to 2 days	2 to 3 months
Fresh Poultry		
Chicken or turkey, whole	1 to 2 days, use-by date	1 year
Chicken or turkey, pieces	1 to 2 days, use-by date	9 months
Giblets	1 to 2 days, use-by date	3 to 4 months
Cooked Poultry		
Fried chicken	3 to 4 days	4 months
Cooked poultry casseroles	3 to 4 days	4 to 6 months
Pieces, plain	3 to 4 days	4 months
Pieces covered with broth, gravy	1 to 2 days	6 months
Chicken nuggets, patties	1 to 2 days	1 to 3 months
Pizza		
Pizza	3 to 4 days	1 to 2 months
Prepackaged	use-by date	1 to 2 months
Stuffing		
Stuffing—cooked	3 to 4 days	1 month
Beverages, Fruit		
Juices in cartons, fruit drinks, punch, unopened	3 weeks	8 to 12 months
Opened	7 to 10 days	8 to 12 months
Dairy		
Butter	1 to 3 months	6 to 9 months
Buttermilk	7 to 14 days	3 months
Unopened	use-by date	3 months

Product	Refrigerator (4°C/40°F)	Freezer (-18°C/0°F)
Cheese, hard (such as Cheddar, Swiss), unopened	6 months, use-by date	6 months
Opened	3 to 4 weeks	6 months
Cheese, soft (such as brie, bel paese)	1 week	6 months
Cottage cheese, ricotta	1 week	Doesn't freeze well
Cream cheese	2 weeks	Doesn't freeze well
Cream—whipped, pasteurized	1 month	Doesn't freeze
Cream—whipped, sweetened	1 day	1 to 2 months
Cream—aerosol can, real whipped cream	3 to 4 weeks	Doesn't freeze
Cream—aerosol can, non-dairy topping	3 months	Doesn't freeze
Cream, half and half	3 to 4 days	4 months
Eggnog, commercial	3 to 5 days	6 months
Unopened	use-by date	6 months
Margarine	4 to 5 months	12 months
Milk	7 days	3 months
Unopened	use-by date	3 months
Pudding	use-by date; 2 days after opening	Doesn't freeze
Sour cream	7 to 21 days	Doesn't freeze
Unopened	use-by date	Doesn't freeze
Yogurt	7 to 14 days	1 to 2 months
Unopened	use-by date	1 to 2 months
Dough		
Tube cans of rolls, biscuits, pizza dough, etc.	Use-by date	Don't freeze
Ready-to-bake pie crust	Use-by date	2 months
Cookie dough	Use-by date, unopened or opened	2 months
Fish		
Lean fish (cod, flounder, haddock, sole, etc.)	1 to 2 days	6 months
Fatty fish (bluefish, mackerel, salmon, etc.)	1 to 2 days	2 to 3 months
Cooked fish	3 to 4 days	4 to 6 months
Smoked fish	14 days or use-by date	2 months
Shellfish		
Shrimp, scallops, crayfish, squid, shucked clams, mussels and oysters	1 to 2 days	3 to 6 months
Live clams, mussels, crab, lobster and oysters	2 to 3 days	2 to 3 months
Cooked shellfish	3 to 4 days	3 months

IX · NUTRIENT ANALYSIS OF RECIPES AND MENUS

....

Analysis of the recipes was based on Imperial measures and weights (except for foods packaged and labelled in metric amounts) and on the specified number of servings.

Actual cooked weights were used where applicable.

Whenever appropriate, menus were analyzed using portion sizes specified in *Beyond the Basics: Meal Planning for Healthy Eating, Diabetes Prevention and Management*, published by the Canadian Diabetes Association (2006).

Lower-fat dairy products were used in all recipes and menus. Low-fat milk used in recipes as ingredients and in menus as beverages was analyzed as skim unless otherwise indicated.

All menus can be assumed to include 2 tbsp (25 mL) 1% milk for tea or coffee whenever milk is not included as a beverage.

Food Choice Values were assigned according to Canadian Diabetes Association (CDA) guidelines (2006), with carbohydrate based on total carbohydrate minus dietary fibre. Total carbohydrate and dietary fibre are stated separately in recipe nutrition information, and nutrient values are rounded to the nearest whole number.

Menus were planned to reflect current CDA nutritional guidelines: carbohydrate provides 50% of total energy; fat provides 30% or less, with 10% or less from saturated fat and with monounsaturated fats and oils used wherever possible.

Recipes were tested and analyzed using canola or olive oils and soft non-hydrogenated margarines unless otherwise specified.

Optional ingredients were not included in analysis.

Menu items and recipe ingredients were chosen for their fibre content and glycemic effect whenever possible.

Menus and recipes were planned in accordance with *Eating Well with Canada's Food Guide* (2007), with an emphasis on variety, inclusion of whole grains as cereals, breads and other grain products, generous use of vegetables and fruit, and the use of leaner meats and food prepared with little or no fat.

Food Choice Values were determined using the values below:

Food Group	Carbohydrate (g)	Protein (g)	Fat (g)	Calories
Grains & Starches	15	3		70
Fruits	15	1		65
Milk & Alternatives	15	8	variable	90
Other Choices	15	variable	variable	variable
Meat & Alternatives	0	7	3	55
Fats	0	0	5	45
Extras	fewer than 5			fewer than 20

ACKNOWLEDGEMENTS

With the completion of this revised edition of *Choice Menus: Cooking for One or Two*, we wish to recognize the support and guidance many people have given us. We offer our sincere thanks and appreciation to the following:

The very helpful team at Collins Canada, a division of HarperCollins Publishers Ltd: senior editor Brad Wilson, vice-president Lloyd Kelly, designer Sharon Kish, managing editor Noelle Zitzer and production editor Allegra Robinson.

The staff at the Canadian Diabetes Association, especially Sharon Zeiler, Senior Manager, Diabetes Education and Nutrition, for her counsel and guidance.

The dietitians and diabetes educators who volunteered to review the manuscript, ensuring its accuracy: Beverley Harris, PDT, CDE; Linda Mailhot-Hall, RD, CDE; Rebecca Horsman, RD; Michelle Knezic, RD, CDE; Shari Segal, PDT, CDE; Wendy Levin, RD, CDE; and Sharon Zeiler, RD.

Sharon Zeiler, RD, and Rosie Shwartz, RD, as well as Margaret's friend Terri Hope and her New York aunt, Liela Weber, for advice in the development of the Seder menu.

Marian Hebb, for once again providing legal counsel, and John Howard, for providing his editing skills, which frequently clarified and improved our words.

Photographer Hal Roth and assistant Paolo Christante, for making all the pictures so representative of the recipes in the book, and food stylist Julie Zambonelli and prop stylist Maggie Jones, who made each dish look so enticing.

The graduates of TRIDEC (Tri-Hospital Diabetes Education Centre, Women's College Hospital), whose requests for "a month of menus" led to the writing of the first *Choice Menus*.

Our families' support and critiques, which we know are invaluable.

Finally, we're thankful for the happy coincidence that found the two of us in the same class at the University of Western Ontario, which led to a lifelong friendship and this edition of *Choice Menus: Cooking for One or Two*.

RECIPE INDEX

BM = Breakfast Menu; LM = Lunch Menu;
DM = Dinner Menu; SM = Snack Menu;
SOM − Special Occasion Menu

almonds
    Cranberry Almond Crumble, 155
    Pears with Raspberry Sauce, 159
    Power Granola, 31
appetizers
    Curried Lentil Dip, 170
    Fresh Cucumber Salsa, 167
    Fresh Tomato Salsa, 74
    Salsa Cheese Spread, 171
    Tomato and Goat Cheese Crostini, 69
apples
    Apple Cabbage Slaw, 107
    Baked Apple, *DM 3*
    Baked Sliced Apples, 148
    Fresh Cranberry Chutney, 212
    Microwave Cranberry Applesauce, 93
    Poached Apple Slices, 36
    Waffles with Fresh Applesauce, *BM 2*
    Warm Cranberry Fall Fruit Compote, 147
Asiago cheese, 197
Asian Grilled Pork Tenderloin, 122
asparagus
    Cheesy Eggs and Asparagus on Toast, 70
    Crustless Asparagus and Rice Quiche
        for One, 85
    Oven-Roasted Asparagus, 207
    Overnight Ham and Asparagus Bake, 39
    Stir-Fried Vegetables, 191
Autumn Pumpkin Cranberry Muffins, 42

bacon
    Bacon and Egg Muffins, 41
bagels
    Bagel with Cheddar Cheese, *BM 14*
    Tomato Bagel Melt, *BM 6*
baguette
    Baked Eggnog French Toast with Fruit
        Sauce, 37
    Tomato and Goat Cheese Crostini, 69
Baked Bean Tortillas, 65
Baked Eggnog French Toast with Fruit
    Sauce, 37
Baked Fish en Papillote, 128
Baked Fruit with Raspberry Sauce, 37
Baked Layered Tomato and Potato Slices,
    139
Baked Rice, 141
Bakes Sliced Apples, 148
Baker's Dozen Morning Multi-Grain
    Pancakes, 34
balsamic vinegar
    Balsamic Peaches, 157

Balsamic Strawberries, 157
Balsamic Vinaigrette, 84
bananas
    Baked Fruit with Raspberry Sauce, 91
    Fruit Muesli, 30
    Microwave-Baked Bananas, *LM 20*
barley
    Hearty Vegetable Barley Soup, 62
basil
    Fresh Tomato Salsa, 74
    Polenta Pie with Tomato Mushroom
        Pasta Sauce, 134
    Roasted Tomato Pasta Sauce, 75
    Tomato and Basil Baked Eggs, 130
beans. *See also* green beans
    Baked Bean Tortillas, 65
    Sausage and Sweet Potato Chili, 123
    Spicy Beans on Toast, 64
    Tomato and Black Bean Salad, 83
    Tomato, Bean and Mozzarella Salad, *LM 4*
    Turkey Minestrone, 60
beef
    Beef and Vegetable Meat Loaf, 119
    Beef Burgundy, 194
    Beef Strip Loin with Wine Sauce, 120
    Calf's Liver with Onion and Herbs, 125
    Spiced Beef Brisket, 206
beverages
    alcoholic, 182
    Café au Lait, *BM 2*
    Café con Leche, *SOM 5*
    Frozen Melon Smoothie, 169
    Lime Watermelon Splash, 56
    Minted Limeade, 170
    non-alcoholic, 182
    Rhubarb Punch, 184
blueberries
    Baked Eggnog French Toast with Fruit
        Sauce, 37
    Blueberry Sauce, 38
    Flax and Oat Bran Blueberry Muffins, 40
    Fresh Fruit Jelly, 160
    Light Raspberry Blueberry Spread, 47
    Sautéed Spiced Fruits, 154
    Summer Fruits with Yogurt, *BM 12*
bran
    Orange Bran Flax Muffins, 43
    Orange Date and Bran Muffins, 175
    Power Granola, 31
    Rhubarb Bran Muffins, 175
breads. *See also* bagels, English muffins
    Buttermilk Tea Biscuits, 76
    Cinnamon Toast, *SM 16*
    Herbed Cornbread, 173
    Red Pepper Focaccia, 77
Brisket, Spiced Beef, 206

broccoli
    Vegetable Cheese Pie, 86
broth
    Chicken Broth, 185
    Homemade Light Beef Broth, 58
    Homemade Light Chicken Broth, 204
buttermilk
    Bacon and Egg Muffins, 41
    Baker's Dozen Morning Multi-Grain
      Pancakes, 34
    Buttermilk Tea Biscuits, 76
    Oatmeal Date Muffins, 173
    Orange Bran Flax Muffins, 43
    Orange Date and Bran Muffins, 174
    Red Pepper Focaccia, 76
    Rhubarb Bran Muffins, 174

cabbage
    Apple Cabbage Slaw, 107
Caesar Salad Dressing, 82
cake
    Ice Cream Birthday Cake, 188
    Lemon Passover Cake, 209
cake frosting
    Light Whipped Topping, 188
Calf's Liver with Onions and Herbs, 125
cantaloupe
    Baked Fruit with Raspberry Sauce, 91
    Curried Turkey Salad, 81
    Frozen Melon Smoothie, 169
    Seasonal Fruit Plate with Ricotta Cheese,
      88
Cardamom-Scented Rutabaga, 146
carrots
    Beef Burgundy, 194
    Curried Vegetable and Split Pea Soup, 63
    Gingered Carrot Soup, 61
    Golden Harvest Soup, 201
    Minted Carrots and Snow Peas, 142
    Mushroom Squash Bisque, 113
casseroles
    Beef Burgundy, 194
    Herbed Chicken and Vegetables, 115
    Polenta Pie with Tomato Mushroom
      Pasta Sauce, 134
    Sausage and Sweet Potato Chili, 123
cauliflower
    Cauliflower Potato Mash, 145
    Curried Vegetable and Split Pea Soup, 63
celery
    Curried Vegetable and Split Pea Soup, 63
cereals
    Cooked Multi-Grain Porridge, *BM 10*
    Creamy Rolled Oats, *BM 8, SM 16*
    Dry Cereal Mix, 28
    Fruit Muesli, 30
    Hot Cereal with Multi-Grains, 28
    Power Granola, 31
    ready-to-eat cereals, 223
    Summer Fruits with Yogurt, *BM 12*

cheese. *See also* Asiago cheese; cottage
    cheese; ricotta cheese
    Bacon and Egg Muffin, 41
    Bagel with Cheddar Cheese, *BM 14*
    Baked Bean Tortillas, 65
    Cheese and Spinach Lasagne Roll-Ups, 133
    Cheesy Eggs and Asparagus on Toast, 70
    Crustless Asparagus Quiche for One, 85
    Grilled Cheese French Toast Sandwich, 66
    Individual Turkey Quesadilla, 78
    Open-Face Baked Cheese Tomato
      Tortillas, 73
    Overnight Ham and Asparagus Bake, 39
    Pineapple and Cheese English Muffin,
      BM 4
    Polenta Pie with Tomato Mushroom
      Pasta Sauce, 134
    Pork Chops Marinara with Mozzarella
      Cheese, 121
    Salsa Cheese Spread, 172
    Three Cheese Mushroom Risotto, 196
    Toasted Tomato and Cheese Sandwich,
      DM 30
    Tomato and Black Bean Salad, 83
    Tomato and Goat Cheese Crostini, 69
    Tomato Bagel Melt, *BM 6*
    Vegetable Cheese Pie, 86
chicken
    Chicken and Matzo Ball Soup, 204
    Chicken Breast in Wine Sauce, *DM 5*
    Chicken Caesar and Potato Salad, 82
    Chicken in a Pita, *LM 9*
    Crispy Baked Chicken, 113
    Herbed Chicken and Vegetables, 114
    methods for cooking and handling,
      185, 210
    Poached Chicken Breasts, 185
    Roast Cornish Hen with Wild Rice
      Dressing, 202
chickpeas
    Pasta with Chickpea Garlic Sauce, 135
chili
    Sausage and Sweet Potato Chili, 123
chocolate
    Chocolate Chip Oatmeal Cookies, 176
    Mocha Soufflé Dessert, 195
Chutney, Fresh Cranberry, 212
Citrus Yogurt Jelly, 149
coconut milk
    Fragrant Rice, 192
cookies
    Chocolate Chip Oatmeal Cookies, 176
    Peanut Butter Granola Cookies, 177
corn
    Corn and Zucchini Sauté, 144
    Tomato and Black Bean Salad, 83
    Vegetable Cheese Pie, 86
Cornish hen
    Roast Cornish Hen with Wild Rice
      Dressing, 202

cornmeal. *See also* polenta
  Baker's Dozen Morning Multi-Grain
    Pancakes, 34
  Herbed Cornbread, 173
cottage cheese
  Cheese and Spinach Lasagne Roll-Ups,
    133
  Cottage Cheese Pancakes, 87
  Creamy Ranch Dressing, 109
  Mocha Soufflé Dessert, 195
  Salsa Cheese Spread, 171
cranberries
  Autumn Pumpkin Cranberry Muffin, 42
  Cranberry Almond Crumble, 155
  Cranberry Citrus Coulis, 186
  Fresh Cranberry Chutney, 212
  Light Cranberry Sauce, 111
  Microwave Cranberry Applesauce, 93
  Naturally Fresh Fruit Sorbet, 92
  Warm Cranberry Fall Fruit Compote, 147
Creamy Ranch Dressing, 109
Crispy Baked Chicken, 113
Crustless Asparagus Quiche for One, 85
cucumber
  Fresh Cucumber Salsa, 168
  Gazpacho, 198
curry
  Curried Lentil Dip, 171
  Curried Turkey Salad, 81
  Curried Vegetable and Split Pea Soup, 63

dates
  Oatmeal Date Muffins, 174
  Orange Date and Bran Muffins, 175
desserts
  Baked Apple, *DM 3*
  Baked Fruit with Raspberry Sauce, 91
  Baked Sliced Apples, 148
  Balsamic Peaches, 157
  Balsamic Strawberries, 157
  Citrus Yogurt Jelly, 149
  Cranberry Almond Crumble, 155
  Fresh Fruit Jelly, 160
  Gingered Fruit Parfait, 161
  Ice Cream Birthday Cake, 188
  Lemon Flan, 200
  Lemon Passover Cake, 209
  Mango Mint Sorbet, 193
  Microwave-Baked Bananas, *LM 20*
  Microwave Cranberry Applesauce, 93
  Mixed Berry Crisp, 153
  Mocha Soufflé Dessert, 195
  Naturally Fresh Fruit Sorbet, 92
  Nutty Mango Crisp, 153
  Orange Stewed Rhubarb, 89
  Oranges in Yogurt Cream, 152
  Peach Cobbler, 151
  Pear Hélène, *DM 13*
  Pears with Raspberry Sauce, 159
  Pudding Sundae, *SM 3*

Raspberry Bavarian, 156
Raspberry Fool, 203
Rosy Poached Pears, 158
Sautéed Spiced Fruits, 154
Spicy Pumpkin Pie, 214
Strawberry Bavarian, 156
Warm Cranberry Fall Fruit Compote, 147
dips
  Creamy Herb Dip, 109
  Curried Lentil Dip, 171
  Fresh Cucumber Salsa, 168
  Light Whipped Topping (for fruit), 188
dressings. *See also* salad dressings
  Dressing for Roast Turkey Breast, 115
  Vegetable Bread Stuffing, 210
  Wild Rice Dressing, 202

eggs
  Crustless Asparagus Quiche for One, 85
  Bacon and Egg Muffins, 41
  Baked Eggnog French Toast with Fruit
    Sauce, 37, 38
  Breakfast Alaska, *BM 7*
  Breakfast Tortilla Sandwich, *BM 15*
  Cheesy Eggs and Asparagus on Toast, 70
  cooking methods, niçoise,199
  Egg in a Hole, *BM 3*
  French Toast, *BM 16*
  Grilled Cheese French Toast Sandwich, 66
  Matzo Balls, 204
  Mushroom Omelette for One, *BM 11*
  Spanish Omelette, *DM 6*
  Toasted Vegetable Frittata Sandwich, 67
  Tomato and Basil Baked Eggs, 130
  Tortilla Sandwich, *SN 23*
  Tuna Niçoise Salad, 80
  Vegetable Cheese Pie, 86
English muffins
  Overnight Ham and Asparagus Bake, 39
  Pineapple and Cheese English Muffin, *BM 4*
  Tomato and Basil Baked Eggs, 130
evaporated milk
  Frozen Melon Smoothie, 168
  Gingered Carrot Soup, 61
  Light Whipped Topping, 189
  Mushroom Squash Bisque, 113
  Shrimp Chowder, 57

feta cheese
  Greek Salad in a Pita, 79
fish
  Baked Fish en Papillote with Tomatoes
    and Herbs, 128
  Baked Rainbow Trout, *DM 19*
  Dilled Halibut, *DM 14*
  Grilled or Broiled Salmon Fillet, *DM 10*
  methods for cooking, 105
  Mustard Baked Salmon, 127
  Salmon Pecan Sandwich, *LM 22*
  Thai Peppered Shrimp with Leeks, 190

Tuna Niçoise Salad, 80
Tuna Sandwich, *LM 16*
Tuna Sandwich Filling, 72
flaxseed
    Baker's Dozen Morning Multi-Grain
        Pancakes, 34
    benefits of and tips about, 28, 31
    Flax and Oat Bran Blueberry Muffins, 40
    Hot Cereal with Multi-Grains, 28
    Orange Bran Flax Muffins, 43
    Power Granola, 31
Food Definitions and Procedures, 229
Fragrant Rice, 192
French-Style Green Peas with Lettuce, 136
French toast
    Baked Eggnog French Toast with Fruit
        Sauce, 37
    French Toast, *BM 16*
    Grilled Cheese French Toast Sandwich, 66
Fresh Tomato Salsa, 74
frittata. *See* eggs
frozen desserts
    Ice Cream Birthday Cake, 188
    Mango Mint Sorbet, 193
    Naturally Fresh Fruit Sorbet, 92
Frozen Melon Smoothie, 169
fruit. *See also* specific fruits
    Fresh Fruit Jelly, 160
    Fruit Muesli, 30
    Gingered Fruit Parfait, 33
    Naturally Fresh Fruit Sorbet, 92
    Power Granola Fruit Parfait, 33
    Seasonal Fruit Plate with Ricotta Cheese,
        88
fruit spreads
    Light Raspberry Blueberry Spread, 47
    No-Cook Pineapple Orange Marmalade,
        46

garlic
    Curried Lentil Dip, 170
    Pasta with Chickpea Garlic Sauce, 135
    Provençal Garlic Potatoes, 140
    Roasted Tomato Pasta Sauce, 75
    Spiced Beef Brisket, 206
Gaspacho, 198
ginger
    Asian Steamed Green Beans, *DM 27*
    Curried Vegetable and Split Pea Soup, 63
    Fresh Cranberry Chutney, 212
    Gingered Carrot Soup, 61
    Gingered Fruit Parfait, 161
    Stir-Fried Vegetables, 191
goat cheese
    Tomato and Goat Cheese Crostini, 69
    Golden Harvest Soup, 201
grains. *See* barley, cornmeal, kasha, millet,
        polenta, rolled oats
granola
    Power Granola, 31

Power Granola Fruit Parfait, 33
Peanut Butter Granola Cookies, 177
grapes
    Fresh Fruit Cup, *DM 29*
    Seasonal Fruit Plate with Ricotta
        Cheese, 88
gravy
    Light Turkey Gravy, 117
    Greek Salad in a Pita, 79
green beans
    Asian Steamed Green Beans, *DM 27*
    Tuna Niçoise Salad, 80
green peas
    French-Style Green Peas with Lettuce, 136
Grilled Cheese French Toast Sandwich, 60

ham
    Overnight Ham and Asparagus Bake, 39
    Hearty Vegetable Barley Soup, 62
    Homemade Light Beef Broth, 58
    Homemade Light Chicken Broth, 59
herbs, 231. *See also* basil, mint, parsley
    Herbed Cornbread, 173
    Herbed Chicken and Vegetables, 114
high-fibre recipes. *See* fibre
Honey Yogurt Sauce, 44
honeydew melon
    Fresh Fruit Cup, *DM 29*
    Gingered Fruit Parfait, 161
hot cereals
    Cooked Multi-Grain Porridge, *BM 10*
    Creamy Rolled Oats, *BM 8, SM 16*
    Dry Cereal Mix, 28
    Hot Cereal with Multi-Grains, 28

ice cream
    Frozen Melon Smoothie, 169
    Ice Cream Birthday Cake, 188
Individual Turkey Quesadilla, 78

jams. *See* fruit spreads
jelly
    Fresh Fruit Jelly, 160

kasha
    Kasha and Red Pepper Pilaf, 129
kiwi fruit
    Gingered Fruit Parfait, 161
    Naturally Fresh Fruit Sorbet, 92

lasagne
    Cheese and Spinach Lasagne Roll-Ups, 133
leeks
    Golden Harvest Soup, 201
    Thai Peppered Shrimp with Leeks, 190
legumes. *See* beans, chick peas, lentils
lemon
    Citrus Yogurt Jelly, 149
    Cranberry Citrus Coulis, 186
    Lemon Flan, 200

lemon (continued)
    Lemon Passover Cake, 209
    Rhubarb Punch, 184
    Roasted Lemon Potatoes, 143
lentils
    Curried Lentil Dip, 171
light recipes
    Homemade Light Beef Broth, 58
    Homemade Light Chicken Broth, 59
    Light Cranberry Sauce, 111
    Light Raspberry Blueberry Spread, 47
    Light Turkey Gravy, 117
    Light Whipped Topping, 189
lime
    Lime Watermelon Splash, 56
    Mango Mint Sorbet, 193
    Minted Limeade, 170
    No-Cook Pineapple Orange Marmalade,
      46
    Thai Peppered Shrimp with Leeks, 190
liver
    Calf's Liver with Onion and Herbs, 125

Make-Ahead Crispy Belgian Waffles, 35
mango
    Mango Mint Sorbet, 153
    Nutty Mango Crisp, 153
matzo meal
    Chicken and Matzo Ball Soup, 204
    Lemon Passover Cake, 209
    Potato Kugel, 208
meat
    Asian Grilled Pork Tenderloin, 122
    Beef and Vegetable Meat Loaf, 119
    Beef Burgundy, 194
    Beef Strip Loin with Wine Sauce, 120
    Calf's Liver with Onion and Herbs, 125
    Chicken Breast in Wine Sauce, DM 5
    Crispy Baked Chicken, 113
    Grilled Sausage with Mustard Glaze,
      DM 18
    Herbed Chicken and Vegetables, 114
    methods for cooking, 104
    Poached Chicken Breasts, 185
    Pork Chops Marinara with Mozzarella
      Cheese, 121
    Roast Cornish Hen, 118
    Roast Cornish Hen with Wild Rice
      Dressing, 202
    Roast Turkey Breast with Dressing, 115
    Spiced Beef Brisket, 206
    Veal Cutlet in Tomato Basil Sauce, 124
meat alternatives, 105. See also vegetarian
    recipes
Meatloaf, Beef and Vegetable, 119
melon. See cantaloupe, honeydew melon,
    watermelon
microwave recipes
    Microwave-Baked Bananas, LM 20
    Microwave Cranberry Applesauce, 93

Orange Stewed Rhubarb, 89
    Warm Cranberry Fall Fruit Compote, 148
milk. See also buttermilk; evaporated milk
    sour milk, 77
millet
    Baker's Dozen Morning Multi-Grain
      Pancakes, 34
mint
    Mango Mint Sorbet, 153
    Minted Carrots and Snow Peas, 143
    Minted Limeade, 170
Mocha Soufflé Dessert, 195
muffins
    Autumn Pumpkin Cranberry Muffins, 42
    Bacon and Egg Muffins, 41
    Flax and Oat Bran Blueberry Muffins, 40
    Oatmeal Date Muffins, 174
    Orange Bran Flax Muffins, 43
    Orange Date and Bran Muffins, 174
    Pineapple and Cheese English Muffin,
      BM 4
    Rhubarb Bran Muffins, 175
Muesli, Fruit, 30
mushrooms
    Baked Fish en Papillote with Tomatoes
      and Herbs, 128
    Beef Burgundy, 194
    Dressing for Roast Turkey Breast, 116
    Herbed Chicken and Vegetables, 115
    Mushroom Omelette for One, BM 11
    Mushroom Squash Bisque, 112
    Polenta Pie with Tomato Mushroom
      Pasta Sauce, 134
    Sautéed Mushrooms, DM 16
    Three Cheese Mushroom Risotto, 196
    Toasted Vegetable Frittata Sandwich, 67
    Tomato Mushroom Pasta Sauce, 131
    Veal Cutlet in Tomato Basil Sauce, 124
    Vegetable Bread Stuffing, 210
Mustard Baked Salmon, 127

Naturally Fresh Fruit Sorbet, 92
No-Cook Pineapple Orange Marmalade, 46
nuts. See also almonds, pecans, walnuts
    Cranberry Almond Crumble, 155
    Nutty Mango Crisp, 153
    Power Granola, 31
    toasting, 71

oat bran
    Bacon and Egg Muffins, 41
    Flax and Oat Bran Blueberry Muffins, 40
    Hot Cereal with Multi-Grains, 28
    Orange Bran Flax Muffins, 43
    Power Granola, 31
omelettes. See eggs
Open-Face Baked Cheese Tomato Tortillas,
    73
oranges
    Cranberry Citrus Coulis, 186

No-Cook Pineapple Orange Marmalade, 46
Orange Bran Flax Muffins, 43
Orange Date and Bran Muffins, 174
Orange Stewed Rhubarb, 89
Orange Vinaigrette, 187
Orange Yogurt Sauce, 90
Oranges in Yogurt Cream, 152
Rhubarb Punch, 184
Spinach and Orange Salad, 205
Strawberry Orange Sauce, 45
Oven Puff Pancakes with Poached Apple Slices, 36
Oven-Roasted Asparagus, 207
Overnight Ham and Asparagus Bake, 39

pancakes
Baker's Dozen Morning Multi-Grain Pancakes, 34
Cottage Cheese Pancakes, 87
Oven Puff Pancakes with Poached Apple Slices, 36
parsley
Roast Cornish Hen with Wild Rice Dressing, 202
Roasted Sweet Peppers with Parsley, 137
pasta
Cheese and Spinach Lasagne Roll-Ups, 133
Creamy Onion Fettucine, DM 8
"on call," 103
Pasta and Salad Dinner, DM 4
Pasta with Chickpea Garlic Sauce, 135
Roasted Tomato Pasta Sauce, 75
Tomato Mushroom Pasta Sauce, 134
Turkey Minestrone, 60
pastry
Beef Burgundy, 194
Spicy Pumpkin Pie, 214
peaches
Balsamic Peaches, 156
Fresh Peach Sauce, 38
Peach Cobbler, 151
Sautéed Spiced Fruits, 154
Summer Fruits with Yogurt, BM 12
peanut butter
Peanut Butter and Banana Sandwich, LM 2
Peanut Butter Granola Cookies, 177
pears
Pear Hélène, DM 13
Pears with Raspberry Sauce, 159
Rosy Poached Pears, 158
Warm Cranberry Fall Fruit Compote, 147
peas. See chickpeas; green peas
pecans
Dressing for Roast Turkey Breast, 116
Roast Cornish Hen with Wild Rice Dressing, 202
Salmon Pecan Sandwich Filling, 71
pectin, 46

peppers, sweet
Gazpacho, 198
Kasha and Red Pepper Pilaf, 129
Red Pepper Focaccia, 77
Roasted Sweet Peppers with Parsley, 137
Stir-Fried Vegetables, 191
Three Cheese Mushroom Risotto, 196
pies
Polenta Pie with Tomato Mushroom Pasta Sauce, 134
Spicy Pumpkin Pie, 214
Vegetable Cheese Pie, 86
pineapple
Curried Turkey Salad, 81
Fresh Fruit Jelly, 160
No-Cook Pineapple Orange Marmalade, 46
Pineapple and Cheese English Muffin, BM 4
Sautéed Spiced Fruits, 154
pita bread
Chicken in a Pita, LM 9
Fresh Fruit Jelly, 160
Greek Salad in a Pita, 79
Tuna Sandwich, LM 16
plums
Baked Fruit with Raspberry Sauce, 91
Poached Chicken Breasts, 185
polenta
Polenta Pie with Tomato Mushroom Pasta Sauce, 134
pork. See also ham; sausage
Asian Grilled Pork Tenderloin, 122
Pork Chops Marinara with Mozzarella Cheese, 121
porridge. See hot cereals
potato starch
Lemon Passover Cake, 209
potatoes. See also sweet potatoes
Baked Layered Tomato and Potato Slices, 139
Cauliflower Potato Mash, 145
Chicken Caesar and Potato Salad, 82
Golden Harvest Soup, 201
Hearty Vegetable Barley Soup, 62
methods for cooking, 103
Potato Kugel, 208
Provençal Garlic Potatoes, 140
Roasted Lemon Potatoes, 143
Scalloped Sweet and White Potatoes, 138
Tortilla Española, 199
Tuna Niçoise Salad, 80
Turnip Potato Purée, 213
poultry dressing
Roast Cornish Hen with Wild Rice Dressing, 202
Roast Turkey Breast with Dressing, 116
Vegetable Bread Stuffing, 210
Power Granola, 31
Provençal Garlic Potatoes, 140

pumpkin
    Autumn Pumpkin Cranberry Muffins, 42
    Spicy Pumpkin Pie, 214

quesadillas
    Individual Turkey Quesadilla, 78
quiche
    Crustless Asparagus Quiche for One, 85

Ranch Dressing, Creamy, 109
raspberries
    Baked Fruit with Raspberry Sauce, 91
    Light Ice Cream Birthday Cake, 188
    Light Raspberry Blueberry Spread, 47
    Mixed Berry Crisp, 153
    Naturally Fresh Fruit Sorbet, 92
    Pears with Raspberry Sauce, 159
    Raspberry Bavarian, 156
    Raspberry Fool, 203
rhubarb
    Orange Stewed Rhubarb, 89
    Rhubarb Bran Muffins, 175
    Rhubarb Punch, 184
rice
    Baked Rice, 141
    Crustless Asparagus Quiche for One, 85
    Fragrant Rice, 192
    "on call," 102
    Three Cheese Mushroom Risotto, 196
ricotta cheese
    Pears with Raspberry Sauce, 159
    Raspberry Fool, 203
    Seasonal Fruit Plate with Ricotta Cheese,
        88
risotto. See rice
Roasted Lemon Potatoes, 143
Roasted Sweet Peppers with Parsley, 137
Roasted Tomato Pasta Sauce, 75
Roasted Turkey Breast with Dressing, 115
Roast Cornish Hen, 118, 202
rolled oats
    Baker's Dozen Morning Multi-Grain
        Pancakes, 34
    Beef and Vegetable Meat Loaf, 119
    Chocolate Chip Oatmeal Cookies, 176
    Creamy Rolled Oats, BM 8, SM 16
    Fruit Muesli, 30
    Hot Cereal with Multi-Grains, 28
    Mixed Berry Crisp, 153
    Nutty Mango Crisp, 153
    Oatmeal Date Muffins, 174
    Orange Date and Bran Muffins, 174
    Power Granola, 31
Rosy Poached Pears, 158
rutabagas
    Cardamom-Scented Rutabaga, 146
    cooking, 146
    cutting, 146

Hearty Vegetable Barley Soup, 62
    Turnip Potato Purée, 213
rye flakes
    Hot Cereal with Multi-Grains, 28

salad dressings
    Balsamic Vinaigrette, 84
    Caesar Salad Dressing, 82
    Creamy Ranch Dressing, 109
    Orange Vinaigrette, 187
    Red Wine or Raspberry Vinaigrette, 205
    Vinaigrette, 108
    Warm Sherry Vinaigrette, 110
salads
    Apple Cabbage Slaw, 107
    Chicken Caesar and Potato Salad, 82
    Curried Turkey Salad, 81
    Greek Salad in a Pita, 79
    Seasonal Fruit Plate with Ricotta Cheese,
        88
    Spinach and Orange Salad, 205
    Tomato and Black Bean Salad, 83
    Tomato, Bean and Mozzarella Salad,
        LM 4
    Tuna Niçoise Salad, 80
    Tuscan Tomato Salad, 108
salmon
    Grilled or Broiled Salmon Fillet, DM 10
    Mustard Baked Salmon, 127
    Salmon Pecan Sandwich Filling, 71
salsa
    Baked Bean Tortillas, 65
    Fresh Cucumber Salsa, 168
    Fresh Tomato Salsa, 74
    Open-Face Baked Cheese Tomato
        Tortillas, 73
    Salsa Cheese Spread, 172
    Tortilla Española, 199
sandwich fillings
    Salmon Pecan Sandwich Filling, 71
    Tuna Sandwich Filling, 72
sandwiches
    Grilled Cheese French Toast Sandwich,
        65
    Peanut Butter and Banana Sandwich,
        LM 2
    Salmon Pecan Sandwich, LM 22
    Stacked Turkey Sandwich, LM 1
    Toasted Tomato and Cheese Sandwich,
        DM 30
    Toasted Vegetable Frittata Sandwich, 66
    Tortilla Sandwich, SN 23
    Tuna Sandwich, LM 16
sauces, savoury
    Cranberry Citrus Coulis, 186
    Creamy Ranch Dressing, 109
    Fresh Cranberry Chutney, 212
    Fresh Tomato Salsa, 74

Light Cranberry Sauce, 110
Roasted Tomato Pasta Sauce, 75
Tomato Mushroom Pasta Sauce, 131
sauces, sweet
Blueberry Sauce, 38
Fresh Peach Sauce, 38
Honey Yogurt Sauce, 44
Light Whipped Topping, 189
Orange Yogurt Sauce, 90
Poached Apple Slices, 36
Raspberry Sauce, 91
Strawberry Orange Sauce, 45
sausage
Grilled Sausage with Mustard Glaze,
DM 18
Sausage and Sweet Potato Chili, 123
Sautéed Spiced Fruits, 154
Scalloped Sweet and White Potatoes, 138
Seasonal Fruit Plate with Ricotta Cheese,
88
shrimp
Sautéed Shrimp, DM 7
Shrimp Chowder, 57
Thai Peppered Shrimp with Leeks, 190
smoothies
Frozen Melon Smoothie, 169
snow peas
Minted Carrots and Snow Peas, 143
Stir-Fried Vegetables, 191
sorbet
Mango Mint Sorbet, 193
Naturally Fresh Fruit Sorbet, 92
soufflés
Mocha Soufflé Dessert, 195
soups
Chicken and Matzo Ball Soup, 204
Curried Vegetable and Split Pea Soup, 63
Homemade Light Beef Broth, 58
Homemade Light Chicken Broth, 59
Gazpacho, 198
Gingered Carrot Soup, 61
Golden Harvest Soup, 201
Hearty Vegetable Barley Soup, 62
Mushroom Squash Bisque, 112
Shrimp Chowder, 57
Turkey Minestrone, 60
sour cream
Baked Fruit with Raspberry Sauce, 91
Herbed Cornbread, 172
Turnip Potato Purée, 213
Spiced Beef Brisket, 206
spices, 231
Spicy Beans on Toast, 64
Spicy Pumpkin Pie, 214
spinach
Cheese and Spinach Lasagne Roll-Ups,
133
Spinach and Orange Salad, 205

split peas
Curried Vegetable and Split Pea Soup, 63
spreads. See also fruit spreads
Salsa Cheese Spread, 172
squash
Golden Harvest Soup, 201
Herbed Chicken and Vegetables, 115
Mushroom Squash Bisque, 112
steak
Beef Strip Loin with Wine Sauce, 120
Stir-Fried Vegetables, 191
strawberries
Balsamic Strawberries, 157
Fresh Fruit Cup, DM 29
Fresh Fruit Jelly, 160
Fruit Muesli, 30
Gingered Fruit Parfait, 161
Mixed Berry Crisp, 153
Naturally Fresh Fruit Sorbet, 92
Power Granola Fruit Parfait, 33
Seasonal Fruit Plate with Ricotta Cheese,
88
Strawberry Bavarian, 156
Strawberry Orange Sauce, 45
stuffing
Vegetable Bread Stuffing, 210
Wild Rice Stuffing, 202
sweet potatoes
Sausage and Sweet Potato Chili, 123
Scalloped Sweet and White Potatoes, 138

Three Cheese Tomato Risotto, 196
Thai Peppered Shrimp with Leeks, 190
Toasted Vegetable Frittata Sandwich, 67
tomatoes
Baked Fish en Papillote with Tomatoes
and Herbs, 128
Baked Layered Tomato and Potato
Slices, 139
Fresh Tomato Salsa, 74
Gazpacho, 198
Herbed Chicken and Vegetables, 115
Pasta with Chickpea Garlic Sauce, 135
Roasted Tomato Pasta Sauce, 75
Sausage and Sweet Potato Chili, 123
Toasted Tomato and Cheese Sandwich,
DM 30
Tomato and Basil Baked Eggs, 130
Tomato and Black Bean Salad, 83
Tomato and Goat Cheese Crostini, 69
Tomato Bagel Melt, BM 6
Tomato, Bean and Mozzarella Salad,
LM 4
Tomato Mushroom Pasta Sauce, 131
Tomato Salsa, Fresh, 74
Turkey Minestrone, 60
Tuscan Tomato Salad, 108
Veal Cutlet in Tomato Basil Sauce, 124

tortillas
  Baked Bean Tortillas, 65
  Breakfast Tortilla Sandwich, *BM 15*
  Individual Turkey Quesadilla, 78
  Open-Face Baked Cheese Tomato
    Tortillas, 73
  Tortilla Española, 199
  Tortilla Sandwich, *SM 23*
tuna
  Tuna Niçoise Salad, 80
  Tuna Sandwich, *LM 16*
turkey
  Breakfast Alaska, *BM 7*
  Curried Turkey Salad, 82
  Individual Turkey Quesadilla, 78
  Light Turkey Gravy, 117
  Roast Turkey Breast with Dressing, 115
  Stacked Turkey Sandwich, *LM 1*
  stuffing and roasting, 117, 210–211
  Turkey Minestrone, 60
turnip
  Turnip Potato Purée, 213
Tuscan Tomato Salad, 108

veal
  Veal Cutlet in Tomato Basil Sauce, 124
vegetables. *See also individual vegetables*
  Asian Steamed Green Beans, *DM 29*
  Cardamom-Scented Rutabaga, 146
  Cauliflower Potato Mash, 145
  Corn and Zucchini Sauté, 144
  Gazpacho, 198
  French-Style Green Peas with Lettuce,
    136
  methods for cooking, 98–102
  Minted Carrots and Snow Peas, 142
  Oven-Roasted Asparagus, 207
  Roasted Sweet Peppers with Parsley, 137
  Sautéed Mushrooms, *DM 16*
  Stir-Fried Vegetables, 191
  Turnip Potato Purée, 213
  Vegetable Bread Stuffing, 210
  Vegetable Cheese Pie, 86
  Vegetable Kebabs, *DM 1*
vegetarian recipes
  Baked Bean Tortillas, 65
  Cheese and Spinach Lasagne Roll-Ups, 133
  Cheesy Eggs and Asparagus on Toast, 70
  Cottage Cheese Pancakes, 87
  Crustless Asparagus and Rice Quiche
    for One, 85
  Greek Salad in a Pita, 79
  Grilled French Toast Sandwich, 66
  Open-Face Baked Cheese Tomato
    Tortillas, 73
  Pasta with Chickpea Garlic Sauce, 135
  Polenta Pie with Tomato Mushroom
    Pasta Sauce, 135

  Seasonal Fruit Plate with Ricotta Cheese,
    88
  Spicy Beans on Toast, 64
  Toasted Tomato and Cheese Sandwich,
    DM 30
  Toasted Vegetable Frittata Sandwich, 67
  Tomato and Basil Baked Eggs, 130
  Tomato and Black Bean Salad, 83
  Tomato and Goat Cheese Crostini, 69
  Tortilla Española, 199
  Vegetable Cheese Pie, 86
vinegar. *See balsamic vinegar*

waffles
  Make-Ahead Crispy Belgian Waffles, 35
  Waffles with Fresh Applesauce, *BM 2*
walnuts
  Mixed Berry Crisp, 153
  Nutty Mango Crisp, 153
Warm Cranberry Fall Fruit Compote, 147
Warm Sherry Vinaigrette, 110
watermelon
  Lime Watermelon Splash, 56
wheat flakes
  Hot Cereal with Multi-Grains, 28
wheat germ
  Baker's Dozen Morning Multi-Grain
    Pancakes, 34
wild rice
  Roast Cornish Hen with Wild Rice
    Dressing, 202
wine
  Beef Burgundy, 194
  Beef Strip Loin with Wine Sauce, 120
  Chicken Breast in Wine Sauce, *DM 5*
  Rosy Poached Pears, 158
  Spiced Beef Brisket, 206
  Tomato Mushroom Pasta Sauce, 131
  Warm Sherry Vinaigrette, 110

yogurt
  Citrus Yogurt Jelly, 149
  Creamy Ranch Dressing, 109
  Fruit Muesli, 30
  Gingered Fruit Parfait, 161
  Honey Yogurt Sauce, 44
  Oranges in Yogurt Cream, 152
  Orange Yogurt Sauce, 90
  Power Granola Fruit Parfait, 33
  Raspberry Bavarian, 156
  Strawberry Bavarian, 156
  Summer Fruits with Yogurt, *BM 12*

zucchini
  Corn and Zucchini Sauté, 144
  Toasted Vegetable Frittata Sandwich, 67
  Turkey Minestrone, 60
  Vegetable Kebabs, *DM 1*

DIABETES AND NUTRITION INDEX

....

A1C. *See* hemoglobin A1C
acesulfame-K (Ace-K). *See* sweeteners,
    non-nutritive
alcohol
    alcoholic beverages, 182–183
    and hypertension, 182
    and hypoglycemia, 182
amino acids. *See* protein
antioxidant(s), 38, 169, 225
aspartame. *See* sweeteners, non-nutritive

beta carotene, 225
beverages
    alcoholic and non-alcoholic, 182–183
    soft drinks and mixes, 183
Beyond the Basics, 2, 9, 12, 216–222, 237
Beyond the Basics Resource, 182, 219
blood glucose
    goals, 6, 12, 226
    meters or monitors, 183, 226
    testing, 5–6, 12, 18, 183, 226
blood pressure, high. *See* hypertension
Body Mass Index (BMI). *See* weight
    management
breads, 25, 52, 217
breakfast. *See* meal planning
butter, 25, 221

calcium, 26, 71, 166
calories (energy requirements), 17–18, 165
    in alcoholic and soft drink mixes, 183
    reducing, 54
CDA Good Health Eating Guide, 216
CDA Guidelines for the Nutritional
    Management of Diabetes Mellitus,
    11–12, 237
Canada's Food Guide, 9–10, 23–24, 26, 98,
    105, 216, 237
carbohydrate(s)
    amount needed, 9, 11, 13
    available, 12, 217
    choices, 12
    counting, 11–12
    importance of, 6, 11, 225
    in menus, 12, 20
    in vegetables, 6, 98
cereals
    cooked, 24–25, 217
    ready-to-eat, 24, 217
    whole grains, 10, 24, 25, 102
    cereals of your choice, 25, 217
cheese, 219–220
cholesterol
    in blood, 225
    in food, 220
    to lower, 24

cooking methods, healthy, 97, 102
cyclamate. *See* sweeteners, non-nutritive

desserts, healthy, 54, 100
diabetes
    complications, 6
    definition of, 3–4, 225
    gestational, 3, 6
    pills, 3, 183
    pre-diabetes, 4, 6
    prevention of, 2–4
    risk factors, 3
    symptoms of, 2
    treatment of, 4
    type 1, 4, 6, 225, 228
    type 2, 2–4, 6, 228
dietitian, 2
digestion, 7, 11

eating out, 54–55, 182
eggs, 220
exercise, 3–6, 17
Extras. *See* Food Choices

fats & oils, 10, 14–15, 220–221
Fats Choices. *See* Food Choices
fatty acids
    definition of, 225
    monounsaturated, 15, 226
    omega-3, 15, 220, 227
    polyunsaturated, 226
    saturated, 15, 104, 219, 225
    trans fatty acids, 15, 225–226
    unsaturated, 226
fibre
    importance of, 14
    in cereals, 24, 229
    in fruits, 14, 23, 106
    insoluble, 14, 226
    in menus, 14
    recipes, high fibre, 36, 37, 43, 62, 66, 67,
        80, 123, 133, 136, 144, 152, 153, 156,
        158, 159, 175, 203
    recipes, very high fibre, 33, 64, 65, 79,
        83, 135
    requirements, 14
    soluble, 14, 106, 148, 226
    ways to increase, 9, 14
fish, 220, 227
flaxseeds, 28, 31, 229
Food Choice(s)
    CDA Food Choice System, 216
    Extras, 26, 221
    Fats, 20, 26, 216, 220-1, 238
    Fruits, 218, 224
    Grains & Starches, 102–103, 216–217, 223

Food Choice(s) *(continued)*
    Meat & Alternatives, 10, 104–05, 220
    Milk & Alternatives, 26, 218
    Other, 219
    Vegetables, 98
    used in analysis, 237–238
    used in menus, 18
food diary, 5
food groups. *See* Food Choices
food portions
    measuring, 104
    weighing, 25, 52
Free Food(s). *See* Extras under Food
    Choices,
fruit
    healthiest choices, 9, 23
    importance of, 23
    juices, 7, 24, 224
    reduced-sugar fruit spreads, 26
Fruits Choices. *See* Food Choices
Fruits of your choice, 224

gestational diabetes. *See* diabetes
glucose. *See* blood glucose
glycemic index (GI), 7–9, 23, 227
glycogen, 227
glycosolated hemoglobin. *See* hemoglobin
    A1C
Grains & Starches Choices. *See* Food
    Choices

hemoglobin A1C, 225
high blood pressure. *See* hypertension
how to use this book, 17–19
hydrogenation, 226
hypertension (high blood pressure)
    and alcohol, 15, 182
    and diabetes, 4
    and sodium (salt), 15, 228
hypoglycemia
    and alcohol, 182
    and snacks, 165
    definition, 227
    prevention, 165, 183
    symptoms, 183, 227
    treatment , 183

insulin
    action, 3
    definition, 227
    type 1 and 2 diabetes, 3

labels, food. *See* Nutrition Facts
lactose intolerance, 218

margarine, 10, 15, 25, 221, 226
meal planning
    breakfast, 23, 27
    calories for day, 17
    dinner, 97

    importance of, 6
    lunch, 51
    Plate Method, 11, 97
    snacks, 165
    special occasions, 181
    timing of meals, 9, 18, 165
Meat & Alternatives Choices. *See* Food
    choices
menus
    food choice values used in, 19–20
    nutrient value of, 19–20
milk, 18, 26, 237
Milk & Alternatives Choices. *See* Food
    choices

nutrient analysis of recipes and menus, 237
nutrient value of menus. *See* menus
Nutrient Value of Some Common Foods, 11
Nutrition Facts (on labels)
    breads, 25
    cereals, 24–25, 217, 223
    fruit spreads, 26
    frozen entrees, 106
    how to read, 12
    snack foods, 166
    soups, 51

oils. *See* vegetable oils
omega-3 fatty acids. *See* fatty acids
Other Choices. *See* Food Choices

parboiled rice, 85, 102
physical activity. *See* exercise
potassium, 106, 169
prevention of diabetes. *See* diabetes
protein(s)
    amino acids, 104–105, 227
    complementary, 105
    complete, 104
    importance of, 14, 104, 227
    vegetable, 104
proteinuria, 228

saccharin. *See* sweeteners, non-nutritive
salads. *See* vegetables
salt. *See* sodium
sandwiches, 51–52
snacks
    healthy, 166
    importance of, 165
    menus, 18
sodium
    and hypertension, 15
    -reduced broths, 51, 58, 59
    sources of, 15, 101, 228
    ways to reduce, 15, 51, 60
soft drinks. *See* beverages
sorbitol. *See* sweeteners, nutritive
soups, 51–52
soy beverages, 26, 218

sucralose. *See* sweeteners, non-nutritive
sugar(s). *See* sweeteners, nutritive
supermarket meals, 105–106
sweetener(s), non-nutritive
    acesulfame-K (Ace-K), 221–222
    aspartame, 26, 221–222
    cyclamate, 221–222
    and fruit spreads, 26
    saccharin, 221–222
    sucralose, 26, 221–222
sweetener(s), nutritive
    sorbitol, 26, 228
    stevia, 222
    sugar, 13–14, 219

trans fats. *See* fatty acids
triglyceride(s)
    and alcohol, 182
    definition, 15, 228
    importance of,
Vegetable Choices. *See* Food Choices
vegetable oils, 10, 15, 221
vegetables
    importance of, 9, 98–102, 219
    most fibrous, 98
    most nutritious, 102
    salads, 51–52
    starchy, 217

vegetarian diets, 14, 104–105
vitamins
    A and beta-carotene, 61, 98, 99, 100, 101,
        103, 123, 137, 146, 148, 169, 172, 225
    B, 26, 27, 85, 121, 198, 218, 220
    C, 23, 27, 98, 99, 100, 101, 102, 103, 137,
        146, 156, 169, 193, 225
    D, 10, 26, 27
    E, 28, 220, 225, 229
    folic acid, 99, 101, 102, 137
    supplements, 98

weighing foods. *See* food portions
weight management
    achieving a healthy weight, 4
    body mass index (BMI), 2–3, 11
    in prevention of diabetes, 3–6
    strategies for weight loss, 4
    waist circumference, 4
whole grains. *See* cereals

yogurt, 26–27, 149, 218